PALAEO-
ASIATIC

TURKIC

CAU-
CASIAN

MONGOL

MANCHU-
TUNGUS

KOREAN

JAPANESE

CONGO

CHARI-NILE

M A L A Y O - P O L Y N E S I A N

ALTAIC	DRAVIDIAN	AUSTRO-ASIATIC	FINNO-UGRIC

MILIES OF THE WORLD

SECOND EDITION

Historical Linguistics
An Introduction

SECOND EDITION

Historical Linguistics
An Introduction

Winfred P. Lehmann

THE UNIVERSITY OF TEXAS

HOLT, RINEHART AND WINSTON, INC.

*New York   Chicago   San Francisco   Atlanta
Dallas   Montreal   Toronto   London   Sydney*

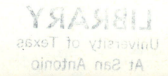

To

R.P.L.

Copyright © 1962, 1973 by Holt, Rinehart and Winston, Inc.
All rights reserved
Library of Congress Catalog Card Number: 72-10305
ISBN 0-03-078370-4
RAMAC 2783702
Printed in the United States of America
456 038 98765432

Preface

The last decade has produced many advances in linguistics research. Many have been in the field of descriptive linguistics, but those affecting historical linguistics have led to a second edition of this book.

The greatest advances have come in the field of syntax. As a result of the work in syntactic typology, historical linguistics now has a framework for explaining many syntactic phenomena. This work has demonstrated the importance of distinguishing between languages with objects consistently found after verbs as in English and languages with objects consistently found before verbs as in Japanese. In each of these types of languages we can expect to find characteristic features, such as the type of relative clauses, the position of adjectives and genitives, the use of prepositions or postpositions and so on. When however we find discrepancies from an ideal framework, we assume that the language in question is undergoing change.

Historical linguistics have long used such a procedure in phonology. For example, because there is so little evidence for Proto-Indo-European *b* in the framework of obstruents, the phonological system of Proto-Indo-European was assumed to be changing. The expectation of such a change was based on the assumption, often tacit, that the phonological component of a language is systematic. By the end of the nineteenth century linguists had determined a framework for phonological systems; only recently have similar achievements been made in understanding the bases of syntactic systems. As a result we now can provide explanations for syntactic change as did our predecessors for phonological change.

Although historical linguists of the nineteenth century, like Verner and de Saussure, made definitive contributions to our understanding of phonological change, recent linguistic study has achieved gains in phonology as well as in syntax. These gains have to do largely with the use of distinctive features and greater formalism. The greater formalism results from the insistence that all linguistic statements be completely specified, that descriptive as well as historical phenomena be stated in rules. The procedures are *generative*. Whether dealing with phonology, syntax or semantics, linguistics should be generative, that is, completely specific.

A complete generative grammar would be highly complex and lengthy. The best is still Pāṇini's for Sanskrit, and this lacks rules for much of the phonology and semantics, even for syntax. For the description and history of English much more needs to be done, in spite of the work of our predecessors. Beside indicating some of the important achievements of the past – the classification of languages, the development of the comparative method and the method of internal reconstruction, the understanding of various kinds of change – a handbook can do little more than point the way to improved procedures. To master such procedures students will have to deal with linguistic data. Examples can be found in articles published in the journals and in historical treatments of individual languages.

In spite of the recent advances, many problems remain to be solved in historical linguistics, problems in understanding how change is carried out in language, in specific language groups, and in relation to other cultural phenomena. As one example, the recent analysis of the early Indic script gives us hope that in time the inscriptions at sites like Mohenjo-Daro will be deciphered and provide information about the early linguistic history of India, possibly even about the invasion of the Indo-Europeans into India. Other problems have to do with the earlier history of the Indo-Europeans, the reading of Etruscan and the language written in Linear A, the classification of the languages of the Americas, Australia, New Guinea, and Africa. For those who consider these problems too broad in scope there are endless problems of detail, such as the etymology of English *decoy*, or Latin *persona*, or the source of the Germanic past tense suffix of regular verbs like *lived*, or of syntactic constructions like the -*ing* form.

Work on these and other problems will also contribute to refinement of the historical-linguistic method. Moreover, drawing on improved understanding achieved by work in sociolinguistics, psycholinguistics and descriptive linguistics, as well as on methods developed in other sciences, historical linguistics will continue to fill in the gaps in our understanding of the development of language and the history of man. Advances require a thorough understanding of past achievements, both in subject matter and in methods.

The bibliography is immense. Only some works can be listed here; those selected are in English, for many of the important materials have been translated, and few students can readily use materials in even the commonly known German and French, let alone languages like Russian and Japanese. Students who can however profit from these materials will find access to many important topics in historical and general linguistics.

One of the major gains for an author of a book is the clarification it brings about in his views of the subject. Comments by students, reviewers, and colleagues contribute to such clarification. I would like to express my thanks for many such comments, particularly for the capable, careful recommendations made to the publisher by the nameless reviewers as well as those made publicly by reviewers in the journals. Among others who have contributed to improvements in this second edition I would like to acknowledge especially Dwight Bolinger. Gracious and painstaking comments by some of our most eminent linguists are among the best encouragements for undergoing the tedium of revising a book.

Austin, Texas
August 1972   W. P. Lehmann

Contents

CHAPTER *1*

Introduction

1.1 Language in change; native elements and borrowed elements

Languages change constantly, a fact that becomes most noticeable when we read texts a few centuries old. For instance, various kinds of change are apparent in almost any passage of Shakespeare, such as in these four lines from his Sonnet XI:

> *As fast as thou shalt wane, so fast thou grow'st*
> *In one of thine, from that which thou departest;*
> *And that fresh blood which youngly thou bestow'st*
> *Thou mayst call thine when thou from youth convertest.*

When these lines are read today, lines 2 and 4 do not rhyme. We may suspect that they did for Shakespeare, and our suspicion is confirmed when we find that such a word as the proper name *Clark* is in origin the word *clerk*, that *parson* is in origin the word *person*, and so on. For Shakespeare *convert* rhymed with *depart*. Shakespeare's rhymes give us other information about his pronunciation. We find additional evidence in the puns he uses in his plays, as when he equates *steal* and *stale*, which with our different pronunciation would not make such puns. From such evidence, including nonstandard spellings that reflect actual pronunciation, we can pretty well determine the sound of Shakespeare's speech. From such evidence, too, we know that English sounds have been changing. This change is termed **sound change**, or **phonological change** (see Chapter 10). In comparing earlier and later forms of any language, we find various types of phonological change.

The passage just quoted from Shakespeare also shows changes of form. In contemporary conversation, or even when writing poetry, we no longer use the pronouns *thou*, *thine*, or the accompanying verb forms ending in *-st*, though they have been maintained in Quaker plain speech and in prayer. There is enough material in Shakespeare's plays to determine the system of forms he used, and to note the differences between them and the system of forms used in current English. From a comparison of the two systems, we can note various changes in form. These are called **morphological changes**. Materials in other languages also give data on morphological change and lead to the conclusion that all languages change in their system of forms.

The selection from Shakespeare's sonnet also illustrates alterations in syntax. We no longer use *depart* as a transitive verb, except in archaic religious language; *convert*, on the other hand, is generally used as a transitive. Further examples demonstrate other **syntactic changes** between Shakespeare's English and ours. Because morphology serves to provide syntactic markers and is in this way a subdivision of syntax, syntactic and morphological changes are treated together (see Chapter 11). Languages alter more readily in sounds than in syntax, as we see when we study the history of most languages.

Besides changes in phonology and syntax, we must account for changes in meaning. Elements like *-st* have meaning, of course, for they indicate that the subject is the second person *thou* in words such as *growest* versus *grows*. Such meaning is known as grammatical in contrast to the lexical meaning of words. Changes in meaning, in the usual sense of the word, are termed **semantic changes** (see Chapter 12). The word *convert* in Shakespeare's Sonnet XI meant to "undergo a change"; for us it generally means to "produce a change, often from one belief to another." Since the time of Shakespeare it has been modified in scope, as well as changed in its syntactic use. The word *wane* has almost been lost from the language, except in fixed expressions like the *waning of the moon*. Whole realms of words have been added to English since Shakespeare's day; the large vocabulary of science is an example.

In historical linguistics we study differences in languages between two or more points of time. As we investigate languages, we also find differences between two or more points in space. The pronunciation of *depart* varies considerably in England and America, and in various sections of each country. From texts over several centuries, we know that in standard British English the syllable-final *r* has been lost, with lengthening of the preceding vowel; in most sections of America, an *r* remains. Subdivisions of a language are referred to as **dialects**. The study of variations among dialects of a language is termed **dialect geography** (see Chapter 8). Since dialect differences are closely linked with social groups, the study of dialect geography is included in the broader study known as **sociolinguistics**.

Study of variations in languages from place to place is of great concern to historical linguistics, for changes may be introduced into languages as speakers of one language adopt elements of another, or as speakers of one dialect take on forms of another. The process of introducing such elements is known as **borrowing**. The word *depart*, for example, is French in origin. When speakers of English and French were in daily contact, many words were **borrowed** by English speakers from the French vocabulary. The English *depart* may be traced back to Old French *departir*, and ultimately to Latin *dis-* "away from each other" and *partīre* "to divide." On the other hand, the word *grow* can be traced back to Old English *grōwan* and, as far as we can determine, to earlier stages preceding English, which are referred to as Proto-Germanic and Proto-Indo-European. These are the reconstructed ancestral languages of the various Germanic dialects on the one hand, and of the various Indo-European dialects on the other (see Chapter 2).

In most languages we can determine two sets of words: **native words** and **borrowed words**. Native words are those like NE *grow*, which can be traced back to the earliest form of the language in question. Borrowed words are imported from another language.

The study of the history of individual words is known as **etymology**. Etymological dictionaries may give the history of suffixes and phrases, but essentially they have entries for individual words.

We call *grow* a native word because we find **cognates**, that is related forms of English *grow* in Old High German *gruoen* and in Old Norse *grōa*. These words are related to Modern English *green* and *grass*, and to their equivalents in the other Germanic languages. They are also related to Latin *grāmen* "grass," so that we must assume forms of this group of words for Proto-Indo-European, the language from which Old English and Latin developed. Accordingly we classify *grow*, *green*, and *grass* as native English words.

Since native words and borrowed words often exhibit different patterns, we must distinguish between them when we study the history of languages. Most native English verbs, for example, are monosyllables like *grow*.

Moreover, in contrast with borrowed words like *depart*, they are frequently used with prepositional adverbs, as in *grow up* and *grow out*. Borrowed words may accordingly exhibit different syntactic as well as phonological patterns from those of native words.

We must also distinguish importations from dialects of a language, such as Northern English *kirk* in contrast with standard English *church*. Moreover, we attempt to determine the time of borrowings. NE *wine* and *vine* are both borrowed from Lat. *vīnum*; *wine* was introduced about the beginning of our era, when Lat. *v* was still pronounced [w]; *vine* was introduced some centuries later when Lat. *v* was pronounced [v]. By maintaining the two forms, English provides information about change in Latin. Words derived from the same source are called **doublets**. The study of doublets like *wine*: *vine*, *two*: *dual*, *five*: *Penta(gon)*: *punch* [a drink made ideally with five components] is illuminating in disclosing the history of languages. Investigations of the borrowings in languages, of the interplay between dialects and languages, and of the effect of one language on another inform us about the history of individual languages. Many changes are also ascribed to the effect of one language or dialect on another (see Chapters 8:9, 10:8.1, 12:7).

1.2 Related languages; genealogical classification

The comparison of various languages led to the assumption that some languages are **related**, that they developed from a common source. This assumption came to be confirmed in large part through the linguistic situation in western Europe. For common words in French, Italian, Spanish, Portuguese, and several other languages show consistent similarities and differences. Compare for example the words for *dear* and *field*:

>"dear" Fr. *cher* Ital. *caro* Span. *caro* Port. *caro*
>"field" Fr. *champ* Ital. *campo* Span. *campo* Port. *campo*

The French [š] in these words, spelled *ch*, corresponds consistently with the [k], spelled *c*, in the words of Italian, Spanish, and Portuguese.

From these consistent correspondences we assume that at least some French [š] developed from earlier [k] through phonological change. This assumption is supported by other examples, such as,

>"candle" Fr. *chandelle* Ital. *candela* Span. *candela*
>"house" Fr. *chez* Ital. *casa* Span. *casa*
>Port. *candeia* cf. Lat. *candēla*
>Port. *casa* cf. Lat. *casa*

From these correspondences we also conclude that French, Italian, Spanish, and Portuguese are members of one **linguistic group** or **language family**. The reason for their similarity is their common descent from one earlier language, Latin. Through such comparison we can relate other languages, assume that they developed from an earlier language, and classify them as belonging to a specific language family. Determination of language families is known as **genealogical classification** (Chapter 2).

Such relationships are assumed from observation of systematic differences as well as systematic similarities. Further, the system is essential, for it is difficult to define what is similar, what different, until we analyze the system of any language. The French [š] is in some ways a more trustworthy indication of relationship than are the unchanged sounds of Italian, Spanish, and Portuguese, for it can be systematically related to the [k] of these languages and of Latin.

In establishing relationships, we look in this way for recurrences among both similar and different segments of the systems. If we base relationships merely on similar words, our conclusions may be wrong, for we may find them in languages that are totally unrelated, such as Turkish *futbol* and Japanese *futobōru*, which are borrowed from English *football*, or Persian *bad* and English *bad*, which are chance similarities. Historical linguistics developed only after linguists abandoned the comparison of random words that looked alike from language to language and began instead to determine recurrent similarities and differences in the phonological and syntactic systems, as well as in the vocabularies of the languages they assumed to be related.

The languages that developed from Latin, commonly known as the **Romance languages**, are of great importance to historical linguists because they furnish both the materials for comparison and the earlier language from which the Romance languages developed. In the Romance languages problems of comparison and development are available for solution, and in Latin the solution can be verified. With such verification available to them, historical linguists can test their essential techniques and procedures, which were refined especially through work with the group of languages to which the Romance languages and Latin belong, the **Indo-European family.**

In 1786 Sir William Jones, an English jurist in India, observed that **Sanskrit**, the ancient, learned language of India, was systematically similar to Greek and Latin, to his native language, and to earlier forms of English. This observation had been made before, without widespread effect; after Jones's statement however, scholars in Europe began systematic comparison of older forms of English and German with Latin, Greek, Sanskrit, and other languages. Their work in the nineteenth century led to the classification of these languages into the Indo-European family, and to the development of historical linguistics as a discipline.

1.3   Typological classification

In studying linguistic systems, linguists have observed that languages exhibit certain patterns corresponding to the type of language. For example, languages like English, in which normal declarative sentences have verbs preceding their objects (VO languages), also have relative clause constructions following their antecedents. On the other hand, languages like Japanese, in which objects precede their verbs (OV languages), have relative clause constructions preceding the nouns they modify. Syntactic systems seem in this way to be governed by general abstract principles. Such principles have come to be known as **universals**. Observation of systems by types permits us to understand patterns of change and to classify languages by typological criteria (see Chapter 3).

Typological classification is not as well developed as genealogical classification. The typological classification of the past was based largely on surface features of language. Examining underlying structures to determine the universals that govern the structure of languages is one of the most important of current linguistic activities. As such universals are determined, typological classification will become more secure and useful.

Typological and genealogical classification are quite independent of each other. Hindi, for example, though related to English, is an OV language, while English is VO. The contrasts give us important clues in dealing with the history of each of these languages, as we will observe below in greater detail. Such differences, like other contrasts, are important to know when learning and teaching languages; they are studied in contrastive linguistics.

Whether we analyze languages for their genealogical relationships, or for their typological features, we need accurate descriptions. Such descriptions for languages no longer spoken, like Hittite, or for earlier stages of languages still spoken, like Old English, are dependent on proper interpretation of the texts that have been transmitted to us. Interpretation of texts requires an understanding of the writing systems in which the materials of these languages have been transmitted.

1.4   Interpretation of writing systems

Linguists commonly cite forms in a contemporary transliteration, that is, symbols of the Latin alphabet rather than native symbols, not the alphabets used for Gothic or Greek, nor the characters used for Sanskrit, nor those for Chinese and Japanese. Yet without knowledge of the writing system used for each language, we would have inadequate means for its interpretation. We do not know, for example, the exact pronunciation of many Gothic words, such as Gothic *ains*. Gothic was transmitted in a writing system based on that of Greek of the fourth century A.D. At this time Greek *ai* was pronounced approximately like the vowel in English *men*. We cannot however be sure that this was its only value in Gothic. Many linguists have held that the vowel of *ains*, the Gothic word for "one," was actually a diphthong similar to that of English *mine*. For Gothic and for any language attested in written texts, historical linguists must be able to deal with the written records that have come down to us, or their conclusions may be naïve. The problems involved in dealing with written records are discussed in Chapter 4.

Transliterations for writing systems like the Greek or Russian alphabets are standard and readily interpreted. Transliterations like that for Chinese, however, often present problems of their own. For they are conventionalized and use symbols that themselves need interpretation. The Mandarin Chinese forms are given here in a system named after its originator, Wade, with numerals marking tones: 1 = level tone, 2 = rising, 3 = falling-rising, 4 = falling.

Writing systems, like languages, may be classified by general principles. If a writing system contains a small number of symbols, approximately thirty or fewer, it is alphabetic. If it contains sixty to a hundred, it is syllabic. And if, like Chinese or Ancient Egyptian, it contains several hundred or more, it is logographic; the symbols stand for words. An understanding of the principles underlying writing systems is important in deciphering unknown writing systems. For details, see Chapter 4:6.

1.5   Methods used in historical linguistics

1.5.1. The comparative method. For interpreting data in historical linguistics, two methods are especially important: the comparative method and the method of internal reconstruction. The comparative method (see Chapter 5) may be illustrated by examining selected words from French, Italian, Spanish, and Portuguese. If we examine the words for "eight":

Fr. huit   Ital. otto   Span. ocho   Port. oito

it would seem difficult to derive them from a common source. By assembling additional examples, we can however derive them from a specific Latin word and explain the differing development in each of these languages. Compare:

| "milk" | Fr. *lait* | Ital. *latte* | Span. *leche* | Port. *leite* |
| "fact" | Fr. *fait* | Ital. *fatto* | Span. *hecho* | Port. *feito* |

Basing our conclusions on observation of changes in language, we reconstruct as the earlier forms of these words: *okto, *lakte, *faktu. These reconstructions by the comparative method can be corroborated by noting the Latin: *octō* "eight," *lactem* (accusative singular of "milk"), *factum* "fact"; moreover, we can account for the changes in these four languages and also see their essential regularity. In French and Portuguese the Latin [k] has been absorbed in the vowel; in Italian it has been assimilated to the following [t]; in Spanish it has been changed to the affricate [tš] with loss of the following [t]. In four different geographical areas a sequence originally the same developed into four different sequences. Through comparison of such forms, knowledge of possible phonetic changes and of the earlier forms, we can determine the earlier shapes and those of most forms in French, Italian, Spanish, and Portuguese.

Study of the relationships among English [f θ h b d g p t k] and corresponding consonants in the other Indo-European languages was important in developing the comparative method. In the earliest period of historical linguistics, Jacob Grimm noted the systematic relationships among these consonants. Thereupon the Indo-European consonants from which they developed were reconstructed by means of the comparative method. We list these, with examples from Gothic and Sanskrit:

PIE p	PIE t	PIE k
Go. fadar "father"	Go. þrija "three"	Go. haurds "(woven) door, hurdle"
Skt pitá "father"	Skt tráyas "three"	Skt kṛṇatti "spins"

PIE bh	PIE dh	PIE gh
Go. broþar "brother"	Go. doms "fame, (doom)"	OE gūþ "battle"
Skt bhrátā "brother"	Skt dháma "glory"	Skt ghnánti "they strike"

PIE b	PIE d	PIE g
NE pool	Go. taihun "ten"	Go. aukan "increase, eke"
Lith balà "swamp"	Skt dáśa "ten"	Skt ugrás "powerful"

The systematic relationships between:

PIE *p t k*,   Skt *p t k*,   and Germanic *f* þ *h/χ*;
PIE *bh dh gh*, Skt *bh dh gh*, and Germanic *b d g*;
PIE *b d g*,   Skt *b d g*,   and Germanic *p t k*

were stated by Grimm in rules that have subsequently become known as Grimm's Law. Because of the importance of Grimm's Law in the development of historical linguistic theory, the data will be discussed more fully in later sections.

The comparative method can also be illustrated by comparison of other words, such as the numerals from one to ten in some of the Indo-European languages (see Table 1). The numerals in the unrelated languages, Chinese and Japanese, are given for contrast. Again we cite Gothic forms rather than Old English, in part because they are attested several centuries before Old English.

Although a complete account of the similarities and differences between the words of the first six columns of Table 1 would require considerable space, we can readily note a few examples of consistent similarities and differences, such as the *t-* in columns 1 and 2 of the words for 'two' and 'ten' corresponding to *d-* in columns 3 through 6. By comparison the Chinese and Japanese words permit no assumption of correspondences with any of the columns. Japanese *tō* like NE *ten*, to be sure has initial *t*, but the Japanese word corresponding to NE *two* has initial *f*; accordingly we cannot find consistent similarities or differences between English and Japanese.

We also note the systematic difference in vowel between Sanskrit *a* and Latin and Greek *e* in the first syllables of the words for "six," "seven," and

TABLE 1   (For data on pronunciation, see Appendix 1)

ENGLISH	GOTHIC	LATIN	GREEK	OLD CHURCH SLAVIC	SANSKRIT	CHINESE	JAPANESE
one	ains	ūnus	heîs	jedinŭ	ekas	i[1]	hitotsu
two	twai	duo	dúō	dŭva	dvā	erh[4]	futatsu
three	þrija acc.	trēs	treîs	trije	trayas	san[1]	mittsu
four	fidwor	quattuor	téttares	četyre	catvāras	ssu[4]	yottsu
five	fimf	quīnque	pénte	pęti	pañca	wu[3]	itsutsu
six	saihs	sex	héks	šestĭ	ṣat	liu[4]	muttsu
seven	sibun	septem	heptá	sedmĭ	sapta	ch'i[1]	nanatsu
eight	ahtau	octō	oktṓ	osmĭ	aṣṭā	pa[1]	yattsu
nine	niun	novem	ennéa	devęti	nava	chiu[3]	kokonotsu
ten	taihun	decem	déka	desęti	daśa	shih[2]	'tō

"ten." Analysis of all the systematic similarities and differences between the Indo-European languages in accordance with the comparative method required the work of many linguists during the nineteenth and twentieth centuries, and it is still not complete. But even with as little material as the numerals from "one" to "ten," we can assume with confidence that English, Gothic, Latin, Greek, Old Church Slavic, and Sanskrit belong to one language family, and that they developed from a common source.

1.5.2 The method of internal reconstruction.

The comparative method, as just illustrated, is the most common procedure used in determining older patterns of a language. By examining the Japanese numerals cited in the table, we can note another procedure, one especially valuable when we have no large number of related languages. Without using forms other than those of Japanese listed above, we can note a pattern in these numerals: the double of the lower numerals begins with the same consonant as does its half, that is, *mi* "three" and *mu* "six," *yo* "four" and *ya* "eight." After noting this pattern, we might assume that the words for "one" *hi(to)* and "two" *fu(ta)* also had the same initial consonant at one time. By comparing words borrowed into Japanese from Ancient Chinese, we can support this assumption; the Old Japanese initial consonant is often written *F*.

This procedure is referred to as **internal reconstruction** (see Chapter 6). While we use it of necessity in a language like Japanese, which has no proved related languages, we may also apply it to problems in families like the Indo-European, which are widely attested.

Unfortunately the common source of the Indo-European languages was spoken before writing was in use in its geographical area, and we have no attested forms of it. With the methodology developed partly in the study of the Romance languages, linguists have reconstructed the "original" Indo-European language as far as our data permit. To indicate, however, that it is not attested, we label it with the prefix **Proto-** and refer to it as **Proto-Indo-European (PIE)**. (To indicate reconstructed or nonattested forms, we place an asterisk (*) before them; since, however, a form identified as belonging to a proto-language is by definition unattested, when we use P- in a language abbreviation before a cited form, we may omit the asterisk.) We attempt to deal with reconstructed forms as with attested forms. We may accordingly cite them in phonemic transcription, e.g., PIE/dekm/"ten," or in phonetic transcription, e.g., PIE [dékm̥].

By comparing the words for "ten" in all the Indo-European languages we can reconstruct PIE/dekm/ [dékm̥]. We can reconstruct other words, such as PIE/gʷōws/"cow" on the basis of OEnglish *cū*, OIr. *bō*, Lat.

bōs, *bovis*, Gk. *boûs*, Lett. *guovs*, Skt. *gaus*, and so on. We can also reconstruct morphological elements, such as the ending PIE [-ti] from forms like that for "he is" in Gk. *esti*, Skt. *asti*, and many others. When we reconstruct Proto-Indo-European, we are dealing with a language spoken before 3000 B.C. and we obviously do not have the kind of data that is available for Latin. But we can determine the essential elements of the Proto-Indo-European phonological and syntactic systems and even draw some inferences about its vocabulary.

1.5.3 Glottochronology. Swadesh suggested in 1951 that the everyday segments of the vocabulary are replaced at a definite rate, and that the words that have been maintained in related languages may be used for dating in much the same way as radioactive decay has been used in dating the age of the earth. This procedure is referred to as **glottochronology**; in glottochronology, statistical analysis is used for dating and hence it is a kind of **lexicostatistics**. In the use of glottochronology (discussed in Chapter 7), lists of one or two hundred words are gathered from related languages, and the proportion of related words is determined, with no closer attention to their similarities. English *cow* and German *Kuh* would be adequately similar, but not *dog* and *Hund*. Though glottochronology has not lived up to the hopes originally held for it, it is still used in attempts to solve questions on the interrelationships between languages attested only in recent times, such as the American Indian languages.

1.6 Sound change

The difference between PIE/dekm/ and NE/ten/ can be accounted for by positing various types of change, at the phonological level. PIE/d/ maintained in Lat. *decem* became PGmc./t/; PIE /k/ maintained in Lat. *decem* became PGmc. /χ/, later /h/. Final *m* developed a preceding vowel, and became *n*; *e* remained unchanged. In early Old English the /h/ from PGmc. /χ/ was lost between vowels, though /h/ was maintained in Old Saxon *tehan* and Old High German *zehan*. Having noted these changes, we can relate precisely PIE /dekm/ and NE /ten/.

Languages exhibit changes of all similar sounds of a phoneme, such as that from PIE /d/ to PGmc. /t/, or changes that affect only some words, and these in some of their occurrences, e.g., the colloquial pronunciation of NE *would you* is [wúdžə]. Speakers may use either this pronunciation, or the more formal [wúd yùw]. Because these changes are not applied to every occurrence of [d] followed by [y], they are called sporadic changes.

To understand changes like that of PIE *d* > PGmc. *t* in the etymon of

NE *ten* or [dy] > [dž] in NE *would you*, we need to know articulatory phonetics. Both changes involve only one feature of the sounds in question. PIE *d* became voiceless in Proto-Germanic. NE [y] after [d] may become strident. Sound change generally takes place with the modification of one feature, whether the change affects all like sounds in a language or whether the change is sporadic.

Both kinds of change are stated in rules. In most standard historical grammars these are expressed as follows:

$$\text{PIE b d g} > \text{PGmc. p t k}$$

that is, Proto-Indo-European voiced stops became Proto-Germanic voiceless stops. In recent historical statements they are expressed by means of distinctive features. Since Proto-Indo-European /b d g/ were the only -continuant consonants at the time of the change in pre-Germanic, this rule can simply be expressed:

$$\begin{bmatrix} \text{-resonant} \\ \text{-continuant} \end{bmatrix} > \text{[-voice]}$$

that is, phonemes that were not resonants and not fricatives became voiceless. Rules expressed in distinctive features are designed to indicate precisely the elements of language that have changed. In achieving such precision, they place greater demands on the reader, both through requirements for information about the technical procedures and about the languages under consideration.

1.7 Morphological and syntactic change

When we compare the Modern English plural *ships* with the Old English counterpart *scipu*, we cannot account for the difference in ending through sound change. Rather, we must conclude that the plural ending was remodeled after that in such Old English nouns as *stānas* "stones" from sg. *stān* "stone."

Study of even a small segment of a language leads to the observation that forms similarly used may influence or modify one another. When, for example, we compare the Old Church Slavic word for "nine" with its cognates in the other Indo-European languages, we may assume that, like them, it should have begun with *n*. The simplest explanation for the initial *d* of OCS *devętĭ* is that it was taken over from OCS *desętĭ* "ten." Such influence is called **analogical**; we say that the Proto-Slavic word for "nine" was modified on the **analogy** of that for "ten"; we also say that the *-s* marking the plural of *ship* was spread by analogy. Modification of this sort can be exemplified in sets of forms, such as the ordinal numerals in English. Modern English *fifth* has been modified from earlier *fift* on the analogy of *fourth*. Analogical modification may be based on semantic patterns, as in OCS *devętĭ*, or on syntactic patterns, as in the English *s*-plurals.

Change also takes place in syntactic patterns of order. In the Old English *Beowulf*, most sentences end in verbs; that is, the basic sentence pattern for early Old English has the object preceding its verb, and we must speak of this stage of the language as basically OV. The OV pattern, however, was undergoing change; in Middle English, objects consistently follow verbs, as they do in Modern English. As we will see in Chapter 3, the change to a VO order was accompanied by other syntactic changes, as in comparative constructions.

Moreover, many inflectional endings were lost. For example, early Old English still contains examples of an instrumental case form. By late Old English, the uses of the instrumental were taken over by the dative. Through changes in final vowels, the instrumental was no longer distinct and was lost as a separate case form. In this way, syntactic changes may be brought about by sound changes. Later, as final endings were lost in English, the dative case itself was no longer distinct; most of its former functions are now expressed by prepositional phrases.

As we will note in greater detail in Chapter 11, syntactic changes in this way involve modifications in forms available for indicating syntactic categories. Many of the modifications are brought about by internal changes; others result from influences of other languages.

1.8   Semantic change

Besides sound change and syntactic change, languages also undergo change of meaning. The meanings of single words may be modified. Gothic *haurds*, for example, meant 'door,' apparently because some doors were woven of reeds or withes; the underlying verb meant "spin, weave," as illustrated in the examples in Chapter 1:5.1. Modern English *hurdle* is not used of doors, but rather for an obstruction in a sport. From this use it came to have an abstract meaning "obstacles." The change of meaning was affected on the one hand by a change in culture, when doors were no longer woven. And subsequently the meaning was affected by internal change, when the word came to be used primarily in contexts referring to social and mental rather than physical activities.

Semantic change may also affect sets of words, or word-fields. Examples may be found in kinship terms. In Old English, for example, a distinction was made between uncles on the father's side, OE *fædera*, and uncles on the mother's side, OE *ēam* (see *eme* in the Oxford English Dictionary). The distinction was subsequently lost, so that the English kinship system now has only one term *uncle*. The change of meaning did not result from importation of the word *uncle* from Old French *oncle*, but rather from a change of culture. In early Germanic times the maternal uncle occupied a special position in the family, a position that was later lost. Moreover, we cannot say simply that a word was changed in meaning; rather that a feature of meaning was modified in the kinship system. Thus, change in meaning may be comparable to change in phonological and syntactic sets. Such change may also be expressed by means of rules, though few attempts have been made to express semantic change in this way. As we will note in discussing semantic change (Chapter 12), meaning has been studied primarily in relation to individual words, not in relation to semantic sets; accordingly our understanding of semantic change is poorer than our understanding of phonological and syntactic change.

1.9   Explanations for change

Besides identifying change in language, linguists have attempted to account for it. Many modifications in language are superficial. For example, when the exploration of space became a major topic, new terms were introduced and the use of others was modified. These modifications, however, had little effect on the language. No new sound patterns or syntactic categories were introduced; and extended uses of words, as in *lunar landing* or *space shuttle*, did not modify the semantic system of the languages that introduced such terminology. Attempts to account for modifications in linguistic structures cannot deal simply with such superficial innovations but must also deal with change that affects the central structure of languages.

Three major explanations for change have been suggested: (1) The influence of one language on another, the results of which have been termed borrowing; (2) the imperfect learning of language by children; (3) the effects of the system or systems of individual languages.

1.9.1 Borrowing is readily observed in vocabulary.   English has borrowed many words from French, Latin, and Greek and readily takes over words from other languages as well. The extent to which borrowing affects syntax or phonology, however, is still inadequately known. Through bilingual speakers, French syntactic patterns like phrases consisting of noun followed by adjective, e.g., *attorney general*, have been borrowed. Extensive bilingualism may apparently bring about the importation of syntactic patterns more widely than in a few phrases. But when foreign patterns or sounds occur in borrowings, they are generally modified in keeping with the patterns of the borrowing language, as in *menu*, *garage*, and other recent borrowings from French into English. An extended period of influence may, however, lead to different results.

In dealing with borrowing, the attitudes of speakers must be taken into consideration. English has borrowed many words from French but, except in specific periods, German has not. Sociolinguists have examined recently the attitudes of speakers regarding specific characteristics, such as the pronunciation of postvocalic *r* in words like *car* in New York City. The imitations of prestige patterns they found may lead to a better understanding of modifications in the past. In certain situations languages may have been modified in their sound systems and syntactic systems, as well as in their vocabulary, by the impact of neighboring languages.

1.9.2 Change has also been ascribed to the imperfect learning of language by children.   A fundamental problem is noting when such patterns are generally adopted. Everyone who has watched children learn languages has observed inadequacies in pronunciation, syntax, and use of words. But these are gradually eliminated as the child grows up. Moreover, the imperfect patterns of one child often differ from those of another. It is accordingly difficult to establish that these patterns are taken over as innovations in a language. Again, it is crucial to determine the conditions under which modifications are generally adopted.

1.9.3 A tendency toward greater regularization in the system of a language may lead to change.   For although languages are systematic, the systems lack balance. English, for example, has three nasals in final position, as in *bam, ban, bang*, but only two initially, as in *Mab, nab* but not **ngab*. Such imbalances may be eliminated in the history of languages, as the development of /ŋ/ as a separate phoneme indicates. Formerly English had no final /ŋ/ as in *strong*; the /ŋ/ became a phoneme when final *g*, still maintained in *stronger*, was lost. In this way English came to have three nasals pairing with the voiceless and voiced stops:

p	t	k
b	d	g
m	n	ŋ

Effects of a system on morphological sets are also apparent, as in English verbs. Irregular verbs, like *hide*, *hid*, *hid*, have come to distinguish only between the present on the one hand and the past and past participle on the other, like the regular verbs *like, liked, liked*. Few verbs remain that have three distinct forms, like *sing, sang, sung*. And only one verb has two different vowels in the past: *was, were*, in British English.

From examining a single language in this way, we might conclude that irregularities in the system are constantly being eliminated. But Italian, with a system of nasals like those in Early Middle English, has not developed a separate phoneme *η*. Moreover, the German irregular verbs are more complex than are those of English. Because of the varying effects of the system from language to language, we cannot simply ascribe change to simplification of irregularities in a language.

1.9.4. Implications of an improved understanding of change.

We can only conclude that the causes of change in language are highly complex, as they are in other social institutions. Detailed study of individual changes, like that of the pronunciation of American English -*t*- in *butter, bottle, bottom*, will give us a better understanding of how languages change.

As a result we will better understand the structure of individual languages and of language generally. Linguists differ in their analysis of individual languages, and in their theoretical views. For example, the English vowel system has two major analyses. The vowels in *beet, bait, boot*, and so on, are either viewed as long or tense, transcribed /biːt beːt buːt/—/bīt bēt būt/—or diphthongized, /biyt beyt buwt/. Moreover, phonological units have been determined independently as autonomous phonemes, or with reference to the syntactic system as systematic phonemes. In systematic phonemics the assumption of tense vowels is preferred, for as in *repeat: repetitive*, many English derivatives are more readily related by assuming a relationship between tense (long) and short vowels. Historical linguistics may be useful in providing information of importance in the analysis of such patterns and for linguistic theory.

It has often been said that explanation for linguistic forms can only be found in earlier forms. We can understand the vowel variations in *mouse: mice, goose : geese, man : men*, for example, by noting the Old and pre-Old English forms of these words. And the vowel variation in *write : wrote : written, sing : sang : sung*, we can understand by noting the related words in other Indo-European dialects, and in Proto-Indo-European. Understanding the phonological, morphological, syntactic, and semantic structure of any language is an important aim of historical linguistics.

By investigating languages for the changes they have undergone, we can determine their history and their interrelationships with other languages. After a century and a half of investigation, the development of most of the languages in the Indo-European family is well known. The development of other language families has not been so fully determined, partly because data are lacking, especially from earlier historical periods. Furthermore, linguists have been primarily interested in determining the background of their own native languages, which with few exceptions were Indo-European.

The success of historical linguistic study depends largely on the state of descriptive linguistics. Indo-European historical linguistics developed rapidly in the nineteenth century because thorough descriptions were available for Latin, Greek, and Sanskrit; on the pattern of these descriptions, grammars were produced for other early Indo-European languages, such as Gothic, Old Church Slavic, Old Irish, and subsequently for the remaining Indo-European languages, such as Armenian and Albanian. Since equally detailed descriptions were not produced for the languages of other families, the historical grammar of these families is less advanced than that of Indo-European.

Recent advances in many subbranches of linguistics promise additional insights into the development of languages. The greater vigor introduced in phonological study by distinctive feature analysis, and in syntactic study by clearer insights into the relationship between surface and underlying forms, provides improved descriptions of languages from which their history can be determined. Contributions in typological classification, in sociolinguistics, and in fields like language learning permit us to use these improved descriptions for insights into the changes that have occurred.

More complete accounts of the development of specific languages and language families will lead to improvement of historical linguistic theory and of the techniques employed in historical linguistics. In discussing language families, we draw in large measure from data in the Indo-European family. To illustrate the procedures of setting up language families and describing genetic relationships, we shall present the Indo-European language group in some detail.

Selected Further Readings

For an introduction to the problems and methods of historical linguistics, see Holger Pedersen, *Linguistic Science in the Nineteenth Century*, translated by John Spargo (Cambridge, 1931), now reissued under the title *The Discovery of Language*, Bloomington: Indiana University Press, 1962. This book provides a readable, if limited, discussion of the principles of historical linguistics as they were evolved in the course of the nineteenth century.

Otto Jespersen, *Language, Its Nature, Development and Origin* (London, 1922), also discusses the history of linguistics in his Book I, pages 19–99, without however confining himself to historical linguistics.

Carl Darling Buck, *Comparative Grammar of Greek and Latin* (Chicago, 1933) subsequently reprinted with few changes, provides a brief, though clear, introduction to historical linguistics, pages 30–67, and may be used generally with profit.

Another concise but excellent statement on the development and principles of historical linguistics may be found in A. Meillet's *Introduction à l'étude comparative des langues indo-européennes*, 8th ed. (Paris, 1937), Chapter 1 and Appendix I. This edition has now been reissued by the University of Alabama Press.

Some of the important theoretical statements of nineteenth-century linguists have been made available in translation in *A Reader in Nineteenth Century Historical Indo-European Linguistics*, edited by W. P. Lehmann (Bloomington, 1967).

CHAPTER 2

Genealogical classification of languages

2.1 Evidence for genealogical classification

In the previous chapter we noted that many of the languages of Europe and Asia are interrelated. Evidence may be found in all components of these languages. Most apparent is similarity of basic vocabulary: words for lower numerals, kinship, domestic animals, everyday activities. But even more convincing are the similarities one finds in the systems of sounds and forms. From the phonological system we may cite initial *d-* in words of the same meaning in Sanskrit, Greek, Latin, Slavic, as in the words for 'two' and 'ten'; the reconstructed PIE *d* contrasts with *t and *dh, forming a subset of three members in the phonological system of Proto-Indo-European. From the inflection we may cite elements filling the same role in these languages, as the ending in the third person singular indicative PIE [-ti], which contrasts with the first singular [-mi] and the second singular [-si]. From word formation we may cite similar constructions, such as compounds like English *Bluebeard*, meaning 'a man who possesses a blue beard'; as we examine older forms of Indic and Greek, we find many such compounds. In syntax, too, we find similar patterns, such as the distinct parts of speech: nouns versus verbs. Such similarities cannot be due to chance. The only explanation for them is common origin of the languages in which the similarities are found. We say that languages having a common origin are related, and classify them in a common genealogical group or family.

The Romance languages, which developed from Latin, provide proof for such an explanation. Since French, Italian, Portuguese, Spanish, and the other Romance languages developed into independent languages only after the collapse of the Roman Empire, they furnish evidence on how languages develop, on how we can establish relationships between languages that developed from a common source, and on how we can group languages by degrees of relationship. The words listed on pages 4 and 5 for 'dear, field, candle, house' are so similar that we can derive them without question from attested Latin words. Yet they also exhibit changes from the Latin words, such as some losses of final elements, and modifications of consonants and vowels. These similarities and differences, as well as similarities and differences in morphology and syntax, give us evidence for assuming separate developments in the different areas in which Latin was once the common language. Subsequent study has provided evidence for such processes in all languages, and for the most widely used method of classifying languages.

In Chapter 1 we also noted that evidence can be found for proposing that Latin in turn is related to Greek, Sanskrit, and a number of other languages. Some of the evidence was apparent to linguists a century and a half ago. They examined the interrelationships to the extent their evidence permitted and proposed the large linguistic group known today as the **Indo-European family.**

Detailed study of the Indo-European family is important for understanding historical linguistic method as well as for knowledge of the interrelationships of some of the world's most widely spoken languages. For the methods applied in dealing with the Indo-European languages may also be applied to other language groups. Moreover, because of the political and economic role of the speakers using languages belonging to it, the Indo-European family is probably the most important and the most widely used today. (For its distribution, and the location of other language families, see the map inside the cover.)

In attempting to set up any language family, the oldest known forms of a language are of great importance, as is identification of the period to which they belong. Accordingly, for any historical study, we attempt to date the materials with which we are dealing. Approximate dates at which the oldest Indo-European materials are attested will therefore be given here.

An understanding of linguistic development also requires that we determine the interrelationships of language subgroups and languages within a family. The data involved in establishing such classifications are often complex. Details will generally be omitted here but can be found in grammars devoted to individual languages, such as Old English, or to individual subgroups, such as Germanic, the group to which Old English belongs. Moreover, successive stages of any language have been only approximately determined. Most proposed stages are based on non-linguistic evidence. The division between Middle High German and New High German, for example, has often been dated at the time of the Reformation. Other criteria used have been the introduction of printing or political developments, as for the terminal date of Middle English, or simply the turn of a century. Although external forces on the language may have been important in spreading or giving prestige to one form of it, we should use only linguistic criteria for linguistic classifications. Since this has rarely been done, the dates given in handbooks for stages of a language must be checked for the criteria used in proposing them. Even when true linguistic dating is possible, students must note that languages never change abruptly: for the Germans or English of the fifteenth and sixteenth centuries, the period at which we demarcate Middle from New German or English, there were no more apparent differences between their speech and that of their children or parents than for speakers at apparently serene linguistic times like the nineteenth century.

2.2   The Indo-European language family

The discovery that the ancient and modern languages of much of India were related to the Germanic and to the classical languages provided the impetus for much of the historical linguistic study in the nineteenth century. When this discovery was made, scholars were greatly concerned with the origins and the early institutions of mankind. The Indic texts, which are even older than the Greek texts known in the nineteenth century, excited the Grimm brothers, Rasmus Rask, Franz Bopp, and others to devote themselves to understanding the interrelationships between their own languages and those of Greece, Italy, and India, in which materials had been preserved for several millennia.

The name given to the family is a compound composed of one unit representing the easternmost area, India, and one representing the westernmost area, Europe, in which the family is located. Such hyphenated compounds have subsequently been devised for many other language families: Sino-Tibetan, Malayo-Polynesian, Afro-Asiatic, and so on. Since the Germanic family is located farthest to the north and west, many scholars, particularly in Germany, label the family Indo-Germanic. Others, using a term which the early Indic and Celtic authors applied to their own people, called the family Aryan; this name is now in disrepute because of a misuse of it for devious political purposes. Other names have also been proposed, but the one used most widely today is Indo-European.

We will first examine, roughly in accordance with their distribution from east to west, the various subgroups of the Indo-European family of which representatives are spoken today.

2.2.1 The Indo-Iranian subgroup. **Indo-Iranian**, formerly also called **Aryan** or **Indo-Aryan**, is the name of the subgroup that was carried to the area of Iran and India in migrations more than three millennia ago. It consists of two subgroups, of which **Indic** is the more important; for **Iranian** texts date from a considerably later period and are less abundant.

The earliest Indic text is the *Rigveda*, a collection of hymns as large as the *Iliad* and *Odyssey* combined. The oldest hymns are cosmological poems, composed somewhat before 1000 B.C. Materials used for transmitting texts disintegrate in the Indian climate, and accordingly we have no early records. But since the poems of the *Rigveda* and the other *Vedas*, that is, collections of hymns, were considered sacred, they were memorized and transmitted orally for many generations. We can vouch for the accuracy of the transmission, for most lines of the poems still conform to the metrical forms in which they were composed.

The veneration accorded the *Vedas*, which led to their careful preservation, yielded other results of importance to linguistics. As the language of the *Vedas* became obsolete and difficult to interpret, priests, or Brahmans, prepared commentaries. Among these were grammars, which informed later generations of priests how to interpret the hymns, even how to pronounce them—for a faulty pronunciation would scarcely achieve the intended aim of a hymn. The result of such linguistic analysis was a standardized language, so completely described and regulated, in the Indic term *saṃskṛta*, that it underwent few further changes. This *saṃskṛta* is known to us as **Sanskrit**, from the Western pronunciation of the term. We date it from several centuries before 400 B.C., the putative time of its greatest grammarian, Pāṇini. A grammar attributed to him described the language with such authority and completeness that ever after it has been learned by Indian scholars with no essential deviations. To this day Sanskrit is in daily use by a small number of Brahmans, and is thus comparable to Latin, Old Church Slavic, and Classical Arabic as a language maintained for religious purposes.

Beside the *saṃskṛta*, "regulated, cultivated, correct," there existed spoken languages called *prākṛta*, **Prakrits**. We are much better informed on Sanskrit than on the Prakrits, for a great amount of learned material has been produced in India. Many of the learned texts are religious writings: the *Brahmanas* are interpretative tracts in Sanskrit; the *Upanishads* are devotional tracts. Moreover, the classical works of Indian literature were composed in Sanskrit, such as the *Mahabharata* and the *Ramayana*, epics much longer than any composed in Europe. Fortunately Sanskrit dramas include female characters. Since they were not permitted to speak the regulated language, we have in their lines, and those of characters of lower castes, examples of Prakrits. Examples also appear in other materials. Literary Prakrit is dated from about the beginning of our era. In the period before Christ, we accordingly have three stages of Indic: **Vedic Sanskrit** or **Vedic**, the language of approximately 1200–800 B.C.; Classical Sanskrit, following it and standardized at approximately 400 B.C.; and the Prakrits.

Vedic and Classical Sanskrit are often referred to as **Old Indic**, the Prakrits as **Middle Indic**, which we may date from about 400 B.C. to A.D. 1000. The Middle Indic dialect on which we have most information is **Pali**; it is the language in which the Buddhist canon is preserved. We may place it shortly before Christ, though Indic dates are highly uncertain because the Indians were quite unconcerned about history. Fortunately contacts with the Greeks permit us to date a great Buddhist ruler, Asoka, around 250 B.C. The many inscriptions he placed throughout India may be used to determine the state of the Indic dialects before the beginning of our era. At the end of the Middle Indic period, before A.D. 1000, we have materials in languages known as **Apabhramsas** 'off-branchings.' From the Apabhraṃsas developed the modern Indic dialects. Most widely spoken of these is **Hindi**, the official language of the Republic of India; Hindi was also known formerly as **Hindustani**, and in Pakistan is called **Urdu**. Hindi and Urdu differ especially in learned vocabulary, for Hindi bases learned terms on Sanskrit, Urdu on Arabic and Persian. Other modern Indic languages are **Bengali**, **Gujerati**, **Marathi**, **Panjabi**, and numerous less widely spoken languages, such as **Singhalese** in Ceylon, and **Romany**, the language of the Gypsies.

Iranian texts from before 300 B.C. are referred to as **Old Iranian** and are handed down to us in two dialects, **Avestan** and **Old Persian**. The *Avesta* is the sacred book of the Zoroastrian religion. Its oldest poems, the *Gāθās*, are dated approximately 600 B.C. and are as archaic in language as those of the *Rigveda*; because of numerous problems in transmission, the *Gāθās* are very difficult to interpret. Old Persian is preserved primarily in the inscriptions of Darius, 521–486 B.C., and Xerxes, 486–465 B.C. The inscription of greatest importance is a long trilingual text in Old Persian, Akkadian, and Elamite, which was chiseled on a stone cliff at Behistan, Iran. The Behistan inscription recounts the feats of Darius. Written in a cuneiform writing system, it not only preserved for us, until recently, the oldest body of Indo-European texts surviving in their original form, but it also provided the avenue to the understanding of cuneiform. To illustrate the close relationship among Old Persian, Avestan, and Sanskrit, we may cite words like that for 'spear': OPers. and Av. *aršti-*, Skt. *ṛṣṭi-* or OPers. *daiva-*, Av. *daēva-* 'devil,' Skt. *deva-* 'god.'

We may date Middle Iranian from approximately 300 B.C. to A.D. 900. Various representatives of it are attested. **Pehlavi** or **Middle Persian** was the language of the Persian Empire, flourishing from about A.D. 300 to 900. Further east **Sogdian** and to the north **Saka** or **Scythian** were spoken and to this day are not completely described, partly because many of their texts were discovered only recently.

At present various Iranian languages are still in use: **Balochi**, of West Pakistan, **Pashtu** or **Afghan**, the official language of Afghanistan, **Persian**, the language of Iran, **Kurdish**, spoken by various groups in western Iran, Iraq, and Turkey, **Ossetic**, in the northern Caucasus, and many others. Although still spoken by millions, the Iranian languages have been displaced in many areas by Turkic dialects and have a much smaller number of speakers than do the Indian dialects. Since dialects of the two groups are spoken in much of southern Asia, Indo-Iranian has remained one of the most prominent subgroups in the Indo-European family.

2.2.2 The Armenian subgroup. Of **Armenian**, located in the southern Caucasus and western Turkey, we have no materials until the fifth century A.D. We assume from Akkadian and Greek accounts that the Armenians migrated to Armenia some centuries before the beginning of our era. Yet the oldest materials we have were presumably composed in the fifth century A.D. and are almost exclusively translations of Christian writings. A considerable number of Armenian texts have survived; some Christian writers have had their materials preserved only in Armenian. The language of these texts is referred to as **Old** or **Classical Armenian**, which was maintained with few changes as the written language until the nineteenth century. Modern Armenian exists in two branches: the **Eastern**, spoken in the Union of Soviet Socialist Republics and Iran, and the **Western**, spoken formerly in Turkey. Some speakers of Armenian have settled elsewhere, in Lebanon, parts of Europe, and the United States.

Armenian has been so heavily influenced by other languages, notably Iranian, that until late in the nineteenth century there was doubt whether it should not be classed as an Iranian dialect. A. Meillet, in *Linguistique historique et linguistique générale*, 1.95, cited the Gypsy dialect of Armenian as an example of a language that may contain almost no native vocabulary but still maintains the native phonological and syntactic structure. The grammatical structure of Armenian then is Indo-European, and exact correspondences can be set up for the basic vocabulary, such as *hayr* 'father' = Latin *pater*. Yet, in spite of our certainty that Armenian is a language separate from Indo-Iranian, its precise relationship to the other Indo-European languages is not yet agreed on. Occasionally it has been related to the poorly attested **Phrygian**.

2.2.3 *The Albanian subgroup.*

The early history of Albanian is even more inadequately known. Our earliest records are translations of the Gospel of Matthew from the fourteenth century A.D. We have few further materials until 1685, when a Latin-Albanian dictionary was produced, followed by religious translations, and collections of folktales in the nineteenth century. There are two dialects: **Geg** in the north and **Tosk** in the south and extending into Greece and Italy.

Albanian, like Armenian, has undergone many changes in its vocabulary, influenced successively by Latin, Greek, Slavic, and Turkish. Its origins are difficult to determine. It has been considered by some scholars a modern representative of **Illyrian**, by others of **Thracian**. Both Illyrian and Thracian are poorly known Indo-European languages of the period before the beginning of our era. To determine the early position of Albanian, we must either have thorough reconstruction of its early stages, on the basis of descriptive work now being carried on, or we will need new early texts. Reconstruction is hampered by the small proportion of native material in the language; discovery of early texts is a matter of chance. Without one of these aids, however, Albanian of only the past few centuries can be described.

2.2.4 *The Slavic subgroup.*

The **Baltic** and **Slavic** groups are attested only during the past millennium, yet languages in each contain relatively archaic characteristics. Such characteristics are the large number of case forms in the noun declension of Lithuanian, which lacks only one of the cases of Sanskrit, the ablative. In its accentual system Lithuanian preserves for words a pitch accent that Classical Sanskrit had already given up. Yet our oldest extended Lithuanian texts date only from the sixteenth century A.D. Our oldest Slavic texts date from the ninth century A.D. The lateness of texts from both groups has made it difficult to determine precisely their interrelationship. Some scholars class both of them in one subgroup of Indo-European, **Balto-Slavic.** Others maintain that the similarities between the Baltic and the Slavic languages are due to mutual influences exerted during a long period of contact. These scholars set up two independent subgroups of Indo-European, **Baltic** and **Slavic**. A choice between the two depends on the interpretation of selected linguistic characteristics. Given only recent texts, we can scarcely state with assurance whether one subgroup or two are to be posited.

Speakers of Slavic dialects apparently were located in southeast Poland and western Russia at the time of the Romans. They spread out from this area and in the sixth and seventh centuries came into contact with the eastern Roman Empire in Bulgaria. The earliest Slavic documents we have date from the advent of Christianization. Shortly after 850 two missionaries, Cyril (Constantinus) and Methodius, carried Christianity to Slavic speakers and translated the Bible into their language. The language of the translation is known either as **Old Church Slavic** or **Old Bulgarian**. The Russian church has maintained it as its official language, and accordingly it occupied a position in eastern Europe similar to that of Latin in the Roman church.

The Slavic languages spoken today are classified in three groups: **South, West,** and **East Slavic**. **South Slavic** comprises: **Bulgarian, Serbo-Croatian,** and **Slovenian**; **West Slavic** comprises **Czech, Slovak, Polish,** and **Wendish**; **East Slavic** comprises **Great Russian, White Russian** or **Byelorussian,** and **Ukrainian**. Through the political expansion of the Russian Empire, (Great) Russian was spread south into the Caucasus and east to Siberia; it has continued its expansion and today is one of the most widely spoken languages of the world.

Differences among the various Slavic languages are relatively slight, much smaller than those among the Germanic languages. One may assume therefore that there has been no long period of separation; this assumption is supported when we reconstruct Proto-Slavic, for we find it similar to Old Church Slavic.

2.2.5 The Baltic subgroup.   The Baltic group consists of two languages still in use, and **Old Prussian**, which is known through translations from the sixteenth century and became extinct around A.D. 1700. Old Prussian is important for Indo-European studies because of its conservatism, especially in the vowel system. (Prussian was replaced partly by Lithuanian, partly by German; the name was then applied to German speakers of the area in which the Old Prussian language was spoken.) Like Old Prussian **Lithuanian** was first recorded in a translation of Luther's catechism, dating from 1547. Modern Lithuanian is remarkable for its conservative pitch accent, inflection, and retention of formal distinctions, especially in the substantive. The word for 'son' *sūnùs* is like that in Sanskrit, *sūnús*; *eĩti* 'he goes' has undergone fewer changes than has Latin *it*. Lithuanian is accordingly one of the most important Indo-European languages for comparative study. The other surviving Baltic language, **Latvian** or **Lettish,** has undergone many more changes. It, too, is known from the sixteenth century; it no longer has a pitch accent, and many of its inflectional endings have been lost. A few dialects are attested for both Lithuanian and Lettish. During the short extent of the two republics of Lithuania and Latvia, standard languages were established. Neither language has more than several million speakers today.

2.2.6 The satem-centum subdivision.

In dealing with earlier stages of the Indo-European languages the groups we have so far discussed are often classed together as one of the two large subdivisions of Proto-Indo-European. The chief basis for this classification is a contrast of sibilants in these branches versus velars in the remaining branches. For example, in the word for 'ten' we find:

Skt. *daśa* Av. *dasa* Arm. *tasn* OCS *deseti* Lith. *děšimt* versus
Gk. *déka* Lat. *decem* OIr. *deich* Goth. *taihun*

In the word for 'hundred' we find:

Skt. *śatam* Av. *satəm* OCS. *sŭto* Lith. *šiṁtas* versus
Gk. *hekatón* Lat. *centum* OIr. *cēt* Goth. *hund*

The eastern languages are labeled **satem** after the Avestan form for 'hundred'; the western are labeled **centum.** When this classification was first proposed, scholars assumed that the speakers of Proto-Indo-European had split into two groups and that in the eastern group a sound change took place that differentiated the eastern from the western dialects.

Questions have been raised concerning this division, largely as a result of observations about dialect classification. If there had been a fundamental split between Eastern Indo-European and Western Indo-European, we should expect it to be reflected in a number of differing characteristics for each group. Since we do not find such additional characteristics, we do not hold today that there was once a single predecessor of the satem languages. We interpret the distribution of velars in centum languages and sibilants in satem languages by assuming that by a sound change some velars became sibilants in the eastern section of the Indo-European speech community. Results of the change spread through Indo-Iranian, Armenian, dialects poorly known, Slavic, and into Baltic; but in Baltic not all velars that show up as sibilants elsewhere were changed. The satem situation is therefore typical in a speech community after a sound change has taken place and the effects have spread. It did not affect the Anatolian languages or Tocharian, possibly because they had left the Indo-European speech community before the sound change took place, possibly because they were on its periphery (see Sections 2.2.11–12). We may continue to speak of satem languages because the change of velars to sibilants provides one of the foremost Indo-European isoglosses, but we no longer assume that the Indo-European speech community early split into two parts.

2.2.7 The Greek subgroup.

2.2.7 The Greek subgroup.   Although it has relatively few speakers today, **Greek** or **Hellenic** is important historically. Its spread into its current area, and its further expansion and contraction, is also highly interesting for general historical linguistics.

We assume from Greek history, supported by deductions based on linguistic evidence, that the present region of Greece was inhabited by non-Indo-European speakers before 2000 B.C. Place names like that of *Corinth*, with an element consisting of *n* plus dental consonant, are found also in Asia Minor; they are pre-Greek and were maintained by Greek speakers as were Indian place names in the Americas. Around 2000 B.C. Greeks, or Hellenes, began a southward invasion and in successive migrations gradually occupied the present area of Greece, the islands and adjoining areas in the Mediterranean, and the west coast of Asia Minor. Greek historians tell about the last of these waves, the Doric migration of around 1200 B.C. From the introduction of Greek speech, we can suggest how Indo-European languages may have been spread also in areas of which we have less knowledge, such as India and Italy.

The gradual increase of our knowledge of early Greek is also of great interest for historical linguistics. Until a short time ago the earliest datable Greek material was from the seventh century B.C. Vase inscriptions and poetry—the *Iliad* and the *Odyssey*—were older but uncertain in date. (Although the fall of Troy is dated roughly at 1200 B.C., there has been little agreement on the date of the Homeric poems.) During the past half-century, tablets were found on Crete and the mainland, which for some time could not be deciphered; they were classified by their scripts as **Linear A** and **Linear B.** A number of scholars worked on Linear B after World War II, employing the methods of cryptography toward its decipherment. In 1952 one of these, Michael Ventris, published his conclusions, which demonstrated that the language used in the Linear B tablets was Greek. This variety of Greek is usually referred to as **Mycenaean Greek**. The tablets date from 1450 to 1200 B.C. Accordingly, we now have very early texts for Greek, even earlier than those for India. With the new material our views of the dialect situation of Greek have been modified, as well as those on the development of Greek from Proto-

Indo-European and the importance of Greek in the second millennium B.C.

Many problems in the interpretation of Mycenaean Greek result from the imperfect script in which it was written. Linear B is syllabic. Consonant groups are either broken up, or simplified. Only the cumulative weight of evidence persuades us that Ventris' decipherment must be accepted. A Greek word for 'king' *basileús* is spelled in Mycenaean by syllabic symbols that we transliterate *pa-si-re-u*. These forms look quite different, but when we find 'priest' *hiereús* represented as *i-je-re-u*, 'fuller' *knapheús* as *ka-na-pe-u*, we accept the interpretation in spite of the inadequacy of the Linear B writing system for Greek.

In later Greek we have a diversity of dialects subdivided into two large groups: **West Greek** and **East Greek**. To East Greek belongs **Attic-Ionic**, the language of Attica and much of Asia Minor. Historically the most important dialect is that of Athens, **Attic Greek**. Because of the intellectual domination of Athens, its dialect came to be that used throughout Greek-speaking areas and was called the common language, *koinē*, or Hellenistic Greek. This is the dialect spread by Alexander the Great throughout his empire and maintained as the general language far outside the Hellenic peninsula. It is the Greek used in the New Testament.

With the decline of Greek political power, the area over which the Greek language was used also shrank. Today it is largely confined to Greece, though there are still some speakers in other countries, notably Cyprus, Turkey, and the United States. Except for **Tsaconian**, a dialect spoken in old Doric territory, the Peloponnese, modern dialects are descendants of the *koinē*.

2.2.8 The Italic subgroup.

Italic was brought into the Italian peninsula in successive waves during the second millennium B.C., like Greek into the Hellenic peninsula, though probably somewhat later. We know relatively little about the language situation in Italy before about 600 B.C. and can speak with assurance about it only from 250 B.C. We divide the Italic languages attested into two groups, **Oscan-Umbrian** and **Latin-Faliscan**. The subsequent history of the Italic languages provides a dramatic example of language spread and displacement. Latin gradually displaced all the other Italic languages and was spread throughout the Roman Empire. Subsequently a number of dialects developed from it in the various sections of the Empire, and in Italy itself. Since the Renaissance the dialect of Florence has been the basis for the standard language of Italy.

Oscan has come down to us in approximately two hundred inscriptions, from the last two centuries B.C. **Umbrian** is attested primarily through the

Iguvine tablets, dated in the first century B.C. Other related dialects are poorly attested. Oscan is important for Indo-European linguistics because it is conservative in vocalism. Formerly it was assumed without question that Oscan-Umbrian belonged with Latin-Faliscan in the Italic subgroup. Recently differences have been pointed out, largely in vocabulary, in which Oscan-Umbrian differs greatly from Latin-Faliscan. In grammatical structure, however, the two are sufficiently alike to suggest their retention in the Italic subgroup of the Indo-European family.

Only a few **Faliscan** materials have come down to us. Another Italic dialect surviving only in inscriptions is **Venetic**, spoken in northeast Italy before the beginning of our era. **Latin** is attested in an early inscription from Praeneste of approximately 600 B.C., which is instructive because of its archaic language and its content.

MANIOS	MED	FHE	FHACED	NUMASIOI
Manius	mē		fēcit	Numeriō

'Manius made me for Numerius.'

Inscriptions of this sort, labeling maker and recipient, are found on artifacts in other Indo-European dialect areas and give us a great deal of information about changes in the language, as the comparison above with classical Latin indicates.

We have relatively few Latin texts from before 200 B.C. Subsequently there are many literary texts, and also inscriptions giving us information on the spoken language. The spoken Latin, or **Vulgar Latin**, was spread throughout the Roman Empire and was the basis from which the Romance languages developed. Since Vulgar Latin is not as completely attested as we might like, recent work has been devoted to reconstruction of Proto-Romance from modern dialects.

Classical Latin was long maintained as the written language throughout the Roman Empire. Accordingly we have evidence for the emerging Romance languages only long after the collapse of the western Roman Empire: **Italian** from the tenth century; **Provençal** from the eleventh; **French** from 842, in the Oaths of Strassburg; **Spanish**, **Catalan**, and **Portuguese** from the tenth and eleventh centuries; **Rumanian** from the sixteenth. Besides these seven important languages, three minor ones are attested from modern times: **Sardinian**; **Rhaeto-Romance**, **Romansch** or **Ladin**, spoken by approximately 100,000 speakers in Switzerland and Italy; **Dalmatian**, of which the last speaker died in 1898.

Through its spread to Central and South America, Spanish has become one of the most widely spoken languages; forms of it, differing from area to area, are used throughout this huge area except for Brazil, where Portuguese is the national language.

2.2.9 The Celtic subgroup.
Celtic has many characteristics in common with Italic. Yet we cannot be certain of the relationship between the two subgroups, for no Celtic materials of any extent have been preserved from before our era. From place names, like *Bohemia* ('home of the Boii,' a Celtic tribe), we assume that Celts early inhabited central Europe. We know that they expanded greatly in the second half of the first millennium B.C. They established themselves in Spain, in northern Italy, and almost captured Rome. They penetrated into Asia Minor, as far as the present-day city of Ankara, and must have been distinct from other groups at the time of St. Paul's missionary journeys, as we may note from his "Letter to the Galatians". Moreover, St. Jerome reported that they maintained their Celtic speech to his day, in the fourth century A.D. During their expansion they became predominant in Gaul, Britain, and Ireland. Since the beginning of our era, however, the Celtic languages have been steadily receding.

The Celtic languages are classified into two groups, one in which PIE /k^w/ has become *p*, **p-Celtic** or **Brythonic**, the other in which it is a velar, **q-Celtic** or **Goidelic**.

Gaulish, attested in names and inscriptions from before our era, was a continental Brythonic dialect; it is no longer spoken. The remaining Brythonic dialects, **Welsh, Cornish**, and **Breton**, are continuations of dialects spoken in England before the Roman invasion. Our earliest manuscript materials are *glosses*, words written in manuscripts to translate difficult words in the original, much as language students do today. We have glosses from around 800 A.D. for Welsh and Breton. Literary materials in Welsh survive in considerable quantity from the twelfth century. Today Welsh is the Celtic language with the greatest number of speakers. Breton, which was taken to the continent in the fifth and sixth centuries A.D. as a result of the Germanic invasion of England, is still maintained in Brittany. Cornish became extinct in the eighteenth century.

Of Goidelic two languages are attested, *Irish*, and *Manx*, of the Isle of Man, now extinct. We have Irish materials in ogam inscriptions (see Chapter 4:5) from around the fifth century A.D., followed by glosses written by Irish monks on the continent in the eighth century. From the eleventh century a large amount of literary material is attested. Irish was taken to Scotland from the fifth century; the language there is referred to as **Scots Gaelic**. In Ireland itself, several dialects developed, some of which have been completely supplanted by English. With the establishment of

Eire, an attempt was made to establish one of these, **Munster**, as the national language, but the attractiveness and usefulness of English have thwarted the government's efforts. Celtic, an important subgroup several millennia ago, seems destined soon to disappear.

2.2.10 The Germanic subgroup.   Much of the displacement of Celtic has been brought about by the **Germanic** languages. Speakers of Germanic languages began their migrations in the last centuries before our era, and continued them more than a millennium, with penetration westward to Iceland, Greenland, and America, eastward into former Baltic and Slavic territory, and southward as far as Africa. In a second expansion from the sixteenth century, Germanic languages were again carried westward to North America, southward to South Africa, India, and Australia, and to lesser land masses of the world. The expansion of the Germanic languages, occasioned in the centuries around the beginning of our era by the Völkerwanderung [migration of peoples], may provide an example of how various less thoroughly documented languages were spread, such as Chinese and Semitic in the centuries before the beginning of our era.

Our first information about the Germanic tribes comes from classical writers; Caesar and Tacitus have given us especially valuable reports. The Romans seem to have confused Germans and Celts. The name, German, may have been taken over from that of a small Celtic tribe; many fanciful explanations of the past on its origin reflect more romantic speculation than linguistic competence. Apart from Germanic place and personal names, we have no data until the fourth century; our attempts to determine the early history of Germanic must therefore be based entirely on reconstruction. For this reason the classification of the Germanic dialects has until recently indicated their distribution several centuries after Christ rather than their earlier development. Handbooks generally speak of three subdivisions: **East**, **West**, and **North Germanic**. Linguistic indications suggest that we should rather speak of two: a *ggw* group, including the so-called East and North Germanic dialects, in which *ggw* developed from *ww*, and *ddj* or *ggj* from *jj*; a *ww* group, corresponding to the West Germanic dialects, in which *ww* and *jj* were maintained. In the past decades, attempts have been made to distinguish subgroups in the *ww* group, often with greater reliance on cultural than linguistic data. We no longer believe that there was little intercommunication among Germanic subgroups in England, Scandinavia, and northern Europe. Accordingly late mutual influences may have effaced earlier relationships; such intercommunication is especially clear in the Scandinavian area.

Materials from the fourth century A.D. have come down to us in

Norway and Denmark, in the so-called Runic inscriptions. They are composed in a formalized language in which vowels of unstressed syllables are maintained. Among the best known is that on one of the golden horns of Gallehus, Denmark:

Ek HlewagastiR HoltijaR	horna tawido.
'I Hlewagastir of Holt	made the horn.'

Early Runic inscriptions are attested from the various Scandinavian areas, especially Norway, before the eighth century, with little dialect differentiation, probably in part because the inscriptions were composed in a conservative language of priests. From the time of Scandinavian expansion, we speak of two groups: **East Norse**, consisting of **Swedish**, **Danish**, and **Gutnish**, and **West Norse**, consisting of **Norwegian**, **Faroese**, and **Icelandic**. The language of texts composed in Norwegian and Icelandic before the thirteenth century is commonly referred to as **Old Norse**.

Icelandic has a particularly rich and interesting literature from the thirteenth century. Moreover, several grammatical treatises on medieval Icelandic have come down to us, thanks to which Icelandic is thoroughly known from the medieval period on.

Although the other Scandinavian languages are labeled as separate languages, they have continued to influence each other, so that to this day Norwegian and Swedish are mutually intelligible; Danes can readily understand Norwegian and Swedish, though their own speech may cause Norwegians and Swedes difficulties. Technically such mutually intelligible forms of speech are known as **dialects**, and the term **language** is used for mutually unintelligible forms of speech. But for national forms of speech the term dialect is apparently undignified. The Scandinavian languages are therefore excellent examples of the nonlinguistic designation "language" for forms of speech used by a nation rather than for forms of speech unintelligible to native speakers of other languages.

The most extensive early Germanic materials are from a **Gothic** translation of the Bible. The translation, comprising the bulk of our Gothic texts, is ascribed to a Visigoth, Wulfila (311–83). It has been transmitted to us by Ostrogoths, in manuscripts of the late fifth and early sixth centuries. Gothic is relatively archaic, and transparent in grammatical structure; accordingly it is important for comparative Indo-European studies. The Visigoths in Spain and the Ostrogoths in Italy were absorbed by subsequent ethnic groups, and their languages became extinct. Between 1560 and 1562, however, Busbecq, a Flemish ambassador of Charles V to Turkey, took down in Istanbul about sixty words from two natives of the Crimea. Characteristics, such as the *d* in *ada* 'egg' make it unmistakable that their speech was Gothic. It is referred to as **Crimean Gothic**. Before more material than Busbecq's was collected, it passed out of use.

The *ww* group comprises five dialects: **High German**, **Franconian**, **Low German**, **Frisian**, and **English**. For all of them we speak of Old, Middle, and Modern (New) periods. These designations are imprecise, and will remain so until historical linguists define language stages by linguistic criteria. For reference to existing handbooks, however, it is well to know that "Old" generally refers to Germanic languages before the twelfth century, "Middle" from the twelfth to the fifteenth century, and "New" to the subsequent period.

High German is attested first in proper names from the end of the seventh century, in glosses from the eighth, and primarily in religious texts of the ninth. From the earliest times there are distinct dialects. **Alemannic** in the southwest and **Bavarian** in the southeast are generally referred to as **Upper German**. Through the thirteenth century the cultural center of Germany was in the south; our medieval literary materials are thus chiefly in Upper German. During the fourteenth century the political center moved farther to the north. The language spread by the increasingly powerful political units of Middle Germany was also used by the Reformers of the sixteenth century, particularly Martin Luther; it is the basis of modern standard German. Many dialects are still in everyday use. One of these, **Yiddish**, split off from the main body of German in the late medieval period. Lacking the speech of a long-established political center like Paris or Florence, the accepted standard for High German was fixed only at the end of the nineteenth century. The pronunciation was based on that of the stage (*Bühnenaussprache*).

Low Franconian, the dialect of Franconian that has developed into a national language, is known from few documents in the old period. At present it is represented by **Dutch**, and its dialect **Flemish**, which is attested copiously in the medieval period. **Afrikaans** is the form of Dutch that has been established in South Africa.

Before the eighth century there was close association between the dialects on the coasts of England and those of northern Germany. As a result these dialects share common innovations and are often given a special label, **Ingvaeonic**, or North Sea Germanic. From the eighth century, however, High German exerted a progressively stronger influence on the dialects of northern Germany, so that we note a break between the earliest materials handed down to us from the lowlands of Germany, labeled **Old Saxon** and the later **Low German**. Old Saxon is attested from approximately the same time as is Old High German. Middle Low German and Modern

Low German have been constantly receding before High German, especially since the political centralization of Germany in the nineteenth century.

Frisian, spoken on the coast and islands off the Netherlands and western Germany, is attested from the thirteenth century. Not a national language, it is maintained in various dialects by comparatively few speakers.

English is attested first in names from the seventh century. Literary remains, such as Caedmon's *Hymn* and the *Beowulf*, are generally dated somewhat before 750. The early literature was produced in the north, but virtually all materials have come down to us in **West Saxon**, the dominant dialect at the end of the ninth century. In Old English there were three distinct dialects, **Kentish**, **West Saxon**, and **Northern** (or **Anglian**), which was further subdivided into **Northumbrian** and **Mercian**. To distinguish "English Saxon" from the Old Saxon maintained on the continent, Old English was formerly referred to as **Anglo-Saxon**, but this designation is passing out of use.

In Middle English the dialect situation is even more complicated, though we may follow a classification into four subgroups, **Northern**, **West Midland**, **East Midland**, and **Southern**. The dialect of London, on the border between Southern and Midland, came to be the model for standard English. Like New High German, Modern English is therefore not a direct continuation of the prominent language of the older period; both languages have extremely complex histories.

Since approximately 1600, English has expanded continually. It is now the language used most widely as a second language and as an auxiliary language for international communication; as a first language, however, Mandarin Chinese probably has more speakers.

2.2.11 The Tocharian subgroup.   At the close of the nineteenth century, the above-mentioned languages were assumed to be the only members of the Indo-European family from which materials of any extent survived. Explorers then discovered unexpectedly, in Chinese Turkestan, Buddhist writings dating from the sixth to the eighth centuries that are clearly Indo-European. The language was given the name **Tocharian**, as the result of a mistaken identification.

There are two dialects, labeled A and B. Specialists who have been unhappy with these colorless classifications of a misapplied name have attempted with little success to introduce other labels, **Agnean** or **East Tocharian** for **Tocharian A**, **Kuchean**, or **West Tocharian** for **Tocharian B**.

One of the remarkable features of Tocharian is the preservation of palatals as *k* before back vowels; in other Indo-European languages of the East these palatals had become sibilants. This finding dealt a severe blow to the traditional classification of Indo-European into satem dialects in the east and centum in the west.

We know nothing about the provenience of the speakers of Tocharian, and nothing certain about their disappearance. Since most of the basic research on Tocharian has been undertaken only recently, it has contributed little to our knowledge of Proto-Indo-European.

2.2.12 The Anatolian subgroup. The second language of which abundant materials were discovered in this century has also been mislabeled with a name that has been fixed—**Hittite**. Excavations near the Turkish village of Boğaz Köy uncovered in 1905–07 the archives of the Hittite Empire, which flourished from approximately 1700 to 1200 B.C. Many texts from this period were found, and more have been found since. They are written in cuneiform and could be read at once; moreover, many contain Akkadian and Sumerian, so that the meaning of the texts, and of most Hittite words, can be determined. In 1915 Hittite was identified as Indo-European by B. Hrozný.

Twelve years later J. Kurylowicz identified sounds transcribed *ḫ* with reconstructions that Ferdinand de Saussure, solely on the basis of reasoning from internal evidence, had proposed in 1879. Saussure's prediction has been thus proved to be one of the most remarkable in linguistics. Kurylowicz' identification helped add to the great interest in Hittite, and in the early history of the Indo-European languages. Some Indo-Europeanists, notably E. H. Sturtevant, also proposed a reclassification of the family, because of the *ḫ*, other archaisms, and the early time of the records. They suggested that Hittite was a sister language, rather than a daughter language, of Indo-European, and proposed the new label **Indo-Hittite** for the family.

The subsequently deciphered Greek texts written in Linear B have now given us Greek materials contemporary with Hittite. With arguments from linguistic evidence, the Linear B texts have led Indo-Europeanists of today to retain the old label. One may explain the archaic features of Hittite by assuming that Hittite speakers made up the first group to leave the Indo-European community. Assumption of a considerable period of separation would also help to account for the innovations in Hittite.

Among the Hittite texts are found materials in two other related languages, **Luwian** and **Palaic**. Related texts in a different script dating from approximately 1400 to 500 B.C. have been given the name **Hieroglyphic (Hittite)**. The little known languages **Lycian** and **Lydian** are also now assumed to be related to Hittite, with Lycian the continuation of Luwian. The entire group is referred to as **Anatolian**, or **Hittito-Luwian**, and is considered a separate branch of the Indo-European family.

The discoveries in Asia Minor have broadened and deepened our knowledge of Indo-European. Hittite has preserved Indo-European palatals possibly because the change of some of these to sibilants took place after the Hittites left the Indo-European community. Hittite also has a grammatical system much simpler than that of Indo-Iranian and Greek, which earlier were taken as patterns for reconstructing the Indo-European grammatical system. Adequate studies have not yet been completed to modify this view; some Indo-Europeanists, however, have suggested that the complex verb systems of Indo-Iranian and Greek represent later developments rather than a retention from the parent language.

2.2.13 Reconstructed Proto-Indo-European.   With Hittite we are in a position to reconstruct Proto-Indo-European of a period before 3000 B.C. Older attempts to relate Indo-European with other language groups, such as Semitic, are accordingly obsolete. We now construct forms of Proto-Indo-European different from those in the standard handbooks of the late nineteenth-century Indo-Europeanists. A century and a half of work has not solved all problems concerning Indo-European. On the other hand, it has contributed excellent information on the development of the languages used by at least half the people living today. It has also provided the methods for determining and classifying other language families.

One of the most important tools in historical linguistics developed for genealogical classification is reconstruction of prior unattested forms, particularly in the parent language. Yet reconstructions must not be misused. They are merely concise statements of our information on the earliest stage of a language family. As a tour de force one may attempt, as August Schleicher did, to write a tale in Proto-Indo-European. One must then expect to have the tale rewritten as more information is assembled. Hermann Hirt rewrote Schleicher's tale in accordance with his views of Proto-Indo-European. Today, however, we no longer agree with many of Hirt's reconstructions. Discovery of unexpected early materials, like those in Hittite and Mycenaean Greek, has demonstrated the basic accuracy of our reconstructions; but reconstructions smell of the lamp even more than most scholarly products do and are best kept to serve their proper function as concise summaries of our current information.

2.3   Some unrelated languages

Further language families can merely be outlined here. Genealogical classification has become so intricate that a general handbook can aim only at a characterization of the state of research.

Some languages have not been related to any groups, and for lack of information may never be. One such is **Sumerian**, the language of southern Mesopotamia from about 4000 B.C. until it was replaced by Semitic languages. **Etruscan**, spoken in Italy until it was replaced by Latin, cannot yet be fully interpreted, let alone classified. **Basque**, of northern Spain, has no known relatives. Languages related to these either have died out without leaving texts, or they are so remotely connected that genealogical relationship is yet to be discovered.

The classification of other languages is uncertain because of the lack of descriptive studies, for example, those of Australia and Papua. Classification of the languages of South America is not much further advanced. Adequate descriptive materials are beginning to be made available, and accordingly genealogical classification may soon be undertaken with profit. Classification of the languages in other areas requiring considerable descriptive study, for example, those of Africa and Southeast Asia, is being pursued. [For current views one must consult monographs, articles, and reviews, which can be located through bibliographies.]

2.4   The Afro-Asiatic language family

The language family that has been most widely studied, after the Indo-European, is the **Hamito-Semitic**, expanded by Greenberg and renamed **Afro-Asiatic**.

The Afro-Asiatic family comprises five branches: **Egyptian** (1), one of the earliest languages attested, with records from the fourth millennium B.C. Its descendant known as **Coptic** after about the fourth century A.D. survives today as a religious language. **Berber** (2), **Cushitic** (3), **Chad** (4) are known only from recent times. To **Semitic** (5) belong some of the most important cultural languages of the past and present. **Akkadian**, the only representative of **East Semitic**, has been preserved in numerous cuneiform writings from about 2800 B.C. to the beginning of our era. **West Semitic** consists of two groups, **Aramaic-Canaanite** and **Arabic-Ethiopic**. One of the most important Canaanite languages was **Phoenician**, spoken in the area of Lebanon. It was carried to Carthage, and continued in use there as late as the sixth century A.D. Known as **Punic**, it is attested in a few inscriptions and some lines of Plautus.

A second Canaanite language, **Hebrew**, is attested from about 1100 B.C. It was introduced into Palestine, as we may note from *Genesis*, by a small group of nomads who, under the leadership of Abraham, wandered from the north into Palestine. Although Hebrew remained an important religious and literary language, it was largely replaced from the sixth century B.C. by **Aramaic**, which is attested in numerous dialects. In one of these, utterances of Jesus are cited in the *New Testament*, for example, Mark 5:41, *Talitha cumi*. Hebrew was revived as a spoken language around the beginning of this century.

Arabic was the last of the Semitic languages to be widely extended, with the spread of the Moslem religion and civilization. Its dialects are spoken today throughout much of the Middle East and North Africa. Like **Ethiopic**, of which several forms are spoken in Ethiopia, it is attested only after the beginning of our era. **Hausa** of the Chad group is one of the widely used languages of West Africa.

2.5   Other language families of Africa

Classification of the other language families of Africa has been the subject of much recent discussion. Greater assurance will require much careful, detailed work, such as that completed on the Indo-European family.

A large family to the south of the **Afro-Asiatic** is the **Chari-Nile**, or **Macro-Sudanic**, including Dinka and Shilluk. Apart from small or poorly defined groups, most of the other languages of Africa, including the **Bantu**, are classed in the **Niger-Congo** family. One of these, **Swahili**, a trade language, is used for communication through much of eastern Africa by speakers of a great variety of languages. The **Khoisan** family, including **Bushman** and **Hottentot**, is located on the southern borders of the Niger-Congo family.

2.6   Other language families of Asia

A large language family of Asia is the **Dravidian**, whose principal languages are spoken in south India. One of them, **Telugu**, has the second largest number of speakers in India. **Tamil**, with almost as many speakers, **Kannada**, and **Malayalam** are also important. Since the Dravidian language **Brahui** is still spoken in the north of India and in eastern Baluchistan, it has been suggested that Dravidian was the most widely distributed indigenous language family in India when Indo-European speakers invaded it near the end of the second millennium B.C. This suggestion has received support from the recent proposal that the Indus texts are Dravidian (see Chapter 4.10).

A language completely isolated, with no known related languages, is **Burushaski**, spoken in the northwest of India.

In eastern India and areas further to the east are spoken languages whose further classification is uncertain: **Munda**, **Mon-Khmer**, and

Annam-Muong. The leading investigator to concern himself with these languages, Pater Wilhelm Schmidt, grouped them together in an **Austroasiatic** family.

The **Malayo-Polynesian** languages spoken in southeast Asia and islands of the Pacific are divided into four groups, largely on the basis of geographical location: **Indonesian**, **Melanesian**, **Micronesian**, and **Polynesian**. Each has many dialects. **Bahasa Indonesia**, the language being developed into the national language of Indonesia and often known simply as **Indonesian**, is based on **Malay**, a language of Malaya that came to be used as a trade language in Indonesia. Since the Malayo-Polynesian family extends from Madagascar, where **Malagasy** is spoken, to Easter Island, and from Hawaii to New Zealand, it probably had the widest distribution of any language family until the recent expansion of the Indo-European.

Surveying the languages of north Asia, we may note first the Caucasian languages. There are two families, **North Caucasian** and **South Caucasian** or **Kartvelian**. **Georgian** is the most important member of South Caucasian. The North Caucasian family includes languages of great phonological interest because of their many consonants and few vowels.

Finno-Ugric, with an island of **Hungarian** speakers in Europe and nomadic speakers of **Lappish** in Scandinavia, extends eastward from Estonia through Russia far into Siberia, with **Mari** or **Cheremis**, **Mordvin**, and other subbranches. **Samoyedic**, spoken in far-eastern Siberia, is one of these; when Samoyedic is included with Finno-Ugric, the term **Uralic** is used for the family. The Finno-Ugric languages, with the exception of **Finnish** with four million and **Hungarian** or **Magyar** with fourteen million, are spoken by small numbers of speakers, and have been receding before other languages, notably Russian. With Indo-European and Hamito-Semitic, Finno-Ugric was one of the first families described. Subsequently it has been studied in detail and its interrelationships are well known.

Far to the east in Siberia the **Palaeo-Asiatic** or **Hyperborean** languages are spoken. Inadequately described, they may merely be a geographical group. We have not yet determined whether any of them are related to **Ainu**, which is spoken by a distinct cultural group and is apparently the indigenous language of Japan.

In the central belt of Asia we find the **Turkic** languages. Turkic speakers made numerous incursions from this area after the beginning of our era. Through one incursion **Osmanli**, generally known as **Turkish**, was established in Turkey and is today the most widely spoken Turkic language. Approximately twenty other Turkic languages, spoken chiefly in southern Siberia, have been receding before Russian. Of these, **Uzbek** is the predominant language of the area around Tashkent, **Azerbaijani** of the area around Baku.

The Turkic languages are often classified with the **Mongol** and **Manchu-Tungus** languages in the **Altaic** family. With the exception of Turkic inscriptions from the eighth century, languages of these groups are attested from the last millennium. The classification of these three groups into one large family is made in part on the basis of typological criteria. A further hypothesis is sometimes proposed that the **Finno-Ugric** languages are to be related to Altaic, and the combined group is referred to as **Ural-Altaic**. This hypothesis is highly tentative.

To the hypothetical Ural-Altaic group two isolated languages are sometimes joined, **Korean** and **Japanese**. Evidence for demonstrating further relationship, however, is so scanty that they cannot be convincingly related with each other, let alone with the broader group. To illustrate the difficulties, we may review that portion of the Japanese numerals remaining after the classifier has been removed (see page 10). We then are left with:

1 hi(to)	4 yo	7 nana	10 tō
2 fu(ta)	5 i	8 ya	
3 mi	6 mu	9 koko	

It is scarcely remarkable that such short and simple forms would be difficult to relate further, especially since as we noted above *mi mu, yo ya hi fu* may be analyzed as of two morphemes each. Only the **Luchuan** dialects, which are not far removed from the Japanese, can be related to Japanese. The complexity of syllabic structure exhibited by the Indo-European languages has greatly helped linguists to verify their inter-relationships and to assemble the detailed information we have on their history today.

The remaining languages of Asia belong to the **Sino-Tibetan** linguistic family, which is of great importance for its present distribution and for the antiquity of its documents. It consists of **Tibeto-Burman** and **(Thai-) Chinese**. Tibeto-Burman comprises **Tibetan**, which is attested from the seventh century A.D., **Burmese**, and other languages in and near Burma. (Thai-)Chinese includes various languages in Thailand and the area to the east of it, as well as the dialects of China.

Since one writing system is used throughout China, the assumption is sometimes made that **Chinese** comprises one language. Actually, it consists of as many as nine mutually unintelligible languages, each with subdialects. The writing system that enables their speakers to intercommunicate on paper was also adapted for the totally unrelated Japanese; it could be used more widely, but contemporary demands on time seem to make retention of a system of thousands of symbols difficult, and the Chinese have taken steps toward use of an alphabetic system. If an alphabetic system is established, the Chinese will need to select for intercommunication one of their languages, probably a Mandarin dialect.

Starting from the south, the nine Chinese languages are: **Cantonese**, **Kan-Hakka**, **Amoy-Swatow**, **Foochow**, **Wu** (spoken around Shanghai), **Hsiang**, and three subgroups of **Mandarin**: **Yellow River Basin** and **Manchurian** (1), **Southern** (2), and **Southwestern** (3). With the expansion of the Chinese population, it is difficult to know the number of speakers of these languages; Mandarin is probably used as a first language by more speakers than is any other language.

Chinese has been preserved in inscriptions on bone and bronzes from the second millennium B.C.; literary documents of some length, such as the works of Confucius and Lao-tzu, have come down to us from the first millennium B.C. The materials before the sixth century A.D. are generally referred to as **Archaic Chinese**. **Old** or **Ancient Chinese** is dated from the sixth to the tenth centuries, **Middle Chinese** from the tenth to the thirteenth, and **New Chinese** from then to the present. Since Chinese has always been written in logographic characters, even in earliest times, there are problems in determining the spoken form of the languages. For examples, see Chapter 4:9. The spoken forms are posited partly with the help of borrowings into Japanese and Korean, partly with rhyming dictionaries. The borrowings inform us primarily about the beginnings of morphs; rhyming dictionaries, about their ends. In this way it is possible to reconstruct the pronunciation of Archaic Chinese and to use it for comparison with other languages of the family. From the work done we can suggest that the monosyllabism of present Chinese morphs results from the loss of final elements.

In spite of the wealth of material, many problems in (Thai-)Chinese studies have scarcely been touched. There is even doubt about the relationship of Thai to Chinese. Among other suggestions is the classification of Thai with **Laotian** and **Shan** into a separate family, labeled **Kadai**, and related further to Malayo-Polynesian. The resemblances between Thai and Chinese are then ascribed to borrowing. Further study will lead to numerous interesting contributions on historical linguistics, and possibly also on the interrelationship of literate peoples in the second millennium B.C.

The languages of Australia and Papua have been adequately studied only in very recent times. Genealogical classification will accordingly be a task of the future. While the term **Papuan** is used for more than 700 languages, it is simply a geographical designation.

2.7 Genealogical classification of the languages of America

Few of the native languages of America are well known from earlier than the nineteenth century. Spanish invaders preserved texts in Aztec, Mayan, and a few other languages from the sixteenth century. North American missionaries translated the Bible into Alkonkin languages, preserving somewhat earlier forms than those of today. Unfortunately, few Americans advocated study of the indigenous languages of America; one of these few was Thomas Jefferson. In the absence of early texts, we must attempt to classify the families of American Indian languages almost entirely with contemporary materials, which themselves are often inadequate.

Two types of classification have been produced. Under the leadership of J. W. Powell, fifty-four language families were proposed in 1891 in a classification based primarily on lexical evidence.

A different type of classification was introduced by E. Sapir in 1929. Employing bolder methods of determining relationship, Sapir proposed linguistic *stocks*, on the basis of broad structural similarity. He thus reduced Powell's fifty-four families to six stocks: **Eskimo-Aleut**, **Na-Déné**, **Algonkin-Wakashan** (for George Trager **Algonkian-Mosan**), **Hokan-Siouan**, **Penutian**, **Aztec-Tanoan**. Trager subsequently classed together Penutian and Aztec-Tanoan into **Macro-Penutian**. **Navaho**, the native language of the largest group of speakers in North America, belongs to the Athabascan subgroup of Na-Déné.

Such classification is also being attempted for the twenty-three language families of Mexico and Central America. Until recently most of these have been very inadequately known. Of these **Mayan**, with more than twenty languages, is the largest family. Even more poorly known are the languages of South America, of which seventy-five families or more have been proposed. One of these, **Quechua**, is widely used today in Peru and Bolivia. Another, Guaraní, is one of the official languages of Paraguay. But most of the native languages of South America are undergoing the fate of those elsewhere in the hemisphere. Yet on the basis of descriptive work now being undertaken, we will be able to supplement previous classifications and proceed to broader classifications of the type proposed by Sapir for the North American languages.

2.8 Evidence used for genealogical classification

Although we welcome classification of the type proposed by Sapir, it must not be equated with that made on the basis of reconstructions and other techniques relied on by the great historical linguists of the past. Besides reconstructions Meillet laid great weight on characteristic features found only in segments of a system. One such is the alternation between *-r-* and *-n-* in the inflection of some Indo-European nouns; a trace of this survives in the *r* of English *water* versus the *n* of Norwegian *vatn*. Another example is the alternation between the stem vowel *o* in the Indo-European perfect singular and no vowel in the plural; again a trace survives in English, in the alternation of vowels in *was* versus *were*. Individual vocabulary items on the other hand are among the least characteristic features of language, for, as we have seen, they can be readily borrowed. General structural features can also be transferred from language to language. By contrast with earlier genealogical classification, vocabulary and general structure are the chief criteria for the gross classifications used on American Indian and African languages today. There is, accordingly, a difference between the methods; the results must also be viewed differently.

It is doubtful whether genealogical classification like that practiced by Meillet can ever be carried out on languages that separated five or more millennia ago and that are attested only today. If one compares contemporary Hindi with contemporary Russian, evidence for relationship, and bases for genealogical classification are not great. Genealogical classification is admirably suited to determine the interrelationships of languages such as the Indo-European for which we have many records from several millennia. For languages attested only today, we may not be able to trace the genealogical relationships, certainly not in the detail attained for the Indo-European family, and not for such a time-depth.

Selected Further Readings

The most recent comprehensive compilation on language families is *Les langues du monde*, prepared in a second edition (Paris, 1952) by a group of linguists under the direction of Marcel Cohen, though the names A. Meillet and M. Cohen have been maintained from the first edition. There is a set of accompanying maps, and also, on pages xvii–xlii, a useful bibliography. Louis Gray's *Foundations of Language* (New York, 1939) contains the last large scholarly treatment made available in English, with bibliographies, pages 295–418. Pater W. Schmidt's *Die Sprachfamilien und Sprachenkreise der Erde* (Heidelberg, 1926) is notable for a fine atlas.

For a statement of the Proto-Indo-Hittite hypothesis, see the last chapter of *An Introduction to Linguistic Science* by E. H. Sturtevant (New Haven, 1947). A. Schleicher's fable is reprinted in *Die Hauptprobleme der indogermanischen Sprachwissenschaft* by H. Hirt, edited by H. Arntz (Halle, 1939). After presenting Schleicher's fable, page 113, Hirt rewrites it according to his views of Indo-European. Today we would introduce further changes, partly because we would take into account the data provided by Hittite.

For current views on genealogical classifications, one should consult special handbooks, monographs, and articles dealing with individual language families or even individual languages. Encyclopedias should not be neglected. E. Sapir's article reclassifying the Indian languages of North America appeared in Volume 5, pages 138–41, of the fourteenth edition of the *Encyclopaedia Britannica* (1929). Subsequent editions of this encyclopedia, as well as other encyclopedias, have commissioned articles on language families by leading linguists. As an example of a comprehensive attempt at reclassification, J. Greenberg's *The Languages of Africa* (Bloomington, 1966, reprint) will remain fundamental for some time, though for current views on the languages of Africa, subsequent reviews and restatements must be consulted. Because of the great amount of work under way on poorly described languages, because of efforts to classify them genealogically, and because of the introduction of more rigorous classifications, current views on any language family must be determined from recent special books or reports and from the journals. Notable among these is the journal *Anthropological Linguistics*, fascicles of which have been devoted to language families or subgroupings.

CHAPTER 3

Typological classification of languages

3.1 Typological classification in the nineteenth century

From the beginnings of historical linguistics, attempts were made to classify languages by types rather than by their origins and genealogical relationships. In 1818, the year before Jacob Grimm began the publication of his grammar of the Germanic languages, which did much to develop the principles of historical linguistics, August von Schlegel proposed a typological classification that was widely followed and elaborated through the nineteenth century. It still has popular currency.

According to this classification, languages may be **analytic (isolating** or **root**—with no inflection) like Chinese or Vietnamese; or they may be **synthetic (inflectional)** like Latin and Greek. The agglutinative languages, like Turkish and Japanese, were often assumed to make up a transitional class. **Agglutinative** languages are differentiated from inflectional languages because they maintain bases distinct from endings and show little morphophonemic change at morpheme boundaries; moreover, they have few suppletive forms like those in *good, better, best*. Contrast the Turkish inflections of *yol* 'way' and *kuş* 'bird' with those of Latin *via* and *avis*:

Nominative	yol	via	kuş	avis
Genitive	yolun	viae	kuşun	avis
Dative .	yola	viae	kuşa	avī

| _Accusative_ | yolu | viam | kuşu | avem |
| _Ablative_ | yoldan | viā | kuştan | avī |

The Turkish endings can be neatly separated from the stem and are the same for both examples; in Latin the endings have merged with the vowel of the base and can only be determined by historical methods. By means of such methods, we can propose that the stems of 'way' and 'bird' are *via- and *avi-, and that the endings on these two nouns are parallel to each other; but, as in other inflected languages, we cannot sort out the endings as readily as we can those of agglutinative languages.

When we examine Proto-Indo-European, we can separate the endings almost as if they were affixed as in Turkish. This transparency was interpreted by early nineteenth-century scholars as indicating that inflectional languages developed from agglutinative. Although this nineteenth-century view was based on surface phenomena, and hence on externals of language, the intent behind it illustrates the importance of typological classification for historical linguistics. If we can determine specific frameworks to classify the components of various types of languages, we will be able to use them in studying language change.

A framework of sounds has been used for some time in studying phonological systems. In some of the most important linguistic work of the last decade, a framework for syntactic systems has now been produced; with its help we can relate some syntactic characteristics with specific sentence patterns. As a result we now can deal with syntactic change in much the way historical linguists of the past have dealt with phonological change. For just as phonological systems are never completely in balance, so syntactic systems are not completely consistent within a standard framework. Inconsistencies within a syntactic framework may be accounted for as the results of historical change.

A framework for semantic systems would permit us to deal as rigorously with semantic change as we have with phonological change. Until now only partial frameworks have been produced, as for kinship systems. Since these pertain to so little of the language, they will not be discussed in this chapter but will be examined in the chapter on semantic change (see Chapter 12).

3.2   Typological classification based on surface features

The most complete typology based on surface features is that of F. N. Finck. It is instructive to review it in order to understand the achievements of earlier typological studies, and their shortcomings.

Finck viewed man's use of speech as consisting of two essential processes:

1. Analysis, that is, analyzing a real situation into its components.
2. Synthesis, that is, restoring it to a whole by means of the words of language.

We might choose as an illustrative situation a man approaching; this would be analyzed into two components: an actor and an action. In synthesis a Chinese speaker reports this situation by matching each component with a word: $t'a^1$ 'he' lai^2 'come.' A Turkish speaker would use only one word: *geliyor*, combining the two situational elements. An English speaker would use three, *he is coming*, introducing more words than there are components in the situation.

According to the analysis of the situation, Finck assumed eight types, represented by the following languages:

Eskimo (one word includes several elements of the situation)
Turkish
Georgian   (intermediate between Eskimo and Chinese)
Arabic
Chinese (one word corresponds to one element of the situation)
Greek
Samoan   (intermediate between Chinese and Subiya)
Subiya, a Bantu language (one word corresponds to less than one element of the situation)

As with his classification for synthesis, languages are not required to fit these selected types exactly. English, using more words than there are elements in a situation, would fall between Chinese and Subiya.

According to synthesis, these languages are arranged quite differently. Now at one pole stands Chinese, in which each word is isolated, uninflected, and equivalent to a root. At the other pole stands Eskimo, in which a word incorporates a variety of elements, though as in two other types they are not combined with the base. Between these fall the inflected languages.

Isolating	Chinese	root-isolating
	Samoan	stem-isolating
Inflected	Arabic	root-inflected
	Greek	stem-inflected
	Georgian	group-inflected
Elements Not	Subiya	juxtaposing
Combined	Turkish	agglutinative
with Base	Eskimo	polysynthetic or incorporating

Sapir, Finck's most notable successor in typological classification, provided a format based largely on semantic features. His classification resulted in two basic types of languages, *Language* 150–51. 1. Pure-relational languages like Chinese, in which "radical concepts" such as *book*, *give*, *large* and "abstract ideas" such as those expressed by -*s*, -*n*, -*r* in *books*, *given*, *larger* are not "mixed"; 2. those like English in which they are combined. The expression of "derivational concepts," such as -*ish*, -*y*, -*ness* in which the significance of radical elements is not modified by affixes or internal change, distinguishes simple from complex subtypes. In simple subtypes the relational concepts do not modify the radical elements, while in complex subtypes they do. For example, -*ish* added to *book* not only yields a new English word but it also modifies the concept underlying *book*; not everyone who reads books is bookish. Examples of these classifications are:

1.
    A. Simple pure-relational: Chinese
    B. Complex pure-relational: Turkish
2.
    C. Simple mixed-relational: Bantu
    D. Complex mixed-relational: English, Latin, Greek.

Sapir also set up subclassifications and made a start toward quantitative indication of features; but his classifications, like those of Finck, are difficult to compare from language to language. Joseph H. Greenberg attempted to solve this problem by suggesting that classification of languages for their types be replaced by rankings for individual criteria (*IJAL* 1960).

Instead of labeling a language as synthetic or analytic, Greenberg proposed that a synthetic index, among others, be determined for any given language. Greenberg's synthetic index indicates the ratio of morphs per word in a given language. Sapir's sentence (1) *The* (2) *farm* (3) *er* (4) *kill* (5) *s* (6) *the* (7) *duck* (8) *ling* yields a synthetic index of 1.6, for it consists of eight morphs and five words. In selected examples, Greenberg found the synthetic index to be 1.68 for English, 3.72 for Eskimo, 1.06 for Vietnamese.

After such values have been determined, they may be used for comparison between languages, or languages may be given rank orders for any index. But since surface features may not represent the "structure" of languages directly, typological classification based on them has not brought the advantages to historical linguistic study that would result from a typological classification based on underlying features.

3.3   Typological classification based on underlying phonological elements and their arrangements

The primary elements that have been used in phonological classification are phonemes and their arrangements. Among the arrangements studied are configurations of vowel phonemes arranged in accordance with their place and manner of articulation. Some languages have a triangular system of vowels, such as that of the short vowels of some Arabic dialects:

i   u

a

or the system of five short vowels in Classical Latin:

i   u

e   o

a

or the system of seven short vowels of contemporary Italian:

i   u

e   o

ϵ   ɔ

a

Other languages have rectangular systems, such as Tonkawa:

i   o

e   a

or Turkish, with its eight-vowel system:

i   ü   ı   u

e   ö   a   o

or English, with the nine-vowel system proposed by some linguists:

i   ɨ   u

e   ə   o

æ   a   ɔ

Such configurations assist us in understanding rearrangements resulting from sound changes. For example, the Latin system was expanded in Italian, but the basic configuration was maintained. The New High German system, which developed from a short vowel system in Old High German similar to that of Latin, introduced front rounded vowels, *ü* and *ö*, modifying the system in a different way from Italian:

i   ü   u

e   ö   o

a

Yet in both Italian and German the development that led to the new system can readily be understood on the basis of the earlier configuration. Specialists have determined the specific changes in each language that led to the changed system.

Configurations like those given above are based on only a few distinctive features: height, backness, and rounding of vowels. Two degrees of height are evident in Arabic, Tonkawa, and Turkish; three in Classical Latin, English, and German; four in Italian. Two degrees of frontness or backness are evident in Tonkawa and three in English. The apparent four of Turkish are found in a system with three.characteristic features: height, backness, and rounding. For a precise account of the changes in languages, it is advantageous to compare the use of all distinctive features in phonological systems, as we will note below.

Consonant systems too may be classified for configuration of phonemes. English has a relatively large number of fricatives and relatively few stops; moreover, all these obstruents have voiceless and voiced pairs.

p		t		č	k	
b		d		ǰ	g	
	f	θ		s	š	
	v	ð		z	ž	
m		n			ŋ	
w		r	l	y		h

Sanskrit, on the other hand, has a large number of stops, few fricatives, and a symmetrical arrangement of aspirated and nonaspirated stops.

p	t	ṭ	c	k
ph	th	ṭh	ch	kh
b	d	ḍ	j	g
bh	dh	ḍh	jh	gh
m	n	[ṇ	n	ŋ]
	v l r		y	
	s	ṣ	ś		h

If we compare with the current English consonant system that of Old English, we find that the voiced members of the fricative and affricate series developed in late Old English times or subsequently. After they developed, the opposition of voicing is found among all English obstruents. In early Sanskrit, voiceless aspirates were introduced, contrasting with the voiced aspirates, as in the dental position:

t	th
d	dh

As with vowel systems, the configurations of consonants assist us in understanding changes that have occurred.

3.4   Typological classification based on distinctive features

In addition to comparing configurations of phonemes, one may compare the use of all distinctive features in phonological systems. Distinctive features have been proposed for various articulatory and acoustic characteristics. If classified for the distinctive features proposed by Roman Jakobson, the stop systems of Czech and French pattern like the vowel systems of Wichita and Arabic:

	CZECH		FRENCH		WICHITA		ARABIC	
Diffuse	t	p	t	p	i	u	i	u
Compact	c	k		k	æ	a		a
	Acute Grave		Acute Grave		Acute Grave		Acute Grave	

We would expect the systems illustrated here to be subject to different modifications, in accordance with the use of distinctive features.

To illustrate the analysis of an entire phonemic system for its distinctive features, the set of Proto-Indo-European and Proto-Germanic phonemes is presented here. It should be noted that the terms used for distinctive features are still in flux; those used in the charts below are based on Chomsky and Halle, *Sound Pattern*. Further, the binary principle itself has been severely challenged. Even more important in historical linguistics, the specific distinctive features for individual phonemes are uncertain. Thus PGmc. /f θ χ/ have been analyzed as $\langle +tense \rangle$ by some specialists, even though this analysis is unlikely in view of the subsequent developments of these phonemes in the Germanic dialects. These uncertainties, even in the long-studied fields of Germanic and Indo-European linguistics, illustrate the problems faced by historical linguists as they attempt to provide better understanding of phonological developments and sound changes in the past.

With a distinctive feature analysis, one can point precisely to the changes introduced in systems. Proto-Germanic, for example, extended continuant articulation in contrast with Proto-Indo-European. On the other hand, the tense articulation of consonants was reduced, in the changes of PIE /bh dh gh/. Moreover, as we will note further below, the changes from Proto-Indo-European to Proto-Germanic, and from Proto-Germanic to the various Germanic dialects can be carefully described by means of a system based on distinctive features (see Chapters 9 and 10).

Distinctive Features of Late Proto-Indo-European phonological system

	OBSTRUENTS													LARYNGEALS				RESONANTS						VOWELS								
	p	b	bh	t	d	dh	k	g	gh	kʷ	gʷ	gʷh	s	χ	γ	ʔ	h	m	n	r	l	y	w	e	a	o	i	ē	ā	ō	ū	ι
Vocalic	−	−	−	−	−	−	−	−	−	−	−	−	−	−	−	−	−	−	−	−	−	−	−	+	+	+	+	+	+	+	+	+
Resonant	−	−	−	−	−	−	−	−	−	−	−	−	−	−	−	−	−	+	+	+	+	+	+	+	+	+	+	+	+	+	+	+
Consonantal	+	+	+	+	+	+	+	+	+	+	+	+	+	+	+	+	+	+	+	+	+	−	−	−	−	−	−	−	−	−	−	+
High	−	−	−	−	−	−	+	+	+	+	+	+	−	+	+	−	−	−	−	−	−	+	+	−	−	−	+	−	−	−	+	+
Back	−	−	−	−	−	−	+	+	+	+	+	+	−	+	+	−	−	−	−	−	−	−	+	−	+	+	−	−	+	+	+	+
Low	−	−	−	−	−	−	−	−	−	−	−	−	−	−	−	−	+	−	−	−	−	−	−	−	+	−	−	−	+	−	−	−
Anterior	+	+	+	+	+	+	−	−	−	−	−	−	+	−	−	−	−	+	+	+	+	−	−	−	−	−	−	−	−	−	−	−
Coronal	−	−	−	+	+	+	−	−	−	−	−	−	+	−	−	−	−	−	+	+	+	−	−	−	−	−	−	−	−	−	−	−
Round	−	−	−	−	−	−	−	−	−	+	+	+	−	−	+	−	−	−	−	−	−	−	+	−	−	+	−	−	−	+	+	−
Tense	+	−	−	+	−	−	+	−	−	+	−	−	+	+	+	−	+	−	−	−	−	−	−	−	−	−	+	+	+	+	+	−
Continuant	−	−	−	−	−	−	−	−	−	−	−	−	+	+	+	−	+	−	−	+	+	+	+	−	−	−	+	+	−	+	+	−
Voiced	−	+	+	−	+	+	−	+	+	−	+	+	−	−	+	−	−	+	+	+	+	+	+	+	+	+						
Nasal	−	−	−	−	−	−	−	−	−	−	−	−	−	−	−	−	−	+	+	−	−	−	−									
Strident	−	−	−	−	−	−	−	−	−	−	−	−	+	−	−	−	−	−	−	−	−	−	−									

Distinctive features of the Late Proto-Germanic phonological system

	p	f	b	t	θ	ð	k	x	g	kʷ	xʷ	gʷ	s	z	m	n	r	l	y	w	i	e	a	u	ī	ē	ā	ū
Vocalic	−	−	−	−	−	−	−	−	−	−	−	−	−	−	−	−	+	+	−	−	+	+	+	+	+	+	+	+
Resonant	−	−	−	−	−	−	−	−	−	−	−	−	−	−	+	+	+	+	+	+	+	+	+	+	+	+	+	+
Consonantal	+	+	+	+	+	+	+	+	+	+	+	+	+	+	+	+	+	+	−	−	−	−	−	−	−	−	−	−
High	−	−	−	−	−	−	+	+	+	+	+	+	−	−	−	−	−	−	+	+	+	−	−	+	+	−	−	+
Back	−	−	−	−	−	−	+	+	+	+	+	+	−	−	−	−	−	−	−	+	−	−	+	+	−	−	+	+
Low	−	−	−	−	−	−	−	−	−	−	−	−	−	−	−	−	−	−	−	−	−	−	+	−	−	−	+	−
Anterior	+	+	+	+	+	+	−	−	−	−	−	−	+	+	+	+	+	+	−	−	−	−	−	−	−	−	−	−
Coronal	−	−	−	+	+	+	−	−	−	−	−	−	+	+	−	+	+	+	−	−	−	−	−	−	−	−	−	−
Round	−	−	−	−	−	−	−	−	−	+	+	+	−	−	−	−	−	−	−	+	−	−	−	+	−	−	−	+
Tense	+	+	−	+	+	−	+	+	−	+	+	−	+	−	−	−	−	−	−	−	−	−	−	−	+	+	+	+
Continuant	−	+	−	−	+	+	−	+	−	−	+	−	+	+	−	−	+	+	+	+								
Voiced	−	−	+	−	−	+	−	−	+	−	−	+	−	+	+	+	+	+	+	+								
Nasal	−	−	−	−	−	−	−	−	−	−	−	−	−	−	+	+	−	−	−	−								
Strident	−	+	−	−	−	−	−	−	−	−	−	−	+	+	−	−	−	−	−	−								

3.5 Typological classification based on syntactic characteristics

In an important essay in *Universals of Language*, Greenberg pointed out that the normal position of verbs with regard to their objects in a language is correlated with the position of elements in other syntactic patterns, such as relative constructions. If verbs normally precede their objects, relative constructions follow their antecedents, as do adjectives and possessives. Moreover, languages with V(erb)-O(bject) order have prepositions rather than postpositions, and comparatives with the standard following the adjective and the pivot.

If, on the other hand, objects precede their verbs (OV languages), the order in these constructions is reversed.

To illustrate these syntactic arrangements, we may note the cited constructions in a verb-object (VO) and in an object-verb (OV) language, both of which are consistent in type. As our VO example we select Portuguese; as our OV language, Japanese. The constructions illustrated are listed first, followed by the English equivalent of the sentences in Portuguese and Japanese.

1.a Normal word order in declarative sentences. "John saw the dog."
1.b   "Mary saw the cat."
2.   Relative construction. "John saw the dog that ate the meat."
3.   Descriptive adjective. "John saw the big dog."
4.   Possessive construction. "John saw the dog of his neighbor."
5.   Preposition/postposition. "John saw the dog from the window."
6.   Comparative construction. "The dog is bigger than the cat."

	VO	OV
1.a	João viu o cachorro.	Tarō ga inu o mita.
	John saw the dog.	Taro dog saw.
1.b	Maria viu o gato.	Jirō ga neku o mita.
	Mary saw the cat.	Jiro cat saw.
2.	João viu o cachorro que comen a carne.	Tarō ga niku o tabeta inu o mita.
	John saw the dog that ate the meat.	Taro meat ate dog saw.
3.	João viu o cachorro grande.	Tarō ga takai inu o mita.
	John saw the dog big.	Taro big dog saw.
4.	João viu o cachorro do siu vizinho.	Tarō ga kinjo no hito no inu o mita.
	John saw the dog of his neighbor.	Taro neighborhood's man's dog saw.

5. João viu da janela o cachorro.   Tarō ga mado yori inu o mita.
    John saw from-the window the   Taro window from dog   saw.
    dog.
6. O cachorro é maior que o gato.   Inu ga neku yori takai.
    The dog   is larger than the cat. Dog   cat from large.

In applying such frameworks, several cautions are important. The patterns given here are the normal ones; normal patterns, or "unmarked patterns" according to Jakobson's terminology, are often modified for emphasis; they are then said to be "marked". For example, in Portuguese the verb may also be initial in the sentence *Viu João o cachorro*. This order is used to single out the verb. In view of the possibility of reordering sentence elements in marked constructions, it may be difficult to determine the normal order of sentences when we are dealing with languages of the past. The difficulty is compounded by the kinds of texts that have survived; these are often poetic, which make great use of "marked constructions." Therefore, it is advisable to locate constructions that have normal, unmarked word order.

The most secure of these is the comparative; it is never changed for poetic effect; an English poet would never say "He you from is better," even though he might use postposed adjectives, as in "This is the forest primeval," or irregular position of standard and pivot, as in "He than you is better."

Another syntactic construction that is relatively secure is found when two sentences with one of the same elements are coordinated; for example, "John saw the dog (and) Mary saw the cat." When such sentences are coordinated, the repeated verb may be omitted in a phenomenon labeled "gapping"; for example, "John saw the dog and Mary the cat." When gapping involves verbs with objects, as in this example, the verb is maintained in the first sentence of consistent VO languages. In consistent OV languages, on the other hand, it is maintained in the last. Compare the gapping constructions of Portuguese and Japanese for the sentence: "John saw the dog and Mary the cat." *João viu o cachorro e Maria o gato. Tarō ga inu o to Jirō ga neku o mita.* If we can find examples of the comparative construction and of gapping in texts, we may determine the underlying order of sentences, and accordingly the basic type of the language in which the texts are written.

3.6 Syntactic frameworks as a measure of change

As we noted above, not all languages are consistent in type. We must label English as VO on the basis of its comparative construction and the gapping of verbs with objects, and because of the normal VO word order. Yet

English is inconsistent in having adjectives precede nouns. We will discuss this construction in greater detail in the chapter dealing with syntactic change. But here we may note that older forms of English exhibit even more OV characteristics than the position of the adjective. For example, the Old English *Beowulf* even contains examples of OV comparative constructions, as in line 1850: *þæt þē Sǣ-Gēatas sēlran næbben* (that from-you the Sea-Geats a better would not have) 'that the Sea-Geats would have no one better than you.' Moreover, the greater proportion of sentences in the old portion of the *Anglo-Saxon Chronicle* have OV order. We may therefore conclude that English has been changing from an OV language to a VO language, and that some OV characteristics have not yet been eliminated, such as the position of adjectives before nouns.

In much the same way, we may analyze any language for distinctive typological criteria and for inconsistencies. If we find inconsistent constructions, we attempt to determine the reasons for them.

Portuguese, as we noted, is consistently VO; so are the other Romance languages. On the other hand, Classical Latin exhibits many OV characteristics, such as the comparative construction illustrated in *tē major* 'greater than you.' Because of the many OV constructions in Latin and Old English, we conclude that earlier forms of these languages were OV, and that Proto-Indo-European was OV. This conclusion is supported by evidence from the oldest Indo-European texts in Hittite, Vedic Sanskrit, and Greek.

If we examine the modern Indo-European languages, we find that the Asiatic branches are OV in structure (Indo-Aryan and Armenian), the southern European languages are consistently VO (Albanian, Greek and Italic-Romance, as well as Celtic, which have the verb in initial position), and that the northern Indo-European languages, beginning with Iranian, are inconsistently VO (Persian, Slavic, Baltic, Germanic). Determining the bases of these developments will be one of the important areas of study for Indo-Europeanists in the future. And as the methods devised for historical phonology were applied to the study of other languages, in much the same way the methods developed in the study of the syntactic changes of the Indo-European languages will be of importance for general historical linguistic study.

3.7 Prospects of typological classification for historical linguistics

Although the chief aim of typology is classification of languages, it has provided new techniques for historical study. Typological classification applied at selected stages of languages enables us to mark their development on the basis of verifiable criteria. This classification is not based on a selected segment of the vocabulary, but includes borrowings, which hamper genealogical classification. Albanian, Armenian, and English, with their many borrowings, can in this way be characterized as readily as are the more conservative Indo-European languages like Lithuanian or Sanskrit.

The presence of specific characteristics permits inferences about the history of languages. For example, the VSO order of Irish has been ascribed to influence of a non-Indo-European language. The inconsistent feature of adjective order in current English may also be a result of influence from another language. Eventually we may be able to propose a theory concerning the interrelationships between all components of language, dealing with such observations as the remarkable preponderance of agglutinative structure in OV languages. Typological classification has provided important observations for historical linguistic study, which will lead to great improvement in our understanding of change in language.

Selected Further Readings

Introductions to earlier typological classification are given in Edward Sapir's *Language* (New York, 1921), especially Chapter VI, "Types of Linguistic Structures," and in F. N. Finck's *Die Haupttypen des Sprachbaus* (Berlin and Leipzig, 1909). For the typology of phonological systems, a fundamental work is N. S. Trubetzkoy's *Grundzüge der Phonologie* (Prague, 1939), now translated as *Principles of Phonology* by Christiane A. M. Baltaxe (Berkeley and Los Angeles, 1969).

The distinctive features proposed by Jakobson are presented in *Fundamentals of Language*, by Roman Jakobson and Morris Halle (The Hague, 1956), pp. 29–32. More recent treatments are given in *Introduction to Phonological Theory*, by Robert T. Harms (Englewood Cliffs (N.J.), 1968), *The Sound Pattern of English*, by Noam Chomsky and Morris Halle (New York, 1968), and *Preliminaries to Linguistic Phonetics*, by Peter Ladefoged (Chicago, 1971); Ladefoged reviews critically the phonetic analysis proposed by Chomsky and Halle. For syntactic classification, see *Universals of Language*, 2nd ed., edited by Joseph H. Greenberg (Cambridge (Mass.), 1966.

CHAPTER 4

The use of written records

4.1 On the importance of understanding writing systems and their transliteration

Materials of concern in historical linguistics are available primarily through written records called **texts**. In order to interpret texts adequately, a historical linguist must be equipped to deal with the writing system used to record them, even though he generally uses a standard transliteration. These, however, are often inadequate, occasionally even inaccurate; Greek *phi*, *theta*, *khi*, as here, are transliterated with two symbols and, therefore, in transliteration lack parallelism with other Greek consonants, such as *p b t d k g*, even though they are quite parallel with them in Greek writing and phonology. Similarly Sanskrit *bh dh gh* are the traditional transliterations for writing symbols quite parallel to those for Sanskrit *p t k*, etc. The transliteration for Sanskrit aspirated stops has introduced into historical linguistics the further inconvenience of two symbols for some single phonemes in Proto-Indo-European. Such troublesome transliterations can even become misleading to one who does not know their background. We cannot expect revisions that will remove such transliterational shortcomings, for the small number of historical linguists are expected to have enough energy to master oddities in transliteration.

On the grounds that these would complicate the use of older handbooks, historical linguists have persistently rejected most attempts to modify transliterations. Thus, one of the first tasks of a historical linguist is to master the writing systems of the languages with which he is concerned and their standard transliterations.

In addition, historical linguists must understand the principles underlying writing systems. For, in spite of considerable investigation, the interpretation of some symbols, even in languages as thoroughly studied as Gothic, is still disputed. And new writing systems may be encountered, such as those discovered in Crete and now partially deciphered, or that discovered in Mohenjo-Daro and other sites in the Indus Valley, for which a decipherment has been proposed. The writing system used for English, like those used today for all the other Indo-European languages, developed from the Egyptian. By following its development, we can observe the principles of development in writing, and some of the problems we face in dealing with texts.

4.2   The origin of writing systems

The origin of writing is unknown. It may have resulted from attempts at artistic expression, like the animal figures found in caves in Europe and Africa, or from attempts to depict figures for magical or religious purposes. Such figures may be compared with representations still used today, which have no direct relationship with language. Hunters in Africa may prop up a stick to indicate to another party the direction of their chase. Symbols reproduced on wampum belts by American Indians also represented a situation, with no attempt to depict its pronunciation in any selected language. Without understanding Indian languages, the English-speaking William Penn was able to interpret the wampum belt recording his treaty. Such efforts to symbolize situations rather than speech, we consider precursors of writing; we speak of writing systems only when symbols have been devised to represent elements of the language.

In the history of mankind only three writing systems have been devised that have gone through a long series of development and adaptation for various languages: those of Egypt, Sumer, and China. They may actually have a common origin. Our data on their possible earlier relationship are inadequate. Only the Egyptian has been developed to an alphabet, a contribution of the Greeks (see, however, 4.8 and 4.9). From a history of the Egyptian, through its adaptation for West Semitic languages, for Greek, for Latin, and from it to the languages of Europe, the development of writing systems may be noted.

4.3   Development of the Egyptian writing system

The earliest Egyptian texts we know, from the latter part of the fourth millennium B.C., already show the features of an advanced writing system. This consists of approximately 500 symbols, known as **hieroglyphs**. Many of these are pictorial representations of the object represented by the word they stand for: a representation of a head stands for *tp* 'head'; a representation of a hand stands for *drt* 'hand'; a representation of a lotus stands for *sšn* 'lotus.' (Vowels were left undesignated by the Egyptians whenever they used their semialphabetic system. Although Egyptologists have been able to determine the vowels of many words, the transcriptions of hieroglyphs generally do not indicate them.)

Other hieroglyphs are less directly related to the words they stand for. A representation of a seated man with his hand at his mouth stands for *wnm* 'eat'; a representation of a falcon may stand for *nsw* 'king.' Hieroglyphs may therefore represent words for actions or abstractions as well as for objects. Since they represent words rather than ideas, the formerly used terms **pictograms** or **ideograms** are less appropriate than **logograms**. The symbols themselves we describe as **logographic.**

A further characteristic use of hieroglyphs supports this designation. Some homophones came to be indicated by the same hieroglyph. The word for 'ten thousand' *db'*, for example, was a homophone of the word for 'finger' and was represented by the symbol for 'finger.'

In a further development, some hieroglyphs came to be used for just two consonants, because one of the consonants of a word was lost by phonological change. Other words may always have consisted of two consonants. For example, the word for 'a swallow' (bird) was *wr*; this also came to be used for *wr* 'large,' and further as a partial representation of longer words such as *wrd* 'be weary.' As a result of losses of further consonants, some hieroglyphs came to stand for words with only one consonant. The symbol for 'belt' represented *s*, that for 'water' *n*, and so on. In this way twenty-four such symbols came to represent one-consonant syllables. Their use illustrates the furthest development of the hieroglyphic system within Egypt. To the time of its abandonment around the beginning of our era, the Egyptian writing system maintained its full panoply of hieroglyphs, some of which represented syllables, others words.

Although not directly pertinent in the study of the development of our writing system, it is of interest to observe that a cursive script was developed early. When writing systems are used in everyday activities, writers find it difficult to maintain elegance and clarity of representation. With choice of writing materials, wide attempts at use and rapidity of writing are responsible for many changes in the outward shapes of symbols.

Egyptians were no exception; the earliest cursive system is known as **hieratic**. It gave rise to another, more abbreviated system, known as **demotic**. The symbols of both hieratic and demotic are quite different from the handsome hieroglyphs usually depicted in handbooks and often seen on Ancient Egyptian monuments.

The decipherment of the hieroglyphic system, while peripheral to historical linguistics, illustrates the dependence of historical linguistics on gifted philologists and cryptographers. Possibly the most enduring of Napoleon's achievements in Egypt was the discovery in 1799 of the Rosetta stone by soldiers preparing fortifications. For some time, hieroglyphs had fascinated European intellectuals, and there was widespread interest in the Rosetta stone, for it was clearly a means to decipherment since it contained a text in three writing systems, the Greek as well as demotic and hieroglyphic. From copies of the Rosetta stone a French scholar, François Champollion, in 1824 deciphered the hieroglyphic system; the demotic system was deciphered in 1848 by a German, Heinrich Brugsch. The Rosetta stone itself was taken to England in 1802 and is still in the British Museum.

4.4   The Greek development of the Egyptian writing system

It has long been suspected that our alphabet is an offshoot of the Egyptian writing system. At the end of the first century A.D., Tacitus stated this view in his *Annals*, 11:14: "The Egyptians first represented concepts by means of animal figures; these oldest monuments of human memory may still be seen engraved in stone. They claim to be the inventors of writing. From them the Phoenicians are said to have brought the script to Greece because they ruled the seas, and they received the credit for inventing what they only took over." Yet the link between the Western Semitic (Tacitus' Phoenician) and the hieroglyphic system was unknown. In 1904–05 the archeologist, Flinders Petrie, found sixteen inscriptions in the copper and malachite mines of Sinai, which Sir Alan H. Gardiner later deciphered. These provided a link between the hieroglyphs and the Phoenician system; they also showed how the West Semitic twenty-two-syllable system, like the twenty-four-syllable system of the Egyptians, was based on hieroglyphs. Later West Semitic writing systems, like that maintained for Hebrew, modified the forms of symbols. But essentially they remained syllabic systems, although symbols could be added to specify vowels. To understand some of the modifications, one must remember that the Semitic users of the symbols, and later the Greeks, were not consistent in placing the symbols. Some symbols were reversed, leading to a completely different appearance from those of the Egyptians.

Further modifications of shape were introduced when the Semitic system was borrowed by the Greeks, probably in the ninth century B.C. At first, the Greeks wrote either from right to left, like the Semitic peoples, or from left to right, or both alternately (**boustrophedon**). Some characters then were reversed, for example, *B*. The ultimate shape of our alphabet was not fixed until the Latins took it over. Yet the essential modification of the Greeks was the conversion of the syllabic system of the Semites to an alphabetic system, and the introduction of symbols for vowels.

In naming the symbols, the Semites and Greeks used the **acrophonic** principle. The second symbol of the alphabet was called *beta* by the Greeks, after its Semitic name, see Hebrew *beth*—house; the third *gamma*, see Hebrew *gimel*—camel; and so on. The first symbol stood for ', see Hebrew *'aleph*—ox, a consonant not found in Greek. When Greeks took over its name as *alpha*, it began with *a* rather than with a consonant phoneme. Accordingly they used it to represent a vowel rather than a consonant. The symbols for *e* and *o* developed similarly from consonantal symbols in which the initial consonant was lost. A further symbol, *i*, which to the Semitic users represented a vowel as well as a consonant, was used solely as a vowel by the Greeks, for the consonantal element had been lost in Greek. In this way the Greeks made the contribution of adding vowel symbols to the alphabet. This advance in writing systems has never been independently duplicated, nor have writing systems developed beyond it.

For a more complete representation of speech, symbols for stress, pitch, and other suprasegmentals are essential. Accent symbols were also developed and used by the Greeks in Alexandria. The use of accents did not, however, gain general currency; they were not adopted for the writing of Latin, nor for the writing systems devised for the various European languages. Only in modern times have linguists introduced them, to bring about the remaining essential of an accurate writing system.

Other modifications introduced by the Greeks are of interest, though not of fundamental importance to the structure of the alphabet. Among these are introduction of symbols for open *e* and *o* beside those for *epsilon* and *omikron* (close *e* and *o*). In Ionic Greek, *h* was not pronounced; the symbol for it, *H*, was taken over for *eta*, open *e*, comparing with the symbol *E* for close *e*. An open *Ω* for *omega* was introduced beside *O*. These modifications illustrate the Greek readiness to modify the alphabet.

The Greeks introduced four additional characters to the Semitic alphabet, those for *upsilon*, *phi*, *khi*, and *psi*. We do not know the sources for these. *Upsilon* and *khi* may have been taken from symbols in the sylla-bary of Cyprus. The recent discovery that Linear B was used to write Greek from as early as 1450 B.C. and our consequently increasing know-ledge of early Greek culture may help us to answer such problems in the development of the Greek alphabet.

4.5   Offshoots of the West Semitic and Greek writing systems

There are three other offshoots of the West Semitic syllabary, each with various developments: Aramaic with developments leading to Pehlevi; Syrian with developments like Mongol and Manchu; and the Arabic writing system. All of these introduced vocalic writing only late. Another, the Indic **Brāhmī**, from which developed **devanāgarī** and many other south Asian scripts, remained syllabic, though the indication of specific vowels was obligatory.

Based directly on Greek were, among others, the Gothic system, developed in the fourth century, and the two Slavic systems, the **Cyrillic** and **Glagolitic**, both of the ninth century. Cyrillic was based on majuscules, capitals; Glagolitic probably on minuscules, small letters. Cyrillic is the system used for Russian. It has also been adapted for a wide array of other Slavic, and also non-Slavic, languages.

The major offshoot of the Greek alphabet was the Latin. It was transmitted to the Romans by the Etruscans. In Etruscan the voiced: voiceless distinction between *g* : *k* was not made; accordingly the third letter of the alphabet came to stand for [k], as it still does in English before *a o u*, as in *cat, cot, cut*. Modifications of the alphabet by the Romans were slight; the most important is the introduction of a modified *C* for the *G* sound.

Another modification is of interest in illustrating the dual function of the alphabet to represent numerals as well as sounds. When the Greek alphabet was imported for Latin, some symbols were maintained for numerals: ↓ or ⊥ for fifty (Greek *khi*); ⊙ , ᄃ for hundred (Greek *theta*); ◑ , ᄆ for thousand (Greek *phi*). The source of these eventually became unclear, and they were replaced by the common letters *L C M*, which we use today when writing Roman numerals. A fourth of our Roman numerals, *D* for five hundred, represents half of ◑ . The three other symbols of the Roman numeral system, *I V X*, apparently had their origin in gesture like signs.

Proper understanding of the dual use of the alphabet is essential in dealing with its history. When the Greek alphabet was taken over for

Gothic, for example, the numerical values of the symbols were maintained, but some symbols had new phonological values assigned to them. Wulfila, for example, used the first six letters for the numerals 1 through 6. The symbol for 1 also stood for A, that for 2 for B, 3 for G, 4 for D, 5 for E. But the symbol for 6 did not correspond to a Gothic sound. Quite arbitrarily Wulfila used it for the value [kw]. Accordingly the value for 6 was primary; that for the sound, an adaptation of Wulfila's.

Modifications of the alphabet after its use for Latin are superficial. With the breaking up of the Roman Empire, various "national hands" were developed in its political subdivisions. A ready example survives today for Irish.

Cursives were also introduced. The study of these is the subject of **paleography** and is not of direct concern to linguistics; paleography, however, is essential to linguists dealing with medieval texts.

When scripts came to be too troublesome and unclear, reforms were introduced. The most important of these was the Carolingian, of about A.D. 800. Its importance results from the prestige the Carolingian script enjoyed at the time printing was introduced in Europe. The favored form of letters was the Carolingian minuscule; our printed fonts continue this today. Other modifications, the selection of varying forms of *I* to stand for *I* and *J*, and of *U* to stand for *U* and *V*, and the formation of *W*, introduced no new principles. Our alphabet today is not very different from the Latin.

Extensive modifications had been introduced in scripts for Germanic and Celtic languages, the bases of which are not wholly clear. The Germanic **runes**, based in part on a North Italian development of the alphabet, differ in order and purpose. The old runic alphabet contained twenty-four symbols, three series of eight, arranged probably according to a magical principle. The first six symbols of the first series are well known, through the name for the entire series, **futhark**. Runic symbols were used only for relatively short inscriptions, many of them on grave markers. The symbols we know from Latin were transparently adapted to simplify carving on wooden tablets, for example, ϝ for *F*, or, because the runes were read in any position, ⴖ for *U*. Runic inscriptions are of interest to linguists as they provide our earliest Germanic texts, to philologists because they yield information about Germanic culture, covering especially the fifth to the tenth centuries, and to the general reader because of forgeries, a number of which have attracted attention. The most notable of these is the Kensington Stone, which purported to prove that Vikings had penetrated to Minnesota in the Middle Ages. Like other forgeries it illustrates that a linguist needs to know the basis of his texts.

The **ogam** inscriptions, used for early Celtic, were made by putting notches or lines on the corners of posts. Series of one to five dots, or one to five lines extending to the right, to the left, or in both directions of an edge, provided twenty symbols, five for vowels, fifteen for consonants. Although particularly subject to weathering, the ogam inscriptions when legible are valuable in giving us our earliest Irish texts.

4.6   Types of writing systems

Writing systems, like those surveyed, may be classified into three groups, with transitional types:

1. **logographic**—symbols represent words, e.g., early Egyptian
   a. **logo-syllabic**—symbols represent words or syllables, e.g. later Egyptian.
2. **syllabic**—symbols represent syllables, e.g., Japanese kana
   b. **syllabic-alphabetic**, e.g., West Semitic, in which symbols represent consonants with varying vowels
3. **alphabetic**, e.g. Greek.

The systems in use at any time are rarely pure representatives of one of these types. In contemporary English, numerals indicate words or morphemes such as 2, 4th, and are accordingly logographic, though the basic writing system is alphabetic.

Moreover, writing systems are rarely ideal. The alphabetic system used in English is uneconomical, for several entities may be used to indicate units otherwise represented by one entity: *ig* in *sign*, *i-e* in *sine*, *igh* in *sight*, *i* in *I*.

Worse still, English has the rare distinction of using the same combination of symbols to represent now two separate phonemes side by side, now a given single phoneme, now a given other phoneme; the *th* of *porthole*, *this*, and *thin* represent /th/, /ð/, and /θ/, respectively. Possibly the restriction of /ð/ primarily to a small set of morphemes similar in use, and to initial position in these has permitted this unusual situation to persist; when found medially referring to /ð/, as in *father* and *neither*, *th* represents few minimally contrasting pairs, such as *either* : *ether*.

Writing systems may also represent morphological units, as do many spellings in English. The *-s* of *cats*, *dogs*, *horses*, for example, represents the plural morpheme rather than any phonological unit.

4.7   Interpretation of writing systems, and
supplementary evidence for linguistic purposes

When any written material is analyzed, the type of writing system must be determined, and its degree of correspondence with the language spoken at the time. Often, as in *sight* (see the German cognate *Sicht* [ziçt]) writing systems reflect an earlier stage of the language. Obsolete spellings are helpful for historical study, though possibly difficult to interpret. It requires some study to determine when postvocalic *gh* in English no longer represented a fricative. Our best evidence is derived from inverse spellings like Spenser's *whight* for *white*. This spelling would have been impossible when the fricative was still pronounced; from it, therefore, we receive information about the phonological development of English.

The most frequent imperfection in writing systems is failure to indicate some of the phonemes in a language. The writing system used for English is inadequate in failing to indicate pitch, stress, and juncture; punctuation marks, unsystematically introduced from about the beginning of our era, and capital letters are only approximate indications for these. Another feature poorly indicated is quantity. No provision was made for indicating long vowels in Latin, and when the Latin alphabet was adapted for Germanic languages, long and short vowels were not distinguished.

When writing systems provide insufficient information, we attempt to supplement it in various ways, most commonly by the analysis of poetry. Possibly our best means to determine Germanic quantities are based on the use of words in Germanic poetry. The following lines from the *Beowulf* illustrate how analysis of poetic texts adds information not provided by the Old English writing system.

710   Ða com of more   under misthleoþum
      Grendel gongan,   Godes yrre bær;
             Then came from the moor   under cover of darkness
             Grendel walking,   God's anger he bore;

Since the *Beowulf* manuscript does not use different symbols for short and long vowels, we cannot determine from it whether the *o*'s of *com, of, more, gongan, Godes* are short or long. But in Germanic poetry certain requirements were placed on the poet: each half-line was required to have two prominent syllables in which the vowels were long. Short vowels were permitted in the less prominent syllables, or in the prominent syllables if the lack of length was compensated for by a following consonant in the same syllable, as in *gongan*, or by an additional weakly stressed syllable, as in *Godes*. Since we know from the *m* alliteration of line 710 that *more* is metrically prominent, we must assume that its *o* is long; by converse reasoning we would assume the *o* of *of* to be short. Analysis of Old English poetry thus provides us with information about quantity and accentuation in Old English.

In this way, study of poetry may give us information beyond that provided by a writing system. Yet poetry manipulates phonemic patterns; it does not use them without modification. Therefore, it must be interpreted with the same care as writing systems. Alliteration in Old English poetry permits us to assume that the *g*'s of *Grendel, gongan,* and *Godes* were similarly pronounced. From alliteration we may also determine which other consonants were classed together by the Old English poets. But it tells us nothing about Old English vowels, for in Germanic verse all the vowels alliterated with one another; further, when *g* became palatalized in Old English, as in *gieldan* 'yield,' it continued to alliterate with velar *g*. Poetic conventions like writing conventions must be understood before they can be utilized to provide linguistic information.

Writing systems may also be inadequate because of conventions maintained from the area in which they were formerly used. The writing system taken over for Old English presents other problems than the lack of marking for quantity. Old English contained some vowels that could not be represented by the simple symbols used for Latin, such as the *eo* of *misthleoþum.* We have no contemporary description of the sounds it represented; accordingly its exact value is disputed. The compound symbol *eo* may reflect an Irish development. For in Old Irish manuscripts *e* may be used before *o*, especially in weakly stressed syllables, to indicate the pronunciation of the preceding consonant. In Old English *menigeo* 'multitude,' we assume that *e* marked the preceding *g* as a palatal, with a pronunciation [menijo]. The Old English orthographic system is further complicated because it continues conventions of the Old Irish spelling system as well as the Latin.

Since writing systems are conventional and imperfect, we supplement in various ways the information we seek concerning the actual pronunciation. Misspellings help us to determine when conventional spellings do not reflect the spoken language. If humorists and bad spellers write *of* for *have* in modern English, we may infer that *have* is commonly pronounced /əv/. Scribal errors are similarly informative for older materials.

Moreover, languages are rarely isolated. Words adopted from other languages inform us of the sound systems of both languages, as do borrowings out of a language. The Biblical names found in the languages of Europe, from Old Church Slavic to Old English, give us information on them. From any name taken over into the European languages, even one as simple as *Mary*, reproduced as *Marija* in Old Church Slavic, as *Maria* in Old English, we can infer the value of the symbols because we know the Latin and Greek pronunciation. Conversely we determine the pronunciation of names and words in Old Church Slavic, Old English and other languages from the manner in which they are represented when included in Latin and Greek materials.

We may also draw inferences from earlier or later forms of the language with which we are dealing. The Old English *o* in *of* is pronounced differently in Middle English and New English from that of OE *mōd* 'mood.' We may also attempt to determine the pronunciation of Old English forms by comparing them with related forms in the other Germanic languages. But inferences based on related forms must be established with care. English *of* and *mood* have undergone various changes. We cannot insist that the differing vowels in Modern English reflect differences in Old English, although for these two words they do.

If, on the basis of their differing contemporary pronunciations, we assumed different pronunciations for the vowels in the Old English forms of *wood* and *mood*, our inference would be wrong. The vowels were alike in Old English; through subsequent changes they have become different. Because individual languages, and individual words, undergo various changes, etymological evidence must always be used cautiously in attempts to determine the pronunciation of related materials.

In recent attempts to interpret writing systems, increasing use has been made of structural evidence. Graphemic systems may be analyzed for the internal relationship of their elements and for their relationship with the phonemic system of the linguistic material they represent. Writers with no linguistic training are more aware of the phonemes than of the allophones of their language. If therefore we find beside Old English

i	u
e	o
æ	a

a *y*, as in *cyning* 'king' and an *œ* as in *œxen* 'oxen,' we may conclude that these symbols represented phonemes in some stage of Old English. From the composite form of *œ* we assume it represented a front rounded vowel. The symbol *y* fits best into the Old English system of symbols if we assume that at one time it represented a somewhat higher front rounded vowel. Although structural analysis may permit us to make inferences about the phonological system represented by the orthography, in its interpretation we must be aware of possible complications, such as conventions imported from previous writing systems and those developed in the language.

Because of the shortcomings of methods of interpretation, we welcome descriptions of the language or its writing system made in the past. Greek and Latin grammarians provide some indication of the values of the alphabetic symbols they used. A grammarian in medieval Iceland has given us similar information about Old Icelandic. Less explicit but equally valuable help comes from the rare writer like Orm, who modified a traditional system in an attempt to give a better indication of his pronunciation. Various methods have been developed in attempts to determine the pronunciation and phonological systems underlying texts. We may illustrate some of these by noting further systems of writing.

4.8   The cuneiform writing system

The **cuneiform** or wedge-shaped script was developed by Sumerians in the fourth millennium B.C., taken over by Akkadians in the middle of the third millennium, and from them by various neighbors: by the Hittites and other groups in Asia Minor, who produced texts in the second millennium B.C., by the Elamites, with texts in the three last millennia B.C., and by various less well-known groups. It passed out of use in the fourth century A.D., and subsequently became completely unknown, until cuneiform texts were deciphered in the nineteenth century.

Persian inscriptions provided the avenue to relearning cuneiform. By assuming that these inscriptions were to be attributed to the Persian kings, scholars supplied the names of these kings, compared readings of other words with Avestan and Sanskrit words, and eventually mastered the Old Persian texts and in this way deciphered the cuneiform system of writing.

The Old Persian texts themselves were relatively easy to decipher because only thirty-six syllabic characters, with five additional signs, were used to represent Old Persian. Mastery of Old Persian led to the reading of Akkadian, through the trilingual inscription of the Persian king Darius at Behistan, Iran. For the proper names provided ready comparison. Thus, values were determined for the cuneiform characters much as the values of the Egyptian hieroglyphs were determined from the Rosetta stone. Other Akkadian texts were then read, among them lists and grammars indicating the values of symbols in Akkadian. Still other texts were avenues to Sumerian. In this way the reading of cuneiform gave access to the history of the Middle East from the fourth millennium B.C.

The earliest Sumerian texts indicate that the cuneiform system developed from pictures. An early form of the symbol for 'star, god, heaven' is ✳, for 'vegetation' ⚳ , for 'enclosure' ▢ . As these symbols were inscribed with a stylus on clay tablets, they came to be stylized in wedge-shaped forms and shifted ninety degrees as are the two plants in the compound symbol for 'garden' below. Apparently the shift was made to keep the scribe from smudging his copy. Ultimately ✳ was written with

three strokes ⸰⸰千. Compound symbols also were developed; that for
'garden' was ⸰⸰□. Moreover, characters could be used merely for their
phonetic value; ⸰⸰千 was read as the syllable *AN* as well as the word
'god.'

When cuneiform symbols were taken over by Akkadians, another
complexity was introduced: symbols could be read either by their Sumerian
or their Akkadian values. Since 'god' in Akkadian is *ILU* and 'heaven'
ŠAMU, ⸰⸰千 in Akkadian texts may have these readings as well as the
Sumerian *AN*. When taken over by the Hittites the cuneiform system could
be read with Sumerian, Akkadian, or Hittite values, compounding the
complexity further. Without parallel texts and dictionaries, interpretations
of the Hittite texts would have been fantastically difficult.

The reading of cuneiform texts is aided somewhat by the presence of
determinatives, symbols used with nouns to indicate morphological and
semantic classes, such as plurals, gods, men, rivers, wooden articles, and
so on. Determinatives, used also by the Egyptians, are markers that have
no phonetic value themselves, somewhat like capital letters for proper
nouns and adjectives in English or for nouns in German. The symbols used
for them may also be read as word symbols.

The cuneiform system therefore is a combination of a logographic and
a syllabic system. Its offshoot used for Old Persian was virtually an
alphabetic system.

4.9   The Chinese writing system

A third system of writing, the Chinese, has remained logographic. In
Japan, however, a syllabic system, which is generally used in conjunction
with logographs, has been developed from Chinese characters. In Korean
an alphabetic system was designed in the fifteenth century. Like the
Egyptian hieroglyphs and the Sumerian cuneiform symbols, Chinese
characters developed from pictures. In early inscriptions the symbol for
mu^4 'tree' was 米 , for jih^4 'sun' ⊙ , for men^2 'gate' 門 . When
Chinese characters came to be inscribed on wood rather than on bone, the
lines of characters were straightened, and the characters became stylized.
Today mu^4 is written 木 , jih^4 日 , men^2 門 .

A small number of further characters resulted from combinations of
simple characters. That for 'east' is 'the sun rising through a tree' 東 .
Another small group are symbolic pictures: yen^2 'speak' is a mouth producing speech 言 , earlier 𣥐 . The largest group was made up of components, one of which represents the meaning, the other the pronunciation;
the second component is called the "phonetic." A homonym of men^2 'gate'

indicates plurality. The character developed for this consists of a form of 'man' 亻 (to provide meaning) and the character for 'gate' 門 as "phonetic"; the composite character is 們. A similar process gave rise to 悶 men[4] 'mournful' (men plus 'heart') and 捫 men 'feel' (men plus hand).

The large number of characters of this last kind provided the means for the most common arrangement of Chinese dictionaries. Characters are arranged by a characteristic element, called **radical**, and the number of additional strokes. Although in writing rapidly, Chinese produce characters in cursive form, the stroke order and the number of strokes in conventional writing are still keys to their identification. 們 , for example, is listed under 亻 , radical nine, and further classified by its eight additional strokes.

Until very recent times, the system of characters was the sole method of writing Chinese. Since Chinese morphs are monosyllabic and un-inflected, the writing system was efficient, except for the need to memorize thousands of characters. In this century various attempts have been made to develop a simpler system of writing Chinese. None has succeeded in replacing the character system.

Various systems of transliteration have also been developed. Since these use Roman letters, they are called Romanizations. That of Wade and Giles is used most commonly for transliterating Chinese. Western spellings have given rise to pronunciations of Chinese place-names that are some-times far from the original, such as *Peking* for something like (bey ǰiŋ].

When the Chinese system of characters was carried to Japan, means were devised to indicate inflectional syllables and particles. Certain characters were selected to indicate syllabic values, as for the particle *ka*. In the early period a great many such characters were so used, but in the course of time they came to be restricted in number and stylized. The character 加 'add to' was the one selected to indicate the syllable *ka*. Forty-eight such characters make up the Japanese **kana** syllabary. Of this there are two forms: the **hiragana**, used normally; the **katakana**, which compares in use to our italics. Hiragana symbols developed from rapidly written forms of characters; the hiragana for *ka* is か , in which 口 has become a simple stroke. The katakana symbols developed from abbre-viated forms; the katakana for *ka* is 力 , in which the 口 has been entirely omitted.

Japanese is still written in a combination of Chinese characters with kana. In the word for 'walk,' for example, the Chinese character 歩 must be supplemented by the kana symbol for *ku* く to indicate the positive *aruku*; the negative *arukanai* is written 歩かない . This character has a totally different value when used in the compound for 'infantry' 步兵 *hohei*. As a result of these different uses, the Japanese writing system is possibly the most complicated today.

4.10   The development of writing systems

Both the cuneiform system and the Chinese system follow the development that we traced in the Egyptian–Greek system, though neither carried it as far. The farthest developments of them, in Old Persian and Japanese, were to syllabic systems.

The three writing systems we have dealt with started with pictures, as did other writing systems that we will not discuss: the Aztec, Mayan, the Indus Valley script, Proto-Elamite, Cretan, and Hieroglyphic Hittite. Of these only Hieroglyphic Hittite has been securely deciphered, although Mayan and the Indus Valley script are in process of decipherment. Each of the three was conventionalized and modified by the writing materials.

As a further stage, syllabic systems developed. This stage, clear in the twenty-four Egyptian syllables, the Sinitic and West Semitic scripts, the Hittite and Elamite cuneiform, and the Japanese kana, also has representatives in the Cyprian syllabary, in Linear A and B, and in an interesting modern creation, Sequoia's invented syllabary for Cherokee.

Syllabic symbols developed toward alphabetic symbols in the West Semitic area, for example, in Ugaritic and in Old Persian.

The last stage of development, in Greek, led to the creation of a pure alphabet, in which symbols are used for vowels as well as consonants. The Greek alphabetic system was widely adopted and imitated. New writing systems devised today are alphabetic. In a complete writing system, symbols would also be used to indicate suprasegmentals. Although the Greeks introduced symbols for pitch accent, these symbols did not become a standard part of writing systems like that used for English. Only linguists of recent times have introduced symbols for all the phonemic entities in a language.

Selected Further Readings

D. Diringer's *The Alphabet*, 2nd ed. (New York, 1948), furnishes a general introduction, with numerous illustrations, as does Hans Jensen's *Sign, Symbol and Script*, 3rd ed., translated by George Unwin, (London, 1970). Both Diringer and Jensen should be consulted primarily for their data and their illustrations.

For a structural analysis of writing systems, see I. J. Gelb, *A Study of Writing*, 2nd ed. (Chicago, 1963). Gelb presents a typology in accordance with which writing systems developed. When it differs from that of Diringer and Jensen, his identification of the characteristic structure should be accepted.

Statements on writing systems may also be found in the standard handbooks, such as Bloomfield's *Language*, Chapter 17. For a highly readable discussion of writing systems, their interpretation for linguistic purposes and their decipherment, see Holger Pedersen's *Linguistic Science in the Nineteenth Century*. For a good account of an important recent decipherment, see John Chadwick's *The Decipherment of Linear B* (Cambridge, 1958). Information on scripts that remain to be deciphered may be found in P. E. Cleator's *Lost Languages* (London, 1959).

CHAPTER 5

The comparative method

5.1 The Comparative method: a triangulation procedure for reconstructing earlier forms

Analysis of written texts and of modifications in writing systems provides us with one method of determining linguistic change. When in sixteenth-century texts we find *delight* spelled with *gh*, we assume that *gh* no longer indicates a consonant, but that the consonant earlier represented by *gh* has been lost with an effect on the vowel, for *delight* earlier was spelled like *rite* rather than *right*. After the consonant represented by *gh* had been lost, words like *delite* < ME *deliten* < OFr. *deliter* < Latin *dēlectāre*, were respelled on the pattern of words like *light* < OE *lēoht*, compare Germ. *Licht*, in which the *gh* was etymologically justified. Since spelling systems are conservative, this method of determining change is cumbersome. Moreover, it can be applied only when we have a continuous series of texts. A surer method of dealing with change and determining earlier forms has been developed which is known as the **comparative method (CM)**.

In using the comparative method, we contrast forms of two or more related languages to determine their precise relationship. We indicate this relationship most simply by reconstructing the forms from which they developed.

As an example of a problem (for which we know the solution), we may

cite the contrast between the medial consonants used by some speakers of
American English (AE) in words like *atom*, *bitter*, *little* and those used in
other English dialects, such as British English (BE). In some AE dialects
the *-t-* in these words is voiced, so that *atom* and *Adam*, *bitter* and *bidder*
are pronounced alike. If these pronunciations are maintained, a future
historical linguist will find in related languages the forms:

AE /ǽdəm/ : BE /ǽtəm/ for *atom*
AE /bídər/ : BE /bítər/ for *bitter*
AE /lídəl/ : BE /lítəl/ for *little*

He would also find pronunciations like those of British English in
Australian English and various other dialects of English. Setting such
forms side by side, he would posit an earlier form, that is, an **etymon**, in
the following manner:

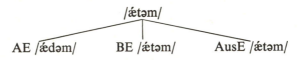

Using the "triangulation" symbolized here, he would propose that the
etymon for these three forms was like the British and Australian English
forms.

This example indicates how the comparative method is used. From this
example we may also note why the comparative method is effective. In
some American English dialects, medial /t/ has been changed to /d/ when it
follows a stressed vowel and stands before /ə/ plus /l/ or /m/ or /r/, or
before /iŋ/ and other weakly stressed syllables. Such sound changes are
generally restricted to certain dialects and to certain environments. If
other dialects can be found in which the change in question has not taken
place, we can compare the contrasting forms and posit the etymon. The
comparative method has been tested on so many such examples that we
are very confident of its effectiveness.

Our confidence in particular uses is strengthened when we find unchanged forms inside the language with the changes. The change from
medial /t/ to /d/ did not take place before /ən/ as in AE *button*. AE *button*
is pronounced very like BE *button*. Since the two dialects have the same
consonants in this pattern, we would assume that it is American English
that has changed the /t/ in *atom*, *bitter*, *little*, even if we did not have
earlier forms.

We also find evidence in related words. Since the change is limited to a
specific phonological environment, /t/ is maintained in the verb *hit*, though
not in the noun *hitter*, which is pronounced [hídər]; it is also maintained

in the adjective *fat*, though not in the comparative *fatter*, which is pronounced [fǽdər]. We may set beside these pairs similar pairs in which the
consonants do not vary, such as *lick* : *licker*, *fast* : *faster*. From such pairs
we assume that the forms with [ər], as well as those with no ending, should
have the same consonants after the accented vowel. To account for forms
like [hídər] and fǽdər], we conclude that in a restricted set of words, that
is, those with medial [t], a change has taken place. For we derive *hitter*
from the underlying form /hit/ plus /ər/, in much the same way as we
derive *licker* from /lik/ plus /ər/.

In this way the intricacies of language change generally provide enough
evidence to support conclusions based on use of the comparative method.

For another illustration we may cite Romance language forms given in
Chapter 1: Fr. *champ*, Ital. *campo*, Span. *campo*, Port. *campo*. If we wished
to reconstruct the earlier initial consonant, we would posit [k]. We could
verify this assumption by noting Latin *campus* 'field', and also by observing
the consistent changes of such initial [k] in French and their maintenance
in Italian, Spanish, and Portuguese.

In a similar way we may determine the forms in a reconstructed
language. As an example we may take the third singular present of the
verb 'be' in Proto-Indo-European. We would compare forms such as
Skt. *ásti*, Lith. *ẽsti*, Gk. *ésti*, and others by the triangulation procedure
illustrated above for *atom*:

In these forms, our chief problem is the Sanskrit *a*; we would propose that
Skt. *a* developed from PIE *e*. This assumption is supported by the finding
that PIE *e* generally developed to Skt. *a*. Moreover, when PIE *k* stood
before PIE *e*, the *k* > *c* in Sanskrit, as in the perfect *cakāra* 'he made' <
*kekore. We must conclude from this change of *k* to *c* that an earlier form
of Sanskrit had maintained *e*. We then reconstruct the Proto-Indo-
European form *ésti*. We will also attempt to verify the reconstructed
forms, using the means illustrated above for English. For Proto-Indo-
European it is manifestly impossible to locate a contemporary form. We
are then limited to examining additional forms, either from the same root or
of the same category.

Examining first singular and plural forms of the root 'be':

1 sg.	Skt. *ásmi*	Lith. *ẽsmi*	Gk. *eimí*
1 pl.	Skt. *smás*	Lith. *ẽsme*	Gk. *esmén*

we reconstruct the two further forms PIE *ésmi* and *smés*. (Detailed analysis of the developments in the various forms cited would require lengthy discussion.) These and still further forms of the verb 'be' lend credence to our reconstruction *ésti*, as would reconstructed forms of other verbs.

We note from the first that the reconstructed forms are limited in validity by the amount of information on which they are based. The comparative method has the serious limitation that it offers no means of reconstructing elements that are completely lost in subsequent stages of the language. Today we reconstruct the Proto-Indo-European third singular *ʔésty*, but with the help of the method of internal reconstruction (see Chapter 6). From the comparative method we could not determine that the Proto-Indo-European form began with a glottal stop, since this is not attested in forms that have come down to us.

Besides comparing the set of forms from one root, we compare phonological sets: the set of vowels in two or more languages, of stops, and so on. To support our reconstructed *s* and *t* in the Proto-Indo-European third singular of 'be', we would attempt to determine the entire Proto-Indo-European obstruent system.

5.2   The comparative method applied to Indo-European obstruents

We may illustrate the application of the comparative method to sets of phonological entities with forms containing Greek and Latin obstruents:

TABLE 2

		1	2	3	4
I	Gk.	patér 'father'	beltíōn 'better'	phrắtēr 'clansman'	
	Lat.	pater 'father'	dē-bilis 'weak'	frāter 'brother'	
II	Gk.	treîs '3'	déka '10'	aná-thēma 'offering'	heptá '7'
	Lat.	trēs '3'	decem '10'	fēci 'did'	septem '7'
III	Gk.	he-katón '100'	génos 'kin'	khamaí '(on the) earth'	
	Lat.	centum '100'	genus 'tribe'	humus 'ground'	
IV	Gk.	a. poû 'where'	baínō 'come'	a. phónos 'murder'	
		b. tís 'who'		b. theínō 'strike'	
	Lat.	a. quō 'whither'	veniō 'come'	dē-fendō 'ward off'	
		b. quis 'who'			

For the first three rows of the first two columns—the voiceless and voiced **orders** of the labial, dental, and velar **series**—the results of our comparison would permit little dispute for the entities with which we are concerned. In both Greek and Latin we find oppositions between voiceless

and voiced stops, among labials, dentals, and velars, and we assume the
same phonemes for Proto-Indo-European. We would posit accordingly for
the system from which the obstruent systems of Greek and Latin developed:

	GREEK		LATIN		PROTO-INDO-EUROPEAN			
	1	2	1	2	1	2	3	4
I	p	b	p	b	p	b	–	
II	t	d	t	d	t	d	–	–
III	k	g	k	g	k	g	–	
IV					–	–	–	

For the last two columns and the last row, however, we would find it
difficult to posit earlier forms on the basis of the material provided here.
We can suggest such forms with greater assurance if we add material from
other Indo-European languages.

The comparative method was sharpened largely by its application to
the obstruent system of Germanic. In Germanic the obstruents had undergone various changes that were not determined before the studies of Rask
and Grimm. By careful comparison these two founders of historical linguistics demonstrated the changes that had taken place in Germanic. Their
work, and that of their successors, led to the development of the comparative method. This work also indicated the need for precise analysis of all
the forms in related languages. Adding to our Greek and Latin examples
cognate words from Germanic and Indic illustrates how these cognates
enable us to fill out our reconstruction of the Proto-Indo-European
obstruents. (Unless otherwise labeled the Germanic examples are from
Gothic. Examples in a wide variety of dialects to support the reconstruction of PIE *b* do not exist. We therefore must cite a cognate from Baltic
and admit that these forms probably come later than Proto-Indo-European,
as do the examples for *b* in Table. 2)

TABLE 3

		1		2		3	4
I	Gmc.	fadar 'father'	Eng.	pool		broþar 'brother'	
	Skt.	pitá 'father'	Lith.	balà 'swamp'		bhrắtā 'brother'	
II	Gmc.	þrija '3'		taihun '10'		doms 'fame'	sibun '7'
	Skt.	tráyas '3'		dáśa '10'		dhāma 'glory'	saptá '7'
III	Gmc.	hunda '100'		kuni 'race'		guma 'man'	
	Skt.	śatám '100'		jánas 'race'		kṣás 'earth'	
IV	OIcel.	hvat 'what'	OHG	queman 'come'	OE	gūþ 'battle'	
	Skt.	kás 'who'		gámanti 'they go'		ghnánti 'they strike'	

The examples cited here support the inferences drawn from comparison of Greek and Latin, and supplement them, especially for column 4. If we posit an obstruent system for Proto-Indo-European based on these four dialects, we reconstruct it as follows:

PROTO-INDO-EUROPEAN

	1	2	3	4
I	p	b	bh	
II	t	d	dh	s
III	k	g	gh	
IV	k^w	g^w	g^wh	

Additional material must be supplied to support convincingly the reconstructions in row IV and column 3. For row IV we base our conclusions on the Latin and the Germanic evidence, such as Lat. *quis* and OHG *queman*. The consonants posited in column 3 are based primarily on Skt. *bh dh gh* but also on Gk. *ph th kh*. We will not offer further evidence here in favor of these conventional reconstructions.

5.3   The comparative method applied to the Germanic obstruents

A review of the study of the Germanic phenomena during the nineteenth century contributes to understanding the development of the comparative method and other methods of historical linguistics. Rask pointed out in 1818 the relationships between the Germanic obstruents and those of the other Indo-European dialects. In 1822 Grimm made the important contribution of indicating the system underlying the relationships. Proto-Indo-European voiceless stops of all four series are represented by voiceless fricatives in Germanic; Proto-Indo-European voiced stops, by Germanic voiceless stops; Proto-Indo-European voiced aspirates, by Proto-Germanic voiced fricatives, which later in most Germanic languages became voiced stops. The consistency of correspondences in other positions, such as medially in the examples of Table 4, indicates its value in historical linguistics.

By means of these and other examples, we may verify the obstruents just posited for Proto-Indo-European. We can most simply state the development of the Proto-Indo-European obstruents into Germanic by using the following formulas. We read > 'became' or 'developed into.'

$$\text{PIE p t k } k^w \qquad > \text{ PGmc. f } \theta \ \chi \ \chi^w$$
$$\text{PIE b d g } g^w \qquad > \text{ PGmc. p t k } k^w$$
$$\text{PIE bh dh gh } g^w h > \text{ PGmc. } \text{b } \eth \ g \ (g^w)$$
$$\text{PIE s} \qquad\qquad\quad > \text{ PGmc. s}$$

TABLE 4

	1	2	3	4
	PIE p	b	bh	
	Gk. anepsiós 'cousin'	—	nephélē 'fog'	
I	Lat. nepōs 'grandson'	Lith. trobà 'building'	nebula 'mist'	
	Skt. nápāt 'descendant'	OWelsh treb 'house'	nábhas 'mist'	
	Gmc. OE nefa 'nephew'	Go. þaurp 'village'	Germ. Nebel 'fog'	
	PIE t	d	dh	s
	Gk. phrátēr 'clansman'	édomai 'I shall eat'	eruthrós 'red'	hestía 'hearth'
	Lat. frāter 'brother'	edō 'I eat'	ruber 'red'	Vesta
II	Skt. bhrátā 'brother'	ád-mi 'I eat'	rudhirás 'bloody'	vásati 'lives'
	Gmc. broþar 'brother'	OE etan 'eat'	OE rēad 'red'	wisan 'be'
	OCS bratrŭ 'brother'	jadętŭ 'they eat'	rŭdrŭ 'red'	
	PIE k	g	gh	
	Gk. déka '10'	agrós 'field'	steíkhō 'climb'	
III	Lat. decem '10'	ager 'field'	vestīgium 'trace'	
	Skt. dásá '10'	ájras 'plain'	stighnoti 'climbs'	
	Gmc. taihun '10'	OE æcer 'field'	steigan 'climb'	
	PIE kʷ	gʷ	gʷh	
	Gk. lúkos 'wolf'	érebos 'underworld'	nípha 'snow'	
IV	Lat lupus 'wolf'	—	nix, nivis 'snow'	
	Skt. vṛkas 'wolf'	rajas 'cloud'	Av. snāežaiti 'it snows'	
	Gmc. OIcel. ylgr 'she-wolf'	riqis 'darkness'	OE snāw 'snow'	

We could state similarly with appropriate formulas the development of the Proto-Indo-European obstruents in the other Indo-European dialects.

If we wish to indicate the relationship of the obstruents from dialect to dialect, we use the sign = in our formulas, reading it "correspond(s) to," for example:

$$\text{Skt. p b bh} = \text{PGmc. f p ƀ}$$
$$\text{Gk. t d th} = \text{OCS   t d d}$$

We could also state our previous formulas in reverse order, for example:

$$\text{PGmc. ƀ ð g (gʷ)} < \text{PIE bh dh gh gʷh}$$

reading < "developed from."

5.4 Relationships examined with the help of the comparative method

In a study of the relationships between two languages, we should make comparisons for all environments, not merely as we have done here for the initial and some intervocalic environments.

In such comparisons we find a variety of interrelationships.

1. The sounds concerned may have been maintained in both languages; Latin *p* in *pater* and Greek *p* in *pater* are examples.

2. The sounds concerned may have been maintained in one language and may have undergone change in the other; Latin *p* in *pater* and Gmc. *f*, as in Goth. *fadar*, are examples.

When only two languages are attested, it may be difficult to determine which maintains the original form. One may find in either language unchanged sounds in certain environments to use as guides, as we did above in AE *set* beside [sedər]. The occurrence of *p* after *s* provides important evidence in reconstructing PIE *p* from Latin and Germanic, for after *s* Germanic has maintained PIE *p*, as in Goth. *speiwan*, see Lat. *spuō* 'spit.' Since Latin has generally maintained PIE *p*, we conclude that Latin *p* more closely represents the Proto-Indo-European sound than does the Germanic *f*; and we find further support for this conclusion in other Indo-European dialects.

3. The sounds concerned may have undergone change in both languages; the *b* in Lat. *nebula* and the *b* in Germ. *Nebel* both come from PIE *bh*. Reconstructing the etymon of such forms may be very difficult. After a century and a half of attention, the etymon of Greek *ph*, Latin *b* or *f*, Sanskrit *bh*, Germanic ƀ has not been determined to everyone's satisfaction. If unchanged items cannot be found in certain environments, as in Goth. *speiwan*, one must rely on knowledge of the various kinds of sound changes. Such information is presented in Chapter 10. When the sounds have changed in both languages, we may find a variety of developments.

a. The sounds concerned may merge completely, as did PIE *d* and *dh* in OCS *jadętŭ* 'they eat' and *rŭdrŭ* 'red.' Such complete mergers cause great difficulties for reconstruction. We cannot determine whether a voiced stop in the Slavic languages developed from a Proto-Indo-European voiced stop or a voiced aspirate.

b. The sounds may merge in part, as did medial *dh* and *bh* in Lat. *ruber* 'red' with *b* from PIE *dh*, and *nebula* 'fog' with *b* from PIE *bh*. By comparing sounds in other orders, for example, the Latin voiceless stops in *frāter* 'brother,' with the medial dental maintained, and *nepōs* 'grandson,' with the medial labial maintained, partial mergers may be cleared up, especially if we have cognates in related languages. The lack of parallelism in the Latin reflexes of PIE *bh dh gh* leads us to suspect changes in this order between Proto-Indo-European and Latin.

c. Moreover, the mergers may be complex, as in the following Greek examples: 1. *poû* 'where' (where Gk. *p* = Lat. *qu* as in *quod*) : *patér* (where Gk. *p* = Lat. *p*), 2. *tís* 'who' (where Gk. *t* = Lat. *qu* as in *quis*) : *treîs* (where Gk. *t* = Lat. *t*), 3. Gk. *k* = (Lat. *qu*) Gmc. *hw* as in *kúklos* 'circle' OE *hweol* 'wheel' : *he-katón* (where Gk. *k* = Lat. *c* as in *centum* '100'). Again, one must sort out the situation in the language concerned. Analysis of standard Greek indicates that the reflexes of Proto-Indo-European k^w, g^w, $g^w h$ show up as labials before *a o* and as dentals before *e i*, and as velars before *u*, as in *kúklos* 'circle', see the English cognate *wheel*. Accordingly the complex set of mergers is the result of a development within Greek. To the extent we can judge from our Linear B materials, labiovelars were still maintained in Greek until approximately 1000 B.C., and even later in some Greek dialects; because of borrowings from dialects, the rules given above do not apply to all words in standard Greek.

These examples of mergers in individual languages illustrate that the comparative method can be used to determine earlier forms, even after a number of changes. By noting carefully the environment in which each change occurred, we can generally reconstruct the earlier situation, unless there has been a complete merger.

5.5   Advantages and shortcomings of the comparative method

The comparative method has been highly successful in permitting us to reconstruct earlier forms than those attested. Although the evidence for the labiovelar order is not clear in the widely known dialects of Indo-European, labiovelars were reconstructed for Proto-Indo-European; when Hittite texts were discovered, evidence was found for velar and labial articulation, supporting the reconstruction of Proto-Indo-European labiovelars. The Hittite form corresponding to Gk. *tís* is written *ku-iš*.

Another reconstruction by the comparative method that was later verified is Bloomfield's Proto-Algonquian cluster *çk*, which he proposed on the basis of Fox and Ojibwa *šk*, Cree and Menomini *hk*, and related clusters. Later in Swampy Cree, he found a distinct reflex of this cluster, *htk*, and other evidence to support his reconstruction; *Language* 5.99–100 (1928). Since use of the comparative method has in this way been demonstrated to be successful, careful application of it is highly trustworthy.

The comparative method, however, has various shortcomings. Reconstructions achieved by use of the comparative method are less precise phonetically than is the information on which they are based. On the basis of Greek *ph*, Germanic *b*, Slavic *b*, Latin *b*, Sanskrit *bh*, and Armenian *bh*, we may posit PIE *bh*, but we cannot determine precisely its pronunciation.

Nor do we know whether the Proto-Indo-European labiovelars were articulated as velars followed by labial rounding, as velars with simultaneous labial closure, or as still other sounds.

We lose information also in the complexity of the language we reconstruct. In normal use of the comparative method, we proceed backward by triangulation and eventually posit for each subgroup a dialect-free phoneme. In reconstructing the Proto-Indo-European voiceless velar stop *k*, for example, we proceed from comparison of Greek *k*, as in *he-katón*, with Italic *k*, as in Lat. *centum*, to comparison with Germanic χ, as in Gothic *hunda*, with Indo-Iranian *ś*, as in Skt. *sátám*, and so on. It is likely, however, that the dialects of Indo-European were not uniform; further, that they reflect a nonuniform situation in the parent language. Some forms, for example, which are expected to contain a sibilant in Baltic and Slavic, have a velar, e.g.,

> Lith. *akmuõ* OCS *kamy* versus Skt. *aśmā*, Av. *asman-* 'stone', Gk. *ákmōn* 'anvil.'

If Proto-Indo-European had been completely regular and dialect-free, all of these forms except Greek should have a sibilant rather than a velar. Although the CM ideally requires us to reconstruct a dialect-free Proto-Indo-European, such irregularities suggest that the parent language already had dialects. With care we may apply the comparative method in all rigor and, from forms like those for 'stone,' assume dialects within the parent language. Yet the method itself is not designed to yield anything other than a dialect-free corpus.

5.6 Refinement of the comparative method by study of the Germanic obstruents

The comparative method was being refined throughout the nineteenth century. We may illustrate its development by observing the increasing precision applied to the description of the obstruent system of Germanic in its relation to that of Proto-Indo-European and those of the other dialects.

In 1822 J. Grimm published general statements on the relations between Germanic obstruents and those in the other languages. Labeling *p t k* **Tenues**, *bh dh gh* (and *f θ* χ, etc.) **Aspiratae**, *b ð g* and *b d g* **Mediae**, he stated that Indo-European **T** > Germanic **A**, Indo-European **A** > Germanic **M**, Indo-European **M** > Germanic **T**, producing a circular scheme:

On the basis of subsequent changes in the High German area, where *t* later became *ts*, as in German *zu* pronounced [tsu] versus English *to*, he assumed that this change repeated itself in the Germanic languages and therefore considered it a law. Subsequently the formulation has been called **Grimm's law**. Although other linguists have gained a somewhat restricted renown through the discovery of a "law" that describes a minute change in some language, there has been considerable objection to use of the label "law" for a statement of correspondences. Today we may retain the label for established laws, like Grimm's, but otherwise we avoid the term in this sense.

Grimm's contemporaries soon discovered "exceptions" to his law, and accounting for these contributed greatly to the development of historical method in the nineteenth century.

The first exception concerned the maintenance of Proto-Indo-European voiceless stops after Germanic fricatives, as in the following examples:

PIE *pt*	Goth. *hafts* 'married'	= Lat. *captus* 'captured'
PIE *sp*	*speiwan* 'spew'	= *spuō* 'spit'
PIE *st*	*ist* 'is'	= *est* 'is'
PIE *sk*	*skadus* 'shadow'	= Gk. *skótos* 'darkness'
PIE *kt*	*nahts* 'night'	= Lat. *nox, noctis* 'night'

In these and other examples the stop after the Germanic fricative did not change. The lack of change was ascribed to the environment. Within decades after Grimm had published his law, scholars accounted for the first exception by stating that voiceless stops remained unchanged when they followed Germanic voiceless fricatives.

· This solution indicated the importance in historical linguistics of examining immediate environments and observing phonetic characteristics. Although Grimm himself showed little interest in phonetics, his successors studied the production of sounds thoroughly. As a result, articulatory phonetics was greatly developed in the nineteenth century, reaching a high level in the works of Eduard Sievers and Otto Jespersen.

Explanation of the second group of exceptions gave rise to a further advance in method. Involved here were Germanic voiced fricatives and stops that seemed to correspond irregularly to Indo-European voiced stops rather than to voiced aspirated stops, as in

PIE *bh . . . dh-*	Goth. *-biudan* 'offer'	= Skt. *bódhāmi* 'notice'
PIE *dh . . . gh-*	*dauhtar* 'daughter'	= *duhitá* 'daughter'
PIE *gh . . . gh-*	*gagg* 'street'	= *jáṅghā* 'leg'

If the correspondences had been in accordance with Grimm's law, the cognates in Sanskrit should have had initial aspirates.

Hermann Grassmann accounted for the lack of correspondence by pointing out that all such forms contained Proto-Indo-European aspirates in two successive syllables; further, that in Indic and Greek one of the two successive aspirates had been dissimilated to an unaspirated stop. Thus, the irregularity was not to be ascribed to Germanic, but rather to the supposedly more archaic Sanskrit and Greek.

We will examine the Sanskrit and Greek dissimilation of aspirates at greater length in the next chapter. Here we are chiefly concerned with the further refinement of the comparative method based on Grassmann's findings. Observing that his explanation was based on examination of the elements in successive syllables, linguists now learned that they could not deal only with entities and their immediate environments, for sounds might be affected by other noncontiguous sounds. Grassmann's observation led them to examine entire syllables and words, as well as individual sounds.

Accounting for the third set of exceptions led to another refinement. These exceptions comprise forms in which a Proto-Indo-European voiceless stop had become a voiced fricative in Germanic rather than a voiceless fricative. Voiced fricatives can be assumed from OS *sibun*, OIcel. *faðer*, OE *sweʒer*; as the other dialects indicate, often these became stops later. Examples are:

PIE *p'* > PGmc. *b*:   Goth. *sibun*   OE *seofun*   OS *sibun*
          OHG *sibun*; Skt. *saptá*   Gk. *heptá* '7'
PIE *t'* > PGmc. *ð*:   Goth. *fadar*   OIcel. *faðer*   OE *fæder*
          OHG *fater*;   Skt. *pitá*   Gk. *patér* 'father'
PIE *k'* > PGmc. *g*:   OE *sweʒer*   OHG *swigur*; Skt. *śvaśrū́ṣ*
          Gk. *hekurá* 'mother-in-law'

A Danish linguist, Karl Verner, noted that the accent in Sanskrit and Greek never preceded the consonants that corresponded in Germanic to voiced fricatives. He formulated a law to account for these developments, as well as for PGmc. *z* < PIE *s'* (this *z* became *r* in all Germanic dialects but Gothic),

PIE *s'* > PGmc. *z*:   OIcel. *snør*   OE *snoru*   OHG *snura*;
                 Skt. *snusá*   Gk. *nuós* < *snusos 'daughter-in-law'

We may restate Verner's law as follows: Proto-Indo-European voiceless stops became Proto-Germanic voiceless fricatives. In voiced surroundings these voiceless fricatives, plus the already existing voiceless fricative *s*, became voiced when not immediately preceded by the accent. Verner's article, "Eine Ausnahme der ersten Lautverschiebung" probably had a greater effect on historical linguistics than has any other single publication.

As one result, linguists noted that they could no longer limit their attention to consonants and vowels but that they had to consider accent as well. The suprasegmentals began to receive attention. In the late decades of the nineteenth century, one observes in linguistic journals a great deal of attention to the suprasegmental patterns manipulated in verse. Many articles attempted to explain sound changes by recourse to suprasegmentals. Although some of these were overly enthusiastic, after 1876 linguists paid attention to the pitch and stress patterns of language, as fourteen years earlier they had learned to take into account entire words, and several decades earlier, immediate environments. Accordingly, after Verner, linguists dealt with all the phonological markers of an utterance.

5.7 The neogrammarian hypothesis, a conclusion based on successful use of the comparative method

Verner's explanation of the last large group of exceptions of Grimm's law had the further effect of giving linguists complete confidence in their laws and rules. Observing that greater attention to the matter of language permitted them to account for residues and for diverse developments, a group of linguists after 1876 proclaimed that "sound change takes place according to laws that admit no exception." These linguists, referred to as **neogrammarians** by somewhat scornful elders, proclaimed that if one assembled all the facts, and analyzed them accurately and thoroughly, one could state exceptionless principles or laws for the development of language.

This assumption is often referred to as the *neogrammarian hypothesis*. It should be noted that the neogrammarians did not assume that sound changes operated without exception in all lexical sets. For example, they excluded nursery words such as Goth. *atta* 'father' and onomatopoetic words such as NHG *kikeriki* 'cock-a-doodle-do.' The extent of such sets has been one of the hotly argued problems of historical linguistics.

The new movement centred around Leipzig. Its leading young scholars, Brugmann, Osthoff, Leskien, and others adopted the label neogrammarian for themselves. Encouraged by their new scientific method, they proceeded to deal with many problems and to publish handbooks that have been in use since their day. Braune's *Gotische Grammatik*, subsequently revised, provided the pattern for most historical grammars of the past century.

For decades the neogrammarians also attracted to Leipzig brilliant young students, such as Leonard Bloomfield. Through their students and their publications, the neogrammarian school exerted a great effect on linguistics. The principle that sound laws operate without exceptions encouraged linguists to uncover all the facts involved in language change, for it assured them that thorough study would yield results. In spite of occasional pedantic excesses, the neogrammarians applied the comparative method with great skill to various problems in language. They also produced handbooks that have not been superseded to this day, such as K. Brugmann's *Grundriss der vergleichenden Grammatik der indogermanischen Sprachen*, 2nd ed. (Strassburg, 1897–1916).

5.8 Rules proposed for changes determined by the comparative method

In the course of historical linguistics, observations and statements have become increasingly precise. We noted above that Grimm's formulation consisted of three major rules, and that the entities of the rules T A M represented general classes. Grimm's classes, especially A and M, do not correspond to sets of similarly articulated sounds. Improved statements of Grimm's law in the half-century after its formulation added greater precision by indicating in each of its rules the actual sounds involved.

These improved statements represent the sounds with phonetic symbols. Thus the rule PIE $p\ t\ k\ k^w$ > PGmc. $f\ \theta\ \chi\ \chi^w$ refers to the subclass of the IE voiceless stops that was found in all environments except after PIE s and PGmc. $f\ \theta\ \chi$ from Proto-Indo-European voiceless stops. The other rules refer to other subclasses of phonemes occurring in specific environments. Such subclasses of phonemes are known as allophones. On the basis of other examples cited in this chapter, we assume that sound change takes place by such subclasses, which are abstract sets in individual languages. Thus the labiovelars must have developed three allophones in early standard Greek. The allophone before $a\ o$ was characterized by labial articulation. The allophone before $i\ e$ was characterized by fronted articulation; the allophone before u was characterized primarily by velar articulation. As these allophones developed the assumed characteristics further, they merged with $p\ t\ k$, $b\ d\ g$, $\phi\ \theta\ \chi$. In Germanic, on the other hand, the labiovelars developed different allophones, as the Germanic reflexes given above indicate.

In standard grammars the Greek changes of the earlier labiovelars are represented by rules like the following:

$$\text{PIE } k^w\ g^w\ g^wh > \text{Gk. p b } \varphi \text{ before a o}$$
$$\text{PIE } k^w\ g^w\ g^wh > \text{Gk. t d } \theta \text{ before i e}$$
$$\text{PIE } k^w\ g^w\ g^wh > \text{Gk. k g } \chi \text{ before u}$$

Although sound changes take place by allophones, only one feature of the allophone is generally modified. Thus the stop [t] became a continuant [θ] in Proto-Germanic. And the labial feature of early Gk. *k* was lost in Greek before *u*. To indicate the specific modifications, rules are now commonly stated in distinctive features.

Such rules have the advantage of representing the general structural principles of the language. For example, when we state a rule for the development of Proto-Indo-European voiced stops to Proto-Germanic voiceless stops, such as PIE *d* to PGmc. *t*, the rule indicates that not only PIE *d* but also every stop is voiceless in Germanic. That is, the rule is valid for Gmc. *t* from PIE *t* as well as for Gmc. *t* from PIE *d*, as well as for PGmc. *p k k*ʷ. This rule might then be stated as follows:

$$\begin{bmatrix} -\text{res} \\ -\text{cnt} \end{bmatrix} \rightarrow [-\text{voiced}]$$

Since the other Proto-Germanic obstruents *f* θ *s* χ χʷ *b* ð *g* *g*ʷ were [+continuant], when this rule applied, it indicates a general feature of articulation in the language as well as a sound change.

The chief difficulty with the precise rules given by means of distinctive features results from our ignorance of the details concerning earlier languages. We know that the three sets: (1) *p t k k*ʷ; (2) *bh dh gh g*ʷ*h*; (3) *b d g g*ʷ contrasted in pre-Germanic. We can even be reasonably sure that set 1 consisted of voiceless stops, set 2 of voiced aspirated stops, and set 3 of voiced stops. But when we propose distinctive features for the members of each set, we have little evidence for these proposed features. Some scholars assume that pre-Germanic *p t k k*ʷ were lenis stops, as in some contemporary dialects of German. Others assume that they were fortis, as in the chart on page 53 above. Assumptions for the distinctive features of *bh dh gh g*ʷ*h* are even less certain. If detailed analysis will permit us to determine the features of earlier sound systems with greater precision, the stating of rules in distinctive features will add to our understanding of earlier languages.

5.9 Use of the comparative method for syntactic phenomena

So far we have discussed the use of the comparative method only for phonological analysis. Recent advances in syntactic study make it possible to apply the method for syntactic analysis also; advances in semantic study make its use possible in that area as well, but we will comment on that extension of its applicability only in the chapter dealing with semantic change.

As we have observed, the comparative method is applied to abstract sets. Until we have a framework, we cannot determine sets. We noted in Chapter 3 that such a framework is now available in syntactic study. Here we will discuss only one set, the comparative construction. We have seen that two distinct comparative constructions may be proposed. The construction like ours in English, e.g., 'higher than a mountain' has the structure: adjective pivot standard. The Japanese construction: *yama yori takai* 'mountain from high' has the construction: standard pivot adjective. A morphological marker, like *-er*, may or may not be used in comparatives.

Examining the early Germanic languages for comparative constructions we find sequences like the following:

ON Voluspá 64 *sólo fegra* 'sun (than) fairer'
OE Beowulf 1850 *þæt þē Sǣ-Gēatas sēlran næbben*
    (that you (than) the Sea-Geats a better do not have)
    'The Geats have no one better than you'
OHG Otfrid 5.18.9 *ist in allen oboro*
    'is them all (than) higher'
Gothic Skeireins *ni þe haldis* 'not than that more likely'

All of these have the structure: standard pivot adjective (SPA). The pivot is generally indicated by the dative case ending. Applying the comparative method to these syntactic constructions in the NW and E Gmc. dialects

SPA   SPA

we reconstruct an OV type comparative construction S P A for Proto-Germanic.

In this way the comparative method can be applied to any syntactic construction that can be identified as a representative of a given framework. Few such applications have been carried out. But future historical grammars will be far more complete than are our current grammars in the presentation of syntactic patterns. For the comparative method can be applied to all components of language in much the way it has been applied to the phonological component.

Selected Further Readings

A. Meillet's *La méthode comparative en linguistique historique* (Oslo, 1925) is still the best introduction to the comparative method. It is now available in English under the title *The Comparative Method in Historical Linguistics*, translated by G. B. Ford, Jr. (Paris, 1967). Good accounts are given in any of the competent handbooks. Among these are Bloomfield's *Language*, Chapter 18, and

E. H. Sturtevant's *An Introduction to Linguistic Science*, Chapter 15. The most recent comprehensive treatment is Chapter 12 of H. Hoenigswald's *Language Change and Linguistic Reconstruction* (Chicago, 1960). Here the comparative method is presented comprehensively and rigorously.

Notable articles in the development of historical linguistics, such as those by Grassmann and Verner, have been assembled and translated in *A Reader in Nineteenth-Century Historical Indo-European Linguistics*, edited by W. P. Lehmann (Bloomington, 1967).

CHAPTER **6**

The method of internal reconstruction

6.1 Internal reconstruction as illustrated by Grassmann's Law

In explaining the second group of exceptions to Grimm's law, Grassmann made use of the comparative method. His decisive evidence, however, was furnished by observation of patterns within Sanskrit and Greek. Application of the comparative method to Germanic, Sanskrit, and Greek data, however, would not indicate which language better reflects the situation in the parent language. Irregularities within Sanskrit and Greek, clearly show that in some environments these languages had made the departure from the Indo-European distinction between aspirates and stops.

Some of the best evidence for the departure is found in reduplicated verb forms of Sanskrit and Greek. The perfect in Sanskrit and Greek is generally marked by reduplication of the first consonant (or consonants) of the root, followed by a vowel, for example:

Skt. *da-daú*, Gk. *dé-dō-ka*, cf. Lat. *de-dī* of the present *dō* 'give'

When, however, in Sanskrit and Greek, roots with an aspirate are reduplicated, the reduplicating consonant does not maintain aspiration, for instance, in perfect forms based on PIE *bhū-*:

Skt. *ba-bhū́-va* 'he has become.' Gk. *pé-phū-ka* of *phŭ́ō* 'develop'

Since the *p* of Greek is an unaspirated voiceless stop while the *b* of Sanskrit is an unaspirated voiced stop, we assume that the loss of aspiration took place separately in Sanskrit and Greek. In accordance with the patterns of reduplication, we expect to reconstruct on the basis of information derived from within each of these languages the starred forms:

Skt. *bha-bhŭ-va   Gk. *phé-phū-ka   on the pattern of
     da-daú   dé-dō-ka

Such a procedure for positing earlier forms, which takes no outside language into account for reconstruction, we call the **method of internal reconstruction** (**IR**).

We do not find the reconstructed forms *bha-bhŭ-va and *phe-phū-ka in Sanskrit and Greek because in each language one of two aspirates of successive syllables was dissimilated. The changes may be described in Grassmann's formulation: the first of two aspirates beginning successive syllables or a syllable that also ended with an aspirate lost its aspiration.

The examples cited from the Sanskrit and Greek perfect indicate one morphological complication resulting from the loss of aspiration. Another is found in inflected forms, when aspirates are modified by contiguous elements. The nominative of 'hair' in Greek, for example, is *thríks*, the genitive *trikhós*. This paradigm seems to select artibrarily from the two possible aspirates. Yet each form is readily explained. In the nominative the aspiration was lost when the nominative marker *s* was appended after *kh* as in *ónuks, ónukhos* 'claw'; accordingly there was no aspirate with which the initial *th* of *thríks* might be dissimilated. In the genitive, on the other hand, the medial *kh* was maintained, and the initial consonant was dissimilated, yielding *trikhós*. Again comparing similar inflections like *kêruks*, gen. *kérūkos* 'herald,' in which the consonants remain unchanged, we could reconstruct internally from Greek alone pre-Greek *dhrigh- < PIE *dhrigh-*.

6.2   Why the method of internal reconstruction discloses earlier forms

The method of internal reconstruction is made possible because of the occurrence of sound changes without regard to morphological sets. As illustrated in Chapter 5, sound changes take place by allophones, regardless of their morphological role. A sound may undergo change in a number of morphs of a morpheme in which it occurs in specific phonological surroundings; in other morphs of the same morpheme it may remain unchanged. Moreover, in parallel morphemes with different sounds, the change may not take place. We must conclude that sound changes do not take place in accordance with morphological sets, or by systematic phonemes, but rather by subsets of autonomous phonemes, which are known as **allophones**.

If we return to the examples in Chapter 5.1, we will note that for some speakers AE *t* has become *d* in specific phonological environments, as in the forms in special type below:

tick	sin	bid	hit
ticker	sinner	bidder	**hitter**
ticking	sinning	bidding	**hitting**
ticks	sins	bids	hits
red	black	fast	fat
redder	blacker	faster	**fatter**

The change occurred only in restricted phonological environments, as when *t* preceded unstressed vowels such as *ə* plus *l m r*, and *i* plus *ŋ*; it did not occur before *s*, nor when *t* was final, and so on. Moreover, there is no such change for other consonants such as the *k* of *tick*, the *n* of *sin*, the *d* of *bid* and *red*. We can therefore propose that the morphological suffixes -*er*, -*ing* and -*er* were added to bases without change of the preceding consonant. When we find an interchange of consonants in a set of forms that generally shows no interchange, as between *t* and *d* in the forms of *hit*, we assume that a sound change has taken place. From varying allomorphs in a later stage of a language, we can hypothesize the earlier form by using the method of internal reconstruction.

In sum, the method of internal reconstruction is applicable because sound change does not take place in specific morphological categories, such as agent nouns in -*er*, gerunds in -*ing*, or comparatives in -*er*. Rather, sound change takes place in phonological sets. The sound change of intervocalic AE -*t*- has affected only allophones of /t/ that occur in specific phonological environments. Because other allophones were unaffected by the sound change, we can reconstruct the earlier situation by noting parallel morphological sets that have allophones of /t/ unaffected by the change.

As with the dissimilated aspirates of Sanskrit and the -*d*- of *bitter*, the new phones generally merge with those of other phonemes. For many speakers of American English, *bitter* is pronounced like *bidder*. Similarly, Sanskrit *b* resulting from the dissimilation of *bh* in *ba-bhū-va* merged with the existing /b/. We may be able to determine such merged phones by their characteristic phonological environment in order to apply internal reconstruction. In Sanskrit, for example, we suspect any /b/ that is initial in its syllable and precedes an aspirate of being a reflex of earlier /bh/. Future students of English will also suspect any /d/ found after a stressed vowel and before an unstressed, especially if it maintains an interchange with /t/.

6.3 Internal reconstruction applied to the Proto-Germanic interchange between voiceless and voiced fricatives

When phonemes are restricted in occurrence to specific allomorphs of a morpheme, as in the illustrated forms of *hit*, we may apply the method of internal reconstruction to determine the basis of the restriction, and the earlier situation. We find such restrictions for PGmc. *s* : *z*. For the Proto-Germanic forms of 'choose,' we posit:

	Inf.	Pret. 3 sg.	Pret. 3 pl.	Pret. ptc.
	kiusan	kaus	kuzun	kuzan-
cf. 'freeze'	friusan	fraus	fruzun	fruzan-

From these forms, occurrences of *z* may seem characteristically intervocalic after *u*. Yet from other forms, such as PGmc. *nesan* 'be saved' : *nazjan* 'save,' we know that the distribution is related not to specific vowels but to the former position of the accent, as may be verified by comparing related Sanskrit forms. The root of the Sanskrit cognate of *choose* is *juṣ-* 'taste, like, attempt' (Skt. *j* indicates a palatalized *g* and is pronounced like the *j* in E. *just*; *ṣ* indicates a retroflex *ṣ*). The perfect singular, corresponding to PGmc. **kaus-* (though with reduplicated *ju-*) is *jujóṣa*; the perfect third person plural is *jujuṣús*. These forms, in which the *s* is maintained without change, demonstrate the validity of Verner's correlation of the Germanic consonant variation with the varying position of the accent. If we compare also the *s* : *z* interchange after other vowels, as in the forms of *wesan* given on page 97, we have internal Germanic evidence to reject an explanation based on occurrence of PGmc. *z* after *u*.

By the time of the individual Germanic dialects, the original distribution was even more obscured, for in Old Icelandic, Old English, Old Saxon, Old High German, and less well-attested dialects, the reflexes of PGmc. *z* had fallen together with those of PGmc. *r*. Of 'choose' we find the following forms in these dialects:

OIcel.	kiōsa	kaus	køron	kørenn
OE	cēosan	cēas	curon	coren
OS	keosan	kōs	kuran	gikoran
OHG	kiosan	kōs	kurun	gikoran

Detailed study of the interrelationships between *r* and *s* in such forms led to reconstruction of the Proto-Germanic situation, and from this of the Proto-Indo-European.

Study of the distribution of similar phonemes is useful. For parallel with the PGmc. *s* : *z* contrast, we find that of *θ* : *ð*, *h* : *g*, and their reflexes, as in PGmc. *θ* > OE *ð*, OHG *d*; PGmc. *ð* > OE *d*, OHG *t*:

OE	sēoðan	sēað	sudon	soden	'boil'
OHG	siodan	sōd	sutun	gisotan	
OE	tēon	tēah	tugon	togen	'pull'
OHG	ziohan	zōh	zugun	gizogan	

As illustrated in the Old English infinitive for 'pull,' later changes may completely obscure the original pattern. Old English poetry, like *Beowulf* 1036b *on flet tēon* 'lead into the hall,' reflects the earlier pattern; this verse must have at least four syllables, requiring us to assume earlier **tēhan*. Moreover, if we had only Modern English and no Old English materials, the only verb paradigm showing the original Proto-Germanic distribution of voiceless versus voiced fricatives would be *was* : *were*. The distribution is maintained also outside of inflectional paradigms, as in *lose* : *forlorn* and in the increasingly rare *seethe* : *sodden*; the last is now used only as an adjective. After languages have undergone further changes, the original patterns may be very difficult to reconstruct from internal evidence.

6.4   Internal reconstruction applied to the vowel interchanges in Germanic strong verbs

The verb forms given here illustrate that internal reconstruction may be applied with greatest assurance in morphological paradigms. Excellent examples are the irregular, or strong, verbs of the Germanic languages. We list forms in Gothic and Old English, though Gothic alone would be adequate for our reconstructions:

1	Go.	beitan	bait	bitun	bitans	'bite'
	OE	bītan	bāt	biton	biten	
2	Go.	kiusan	kaus	kusun	kusans	'choose'
	OE	cēosan	cēas	curon	coren	
3	Go.	-bindan	-band	-bundun	-bundans	'bind'
	OE	bindan	band	bundon	bunden	

Sound changes have obscured some of the relationships. For example, except before *r* and *h*, PGmc. *e* > Go. *i*, as in *kiusan* and *bindan*. The second elements of the vocalic segment of the roots Go. *beit-*, *kius-*, and *bind-* are reflexes of the resonants PGmc. *y w n*, so that for Proto-Germanic we must posit the roots **beyt-*, **kews-*, **bend-*.

If we label the *b t k s d* of the roots Consonants and the *y w n* Resonants, we can derive these three classes of verbs from roots with a pattern of variation for Proto-Germanic:

CeRC-   CaRC-   CRC-   CRC-

(PGmc. *y* > *i*, *w* > *u*, *n* > *un* when between consonants, as in the CRC forms). Accordingly the three different strong verb classes of Gothic and Old English were originally one class.

From analysis of the Gothic materials, we can readily posit the Proto-Germanic variation. From the later Old English materials, in which various sound changes had taken place, e.g., PGmc. *eu* > OE *ēo*, PGmc. *au* > OE *ēa*, internal reconstruction would be somewhat more difficult.

Examining further Germanic verbs, we find the same variation between PGmc. *e* and *a* in the first two forms of classes 4 and 5, which have a Proto-Germanic structure **CeC-** (the preterite plural and preterite participle are different in pattern and will not be accounted for here).

4 Go.	stilan	stal	stēlun	stulans	'steal'
OE	stelan	stæl	stǣlon	stolen	
5 Go.	wisan	was	wēsun	*wisans	'be'
OE	wesan	wæs	wǣron	*wesen	

A highly structured set of forms, like those of the strong verb in Germanic, assists us greatly in reconstruction of prior stages of a language from internal evidence alone. We are also fortunate in having cognate forms in Indo-Iranian, Greek, and other dialects that support our reconstruction of these Germanic verb classes into one original class. Substituting PIE *o* for PGmc. *a*, we posit PIE:

$$\text{Ce(R)C-} \qquad \text{Co(R)C-} \qquad \text{C(R)C-} \qquad \text{C(R)C-}$$

These formulas may be illustrated by the Greek verb forms: *leípō* 'I leave' with *e*-vowel; *lé-loipa* 'I have left' with *o*-vowel; *élipon* 'I left' with only the reflex of the resonant, as in OE *biten*.

6.5   Internal reconstruction applied to canonical forms, such as Indo-European roots

If morphological patterns are adequately structured, even phonemes that have disappeared may be reconstructed by internal evidence. Most Indo-European roots have a structure CeC-, e.g., *bher-* 'bear.' *gʷem-* 'come,' *sed-* 'sit.' (**Root** is a term that has become established for Proto-Indo-European base morphemes, as opposed to derivational and inflectional morphemes. Forms of a specific shape in language, such as roots consisting of two consonants, PIE *bher-*, or in the Semitic languages of three, e.g., Hebrew *k t b* 'write,' are known as **canonical forms**.) A small number of widely attested roots, however, differ by having only one consonant, e.g., *ag-* 'lead,' *dhē-* 'place,' *es-* 'be.' Saussure suggested in 1879 that at an earlier stage of Indo-European, these were parallel with roots of the structure CeC-; the consonants he posited for that stage have subsequently disappeared.

Saussure's suggestion was not widely accepted. When Kurylowicz dealt with Hittite, however, he identified reflexes for some of Saussure's vanished consonants, which subsequently had been called laryngeals. Today, therefore, we reconstruct these roots with two consonants, PIE *heg-* instead of *ag-*, PIE *dheʔ-* instead of *dhē-*, PIE *ʔes-* instead of *es-*. The confirmation of Saussure's brilliant hypothesis through Hittite has added considerably to our confidence in the method of internal reconstruction. The varying forms of Proto-Indo-European roots presented in Section 6.4 represent morphs restricted in distribution. We may make the further assumption that in an earlier stage the three different vocalisms are to be reconstructed as one. We posit the original form as **Ce(R)C-**, assuming that with accentual variation this became **C(R)C-**, as in Skt. *dṛṣtás* 'seen' beside Gk. *dérkomai* 'I see.' We also derive **Co(R)C-**, as in Gk. *dédorka* 'I have seen,' from **Ce(R)C-**, with less assurance about the element conditioning the change of *e* to *o*.

These vowel variations in Proto-Indo-European, which have reflexes in the various Indo-European languages, such as NE *bite, bit, bitten* : *choose, chose, chosen* : *bind, bound, bound* : *steal, stole, stolen* : *was, were*, are known by the term **ablaut**, or **apophony**. They have been accounted for through principles of internal reconstruction developed in the study of historically observable sound changes. The effort that has been devoted to arrive at an understanding of ablaut, and the obscurities still remaining, may indicate the complexities involved in the reconstruction of languages for which we do not have texts going back a thousand years or more. But the reconstructions may also indicate hope of some success, if an adequate number of forms with morphological variation are maintained through subsequent periods of sound changes.

If the sound changes that take place yield a complete merger, the method of internal reconstruction can be used only in situations like the Proto-Indo-European root, where we have clearly definable morphemes. We can, for example, reconstruct an earlier form for the verb **es-* 'be' but not for the first singular pronoun **eg-ō*. By examining the interchanging forms of Proto-Indo-European roots, we can suggest earlier forms. When, however, we find complete merger in morphemes of varying shapes, we cannot apply the method. In Iranian, for example, *bh* and the other aspirates fell together with unaspirated stops, and we have no evidence for Grassmann's law.

If, on the other hand, sound changes result only in a partial merger, as the dissimilated Sanskrit aspirated voiced stops with unaspirated voiced stops, we can apply the method of internal reconstruction, unless the resulting morphophonemic variation has been obscured by subsequent sound changes, or by analogical changes (see Chapters 10 and 11).

Generally, isolated forms like *forlorn* or *sodden* preserve longest the evidence we can use in internal reconstruction. Yet from isolated forms it is very difficult to apply a technique using morphophonemic variations. Alternating morphemes from the most frequent layers of the vocabulary, such as *was* : *were*, are also likely to preserve means for applying the method of internal reconstruction; because they retain the original syntactic variation, as well as the phonological, they are more useful than are isolated forms.

The constant changes and losses in language eventually obscure entirely the morphophonemic variation resulting from earlier sound change. Ultimately they eliminate the morphophonemic contrasts that may be used in internal reconstruction. In the Romance languages, for example, we find very little evidence for the ablaut of Proto-Indo-European.

6.6   Internal reconstruction applied to the findings of phonology

Proponents of transformational grammar assume that phonemes are determined by syntactic classes, the so-called systematic phonemes. Studies of systematic phonemes are similar to studies carried out with the methods of internal reconstruction. The detailed examination of variations in works on generative phonology such as *The Sound Pattern of English* are accordingly valuable to historical linguists in illustrating the retention of phonological interchange in language, and in illustrating the modifications introduced in such interchanges by subsequent sound changes and analogical influences.

Moreover, since generative phonologists make use of distinctive features, the rules provided in the application of the method of internal reconstruction are now stated with greater formal clarity than they were, as we also noted in our discussion of the comparative method. But the cautions given in that discussion also apply. We often do not have sufficient information to determine accurately the distinctive features. Therefore the rules proposed may include poorly supported assumptions.

To illustrate the application of the methods to the material of a contemporary language, we may examine the rules for interchange of English front tense vowels as stated in *The Sound Pattern of English*. On the basis of vowel interchanges like those in

derive	: derivative	[ay] : [i]
serene	: serenity	[iy] : [e]
profane	: profanity	[ey] : [æ]

Chomsky and Halle set up underlying forms with the tense vowels i $\bar{e}$ $\bar{æ}$, that is, $r\bar{i}v$, $r\bar{e}n$, $f\bar{æ}n$. The vowels become lax i e $æ$ when they stand before a nonfinal unstressed syllable as in *profanity*. In the words of the first column, *y* can be automatically predicted after the tense, underlying vowels. The interchanges in the sets above may then be represented as follows:

$$\begin{array}{ccc} \bar{i} & \bar{e} & \bar{æ} \\ \downarrow & \downarrow & \downarrow \\ \bar{æ} & \bar{i} & \bar{e} \end{array}$$

These interchanges may be stated by means of the "Vowel Shift Rule" (*Sound Pattern* 187), which consists of two parts, a and b:

$$\begin{bmatrix} +\text{tense} \\ \\ V \end{bmatrix} \rightarrow \left\{ \begin{array}{ll} [-\alpha\,\text{high}] \Big/ \begin{bmatrix} \alpha\,\text{high} \\ -\,\text{low} \end{bmatrix} & \textbf{a} \\ \\ [-\beta\,\text{low}] \begin{bmatrix} \beta\,\text{low} \\ -\,\text{high} \end{bmatrix} & \textbf{b} \end{array} \right\}$$

By part **a**, the tense high and $-$low vowels i $\bar{e}$, whether [+high] i or [−high] $\bar{e}$, became [−high] $\bar{e}$ and [+high] i, respectively; that is, *-rīv-* becomes *-rēv-*, and *-rēn-* becomes *-rīn-*. By part **b**, the tense low and [−high] vowels $\bar{e}$ and $\bar{æ}$ become $\bar{æ}$ and $\bar{e}$, respectively; that is, *-rēv-* becomes *-ræv-*, and *-fæn-* becomes *-fēn-*.

Accordingly, by diphthongization of tense vowels and by the two-part vowel shift rule the following interchanges are determined (*Sound Pattern* 188):

$\bar{i}$	$\bar{e}$	$\bar{æ}$	
īy	ēy	æy	Diphthongization
ēy	īy (not applicable)		Vowel shift a
æy (not applicable)	ēy		Vowel shift b

In this way other underlying forms are proposed on the basis of contemporary English, such as *-līn-* on the basis of the alternation between *line* and *linearity*; *-mēt-* for *meter* and *metrical*; *grāt-* for *grateful* and *gratitude*.

Although these underlying forms are determined on the basis of variations in contemporary morphological sets, the vowels of the underlying forms are those found in Middle English. For example, the Middle English vowel in *ripe* was i; this vowel was diphthongized in the Great English Vowel Shift. And the Middle English vowel in *see* was $\bar{e}$; this vowel was raised to i in the Great English Vowel Shift, as was ME $\bar{æ}$ (see Chapter 10:2). As these examples may indicate, the precise analysis carried out by

Chomsky and Halle enabled them to construct underlying forms comparable to those used in Middle English approximately six centuries ago.

Here only a few of the rules proposed by Chomsky and Halle are cited. The Vowel Shift Rule also applies to the back tense vowels, as in *abound* : *abundant, cone* : *conic, custody* : *custodian*. Moreover, by examination of other alternations, such as those in *satisfy* : *satisfaction*, Chomsky and Halle construct underlying forms that are modified by additional rules. These rules to some extent parallel historical processes of the past. *The Sound Pattern of English* accordingly provides an illustration of the results obtainable by thorough analysis of the variations in forms of morphological sets. Such results may be used for internal reconstruction. They provide hope of determining the earlier forms of many languages for which we do not have earlier texts.

6.7   Internal reconstruction as applied to syntactic patterns

In discussing the comparative method, we noted how it can be applied also to determine earlier syntactic patterns. Precise syntactic analysis may also permit application of the method of internal reconstruction in syntax, as we may note from observations of D. Bolinger concerning the syntactic patterns in which NE -*ing* is found ("The Nominal in the Progressive," *Linguistic Inquiry* II. 246–50, 1971).

Bolinger establishes patterns of syntactic alternations for adverbial nominals in English, such as the following:

> He is home. : He is at home.
> I was there an hour. : I was there for an hour.

The progressive form may show similar variations, as in some dialects:

> He's writing a book. : He's at writing a book.

Moreover, as Bolinger points out, the preposition must be used in questions that are answered by the progressive if the nominal is omitted, as in:

> I'm writing a book. : What are you at these days?

Furthermore, the preposition is also found in constructions with action nominals paralleling the progressive, such as:

> He's at work. : He's working.

> She's gone for a horseback ride. : She's horseback-riding.

Citing other syntactic patterns in which the progressive is used as a noun comparable to action nominals like *work* and adverbial nominals like *home*, Bolinger observes that the progressive nominal alone of verb forms can be compounded like nouns (except for back formations like baby-sit), as in:

> I'm trout fishing; it's great fun.
> Trout fishing takes skill.

But the infinitive is not used in such compounds; the following sentences are impossible or unusual:

> *It's fun to trout-fish.
> *Do you trout-fish?

As these examples illustrate, syntactic patterns in contemporary English disclose parallels between syntactic uses of the progressive nominal and other nominals.

On the basis of these parallels, Bolinger proposes that the "progressive tenses represent, historically, a combination of *be* with a prepositional phrase." With this assumption we would derive progressive constructions like:

> He is working.
> from: He is on working.

The evidence given here from Bolinger's demonstration illustrates application of the method of internal reconstruction to syntactic patterns. It is not necessarily true that the progressive has its sole origin in prepositional constructions. Bolinger's study of contemporary English has however demonstrated that some uses of the progressive nominal can be derived from prepositional constructions. Support for this conclusion is provided by Bolinger from dialect forms, such as *He is a-working*.

As the comparative method is being used to determine earlier syntactic patterns on the basis of evidence from related languages, so the method of internal reconstruction permits us to propose earlier syntactic patterns on the basis of one language alone. In this way the method of internal reconstruction will lead to syntactic reconstruction for languages attested only today, and for reconstructed languages like Proto-Indo-European. The method may also be applied for semantic reconstruction, as we will note in the chapter on semantic change.

Selected Further Readings

Chapters 7 and 10 of Henry Hoenigswald's *Language Change and Linguistic Reconstruction* deal generally with the method. Additional control over the method can best be secured by study of its use in dealing with specific problems.

It may be of interest to survey in greater detail than is presented here the application of the method to problems in Proto-Indo-European. An introduction may be found in my *Proto-Indo-European Phonology*, especially Chapters 2, 3, 15; additional readings are cited there. Another application, with discussion of the theory involved, may be found in Wallace L. Chafe's "Internal Reconstruction in Seneca," *Language*, 35.477–95 (1959). An application giving statements in the format of rules may be found in "Generative Grammar and Historical Linguistics" by Bengt Sigurd, *Acta Linguistica Hafniensia X*. 35–38 (1966). For a series of extensive applications, see Jerzy Kurylowicz, *The Inflectional Categories of Indo-European*.

CHAPTER 7

Study of loss in language: lexicostatistics

7.1 Glottochronology

The techniques known as the comparative method and the method of internal reconstruction are both applied to selected speech material with the aim of determining linguistic relationships and reconstructing earlier stages of a language. Both methods are based on our knowledge that languages change. Besides undergoing change, linguistic entities are also lost. The phenomenon of loss in language has not been widely explored, but we know from general reading that losses of vocabulary may occur with changes in culture. Today, for example, we find the technical terms used in astrology difficult; few of us could distinguish between horary and judicial astrology, let alone the nomenclature employed in each. The terms went out of use with the practice. Only recently has there been much attention to loss of vocabulary items. The concern arose out of attempts to use rate of vocabulary loss or percentage of retention to determine chronological linguistic relationship, a procedure referred to as **glottochronology**. The broader term **lexicostatistics** is used for statistical study of vocabulary. Several basic assumptions underlie glottochronology. The first is that some items of the vocabulary are better maintained than others: the lower numerals, pronouns, items referring to parts of the body and to natural objects—animals, plants, heavenly bodies, and so on. These items are referred to as the **basic core vocabulary**.

Another underlying assumption is that the percentage of retention of items in the basic core is constant in some respects; conversely, that their rate of loss is approximately the same from language to language if cultural conditions are similar. If then the percentage of cognates in the basic core is determined for two related languages, the length of time that they have been separated can be stated.

In applying glottochronology to two related languages, one compiles the vocabulary items referring to a selected number of elements, determines which are related, and uses the percentages to posit the length of separation. One might, for example, use a list of five items: those for "animal, four, head, I, sun" and compile one's percentages. In standard German, one would elicit for the above-listed items: "Tier, vier, Kopf, ich, Sonne." These show 60 percent agreement with English, for *animal* and *Tier*, *head* and *Kopf* are not related. If there were a standard scale to determine the time of separation expected from 60 percent agreement in basic-core vocabulary, we could apply it and propose the time when English and German separated.

A scale for determining the length of separation for two languages was devised by Lees, *Language*, 29.113–27. By this formula the time of separation, or **time depth**, is equal to the logarithm of the percentage of cognates, **c**, divided by twice the logarithm of the assumed percentage of cognates retained after a millennium of separation, **r**:

$$t = \frac{\log c}{2 \log r}$$

Using our five items from English and German, we determine **t** as follows (assuming for ease of computation a relatively high rate of retention of 85 percent):

$$t = \frac{\log 60\%}{2 \log 85\%} = \frac{-.511}{2 \times -.163} = 1.561$$

By this formula, English and German separated approximately 1.561 times 1000 years ago, that is around the year A.D. 400.

In such a short list the range of error may be great. To reduce it, one would prefer a long, carefully designed list. M. Swadesh has devised several. In most investigations either of his two lists, one of one hundred, another of two hundred words, has been used. (The lists are reproduced at the end of the chapter.) Even with such lists, the range of error must be computed; see Lees, *Language*, 29.124, or Gudschinsky, *Word*, 12.204–5. Typical conclusions are given in length of separation, plus or minus a number of years, determined from the range of possible error. Gudschinsky, for example, concludes that "Ixcatec and Mazatec were a single homogeneous language, 2,200 ± 200 years ago." (*Word*, 12.205)

7.2   Criticisms of glottochronology

The work that has been done in glottochronology has indicated various problems in its use. No common basic core has been found from culture to culture. A. and G. Sjoberg, for example, have shown, *American Anthropologist*, 59.296–300, that in the cultures of South Asia some items referring to natural objects like the sun cannot be included among the basic core; for they belong to the widely borrowed religious vocabulary.

Moreover, considerable duplication has been found within languages for elements posited in the basic core as different. In applying Swadesh's lists to Athapaskan languages, Hoijer noted that over half the items fail to meet Swadesh's criteria (*Language*, 32.53ff). In Navaho, for example, "this, that" corresponds to five items, no one of which can be clearly matched to the items on the English list; similarly, nouns like "tree, seed, grease" and verbs like "eat, kill, know." Gudschinsky has proposed methods that may deal with such problems; they need further study.

It has also been demonstrated that the rate of retention is not constant from language to language. Meillet long ago pointed to a gypsy dialect of Armenian that contained few Armenian lexical items, while showing the central structure of the language. Clearly the rate of loss in English, Lithuanian, and Greek is much lower than that for this Armenian dialect. If different rates of retention must be proposed from language to language, the generality of glottochronology is eliminated, and its usefulness greatly diminished.

Glottochronology accordingly has been dismissed by many linguists who question whether it is a useful procedure. For languages may undergo differing developments in their semantic structure as well as in their grammatical structure. If they do, no universal list can be devised.

If, on the other hand, the aims of glottochronology are reduced, if it is used within a language group and a culture area for the more modest goals of determining relative dates of separation or establishing subgroups of languages, the problems discussed above may be avoided in part. Glottochronology may then give us useful information about languages attested only from recent times that are related and that are spoken in areas of similar culture.

As one of its contributions, glottochronology has focused attention on the problem of loss in language. Though it may be unworkable in the study of time depth because of the diversity of its results, the wider study, lexicostatistics, may be useful in investigating general principles underlying change and loss in language, especially when data-processing techniques are applied to large amounts of material. Numerous instances are attested of languages going out of use: Cornish in the eighteenth century, Dalmatian in the nineteenth, and today many indigenous languages throughout the world. Thorough documentation of the stages leading to their extinction would be of great interest to historical linguistics. Many languages we know about are now extinct; the steps to their extinction may be understood more clearly if we have thorough descriptions of languages now on the way to extinction.

Selected Further Readings

Possibly the best statement describing the use of glottochronology is Sarah C. Gudschinsky's "The ABC's of Lexicostatistics (Glottochronology)," *Word*, 12.175–210 (1956). It contains a bibliography of the work to 1956, including the numerous articles of M. Swadesh, who is to be credited with the recent interest in the subject. His article "Diffusional Cumulation and Archaic Residue as Historic Explanation," *Southwestern Journal of Anthropology*, 7. 1–21 (1951), relates glottochronology to general linguistic and anthropological theory.

Numerous additional articles could be cited. The following provide an introduction to the applications made and varying views on the subject: Harry Hoijer, "Lexicostatistics: A Critique," *Language*, 32.49–60 (1956); John A. Rea, "Concerning the Validity of Lexicostatistics," *IJAL*, 24.145–50 (1958); D. H. Hymes, "Lexicostatistics So Far," *Current Anthropology*, 1.3–44 (1960), with thorough discussion and extensive bibliography. Two years later Knut Bergsland and Hans Vogt published a devastating critique "On the Validity of Glotto-chronology" *Current Anthropology* 3.115–53 (1962), to which many linguists added their views. After this publication, glottochronology has occupied a very low status. Yet the procedure is still used, and for that reason this brief introduc-tion to it has been maintained. In "The Glottochronology of Six Turkic Languages" *International Journal of American Linguistics* 35.183–91 (1969), Rudolph C. Troike found through use of the one-hundred-word list "close correspondence of . . . data to known historical developments, and concluded that his study "adds another test case to the slowly accumulating body of data confirming the validity of the glottochronological method."

The following list of two hundred words is taken from Gudschinsky's article; the list of one hundred used by Rea is set in italic, with additional words appended. In view of the uncertain results of glottochronology, and on the other hand its relative ease of application, students should carry out their own investi-gations to the extent practicable.

1. *all*
2. and
3. animal
4. *ashes*
5. at
6. back
7. bad
8. *bark*
9. because
10. *belly*
11. *big*
12. *bird*
13. *bite*
14. *black*
15. *blood*
16. blow
17. *bone*
18. breathe
19. *burn*
20. child
21. *cloud*
22. *cold*
23. *come*
24. count
25. cut
26. day
27. *die*
28. dig
29. dirty
30. *dog*
31. *drink*
32. *dry*
33. dull
34. dust
35. *ear*
36. *earth*
37. *eat*
38. *egg*
39. *eye*
40. fall
41. far
42. *fat*—grease
43. father
44. fear
45. *feather*
46. few
47. fight
48. *fire*
49. *fish*
50. five

51. float
52. flow
53. flower
54. *fly*
55. fog
56. *foot*
57. four
58. freeze
59. fruit
60. *give*
61. *good*
62. grass
63. *green*
64. guts
65. *hair*
66. *hand*
67. he
68. *head*
69. *hear*
70. *heart*
71. heavy
72. here
73. hit
74. hold—take
75. how
76. hunt
77. husband
78. *I*
79. ice
80. if
81. *in*
82. *kill*
83. *know*
84. lake
85. laugh
86. *leaf*
87. leftside
88. leg
89. *lie*
90. live
91. *liver*
92. *long*
93. *louse*
94. *man–male*
95. *many*
96. *meat–flesh*
97. mother
98. *mountain*
99. *mouth*
100. *name*

101. narrow
102. near
103. *neck*
104. *new*
105. *night*
106. *nose*
107. *not*
108. old
109. *one*
110. other
111. *person*
112. play
113. pull
114. push
115. *rain*
116. red
117. right–correct
118. rightside
119. river
120. road
121. *root*
122. rope
123. rotten
124. rub
125. salt
126. *sand*
127. *say*
128. scratch
129. sea
130. *see*
131. *seed*
132. sew
133. sharp
134. short
135. sing
136. *sit*
137. *skin*
138. sky
139. *sleep*
140. *small*
141. smell
142. *smoke*
143. smooth
144. snake
145. snow
146. some
147. spit
148. split
149. squeeze
150. stab—pierce

151. *stand*
152. *star*
153. stick
154. *stone*
155. straight
156. suck
157. *sun*
158. swell
159. *swim*
160. *tail*
161. *that*
162. there
163. they
164. thick
165. thin
166. think
167. *this*
168. *thou*
169. three
170. throw
171. tie
172. *tongue*
173. *tooth*
174. *tree*
175. turn
176. *two*
177. vomit
178. *walk*
179. *warm*
180. wash
181. *water*
182. *we*
183. wet
184. *what*
185. when
186. where
187. *white*
188. *who*
189. wide
190. wife
191. wind
192. wing
193. wipe
194. with
195. *woman*
196. woods
197. worm
198. ye
199. year
200. *yellow*

94. *breast*   95. *claw*   96. *full*   97. *horn*   98. *knee*   99. *moon*
100. *round*

Note that in eliciting, one must not search for cognates. Exact cognates exist for the words used in 7.2, e.g., *Haupt* for *head* and *cup* for *Kopf*, yet the normal response of a German speaker asked to give the equivalent of head is *Kopf*. Equivalents in usage rather than etymological cognates must be used as the basis for glottochronology.

CHAPTER 8

Broadening of language materials; dialect geography

8.1 The early work in dialect geography

The growing convictions about the regularity of sound change after 1870 led to great interest in the study of various strata of speech, especially geographical dialects. In spite of the clarifications produced by Grassmann and Verner for the first Germanic consonant shift, and by other linguists for such problems elsewhere, some elements in the standard languages still showed irregularities. It was then tentatively assumed by some linguists that standard languages, such as literary English, contained irregularities because they were mixed. To find pure languages, one would have to collect the speech of the everyday people, commonly known as dialect. Interest in dialects prompted by a search for regular language development was supported by interest aroused by the Romantic movement.

Following Jean Jacques Rousseau, scholars and literary figures came to concern themselves with folkways from the end of the eighteenth century. Using more than the occasional phrases of "rustic dialect" found in Wordsworth, writers like Robert Burns and Johann Peter Hebel preferred their native speech to the more general literary languages. In an attempt to show that dialects as well as literary languages had respectable pedigrees, some linguists devoted their attention to dialects. In 1821 J. A. Schmeller, published the first grammar of a dialect, Bavarian. Although other scholars followed Schmeller's example, dialect study before 1875 was more concerned with social and historical than linguistic problems, as scholars attempted to relate contemporary dialects with ancient tribal groups. In nomenclature and popular conceptions, their work has had a lasting effect. Old English is still often referred to as Anglo-Saxon. With this label the suggestion is made that Angles carried to Britain the Anglian dialect, and Saxons the Saxon dialect, where they subsequently merged to form English. Similarly in Germany the labels for dialects continue old tribal names that are still used as area names, such as Bavarian and Franconian. In subsequent dialect study, less colorful, and also less misleading, labels are used, such as Northern, Midland, and Southern in the United States.

Under superficial examination the early dialect study seemed to support the neogrammarian hypothesis that "sound change takes place according to laws that admit no exception." In standard English, for example, initial *v* and *f* both represent Old English *f*, apparently without pattern, as in *vat*, *vixen* versus *father*, *folk*. Yet in the Somerset dialect spoken by Sophie Western's father in *Tom Jones*, every Old English *f-* is a *v-*. Squire Western says *vather* and *volk* as well as *vat* and *vixen*. Although G. Wenker set out to collect similar material in German dialects, hoping to find similar consistencies there, his work led virtually to the converse of his original aim; it has contributed greatly to our understanding of complexity in language.

Wenker's dialect work has the further importance that with the work of his counterpart in France, J. Gilliéron, it furnished the patterns for dialect investigation. Subsequent studies and conclusions have been largely based on the activities of these two men.

After restricted investigation in the Rhineland, Wenker began to collect material from every section of Germany. His procedure was to prepare forty sentences and send them out to schoolteachers in 40,736 localities, later expanded to 49,363. The sentences, which dealt with every-day matters, were chosen carefully to give data on dialect differences. Sentence 1 reads: *Im Winter fliegen die trocknen Blätter durch die Luft herum*. "In winter the dry leaves fly around through the air." (See Mitzka, *Handbuch*, pages 13–14, for the entire set.) Teachers were asked to transcribe the sentences in accordance with the characteristic speech in their districts. Sets were then returned to Marburg for analysis. Each of the sources for material was eventually to be put on a map, and the characteristic features of dialects were to be plotted by the location of their occurrences. Publication of the maps did not get under way until 1927 and is not yet complete. The plotting of dialect distribution on maps, however, led to the terminology used in detailed study of the language data.

The study of the varying forms of speech in one language is known as **dialect geography**, or **dialectology**. In plotting their findings on maps, dialect geographers compiled **dialect atlases** containing maps of the features investigated. Terminology for dialect spread was fashioned after that used in map-making. On the pattern of isobar and isotherm, **isogloss** is a term used for a line drawn from location to location along the outer limits of characteristic features. The interpretation and linguistic significance of varying patterns of isoglosses was developed as the German and French dialect materials were analyzed and described. Moreover, procedures of collecting dialect materials were improved as subsequent dialect geographers profited by the experience of their predecessors.

The advantage of the German collection is its broad coverage. For a relatively small area like that of Germany, close to 50,000 recordings provide great breadth of information. Yet Wenker's dialect project also had shortcomings: for one thing, it has not been completely published. To this day scholars who wish to use the German materials must go to the archives in Marburg. Further, transcriptions were made by untrained observers. Everyone has idiosyncracies in recording; with untrained workers there can be no attempt to correct these, or even to determine them. These shortcomings are especially serious in phonological study, for which the German project was best suited. The forty sentences provide little material on morphological variation, less on lexical differences. When these shortcomings became apparent, efforts were made to repair them.

To provide material collected by trained observers, young scholars undertook the collection and description of speech in various localities. Numerous monographs were published, supplementing the inadequate materials of the atlas. A. Bach, *Deutsche Mundartforschung*, gives a densely printed selection of them, pages 214–26. To provide the deficient lexical material, W. Mitzka in 1938 sent out a second set of materials, questions designed to secure names of everyday items, such as plants and animals. His results are being published in a German word-atlas, and in monographs dealing with individual words. To provide contemporary records of pronunciation, E. Zwirner undertook in the 1950s to collect tape recordings of German dialects from more than 1200 localities. His recordings, although brief, preserve speech for subsequent interpretation. Tape recordings have the further advantage that copies may readily be provided to other investigators. With these supplements ample materials are available for German dialect study, and provision has been made to remedy the deficiences of Wenker's initial undertaking.

Gilliéron, editor of the French atlas, planned from the start to avoid the pitfalls encountered by his German predecessor. He selected and trained one worker, Edmond Edmont, to collect all material for the French atlas. Edmont, who had an excellent ear, provided accurate, reliable, and consistent records. Cycling from point to point, where he established himself in congenial surroundings, he collected material by direct questions rather than through a highly restricted set of sentences. In the years of collecting, 1896–1900, Edmont gathered material from 639 locations, providing less coverage than had the German project. Under its superb organization, however, the French atlas was completely published by 1910. Gilliéron must therefore be credited with providing the pattern according to which the materials of many subsequent projects were published.

8.2   Dialect studies based on findings of the early projects

The advantages that later dialect studies derived from the German and French undertakings may be illustrated by the American project. After consultation with linguists who had directed earlier projects, the project was designed to avoid mistakes made in previous collections. (See the report of Hans Kurath in the *Handbook of the Linguistic Geography of New England.*) Its planning, which resulted in great part from earlier dialect studies, also reflects the growing realization of the complexity of language.

Under the direction of its carefully chosen editor, Hans Kurath, great attention was given to:

1. Selection and training of field workers.
2. Selection of informants and locations to investigate.
3. Preparation of a questionnaire.

The field workers, already highly trained linguists, were given further training in the summer of 1931 under two eminent dialect geographers, Jud and Scheuermeier. To cover an area as large as New England, having a number of field workers is essential in spite of the resultant diversity of recordings. Yet this diversity was not unduly great. Moreover, it provided a check on the characteristics of individual workers that was missing in Edmont's excellent work.

Just as the selection and training of field workers illustrates the increase in precision of dialect geography since 1876, the care in selection of informants indicates the increasing awareness of the complexity of language. Informants were chosen from each age group. Since this was the first large-scale dialect study in the United States, particular care was taken to include speakers more than seventy years old. Moreover, speakers from three selected social groups were included: those with little formal education and restricted social contacts, those with some formal education, and those with advanced education. All information about informants and other pertinent data about speech communities were carefully noted, and are available to analysts.

For the preparation of worksheets comprising the questionnaire, samplings were made to determine points of variation among speakers, which in turn suggested items to investigate. Worksheets were thereupon designed to elicit specific forms but also to allow flexibility. Moreover, field workers were to note if an informant indicated that a form was rarely used, old-fashioned, amusing, or whether it elicited from him other attitudes or responses. Adequate information was collected and made available so that linguistic facts could be understood not only by linguists but also by historians, geographers, sociologists, and others interested in the social and cultural history of New England (Kurath, *Handbook*, ix). Simultaneous tape recordings are now possible, with which other linguists may check transcriptions. In this way dialect geographers collect material of any breadth and precision that scholarly resources, finances, and time permit.

The American project covered New England, with subsequent publication of an atlas, 1939–43. Further collecting in America has been carried out. A concise statement on the state of American dialect study a decade ago has been provided by R. I. McDavid, Jr., in Chapter 9, "The Dialects of American English," of W. M. Francis', *The Structure of American English* (New York, 1958). The work involved in covering a territory the size of the United States is so huge that numerous smaller projects have now been undertaken. Elsewhere as well, the arranging of dialect collections in multiple projects, rather than preparation of national atlases, now forms the general pattern. For unless a language area is small and homogeneous, the results of dialect collection are so huge and diverse that they are not readily accessible. In France, too, numerous studies covering only a section of the country have been undertaken in attempts to provide fuller information than that in Gilliéron's atlas.

Changes in language and costs of publication make it likely that future results will be available in archives rather than in atlases after the French pattern. However the collections are made available, linguists now have access to a broad array of linguistic data. The extent of collections may be determined from Sever Pop's survey of 1400 pages, *La Dialectologie* (Louvain, 1950), and from the listings of subsequent bibliographies. These must now be interpreted for their contributions to our understanding of linguistic development. (See Map 1.)

8.3   Findings of the German dialect project concerning the Old High German consonant shift

The contributions by dialect geographers to our understanding of language were not long in coming. Very early in investigation, it became quite apparent that the boundaries between languages and those between dialects could not be neatly defined. Isoglosses differ from item to item. Since the division between High German and Low German was among the most highly investigated among language interrelationships, many of the procedures of dialect geography were worked out in solving problems concerning it.

The chief items differentiating High German from Low German are the reflexes of Proto-Germanic *p t k*. These remained in Low German, as in English, but have become fricatives and affricates in High German.

A summary of the changes in initial, medial, and final positions may be given as follows:

1. Late Proto-Germanic *p- t- k- -pp- -tt- -kk-* > Old High German *pf ts k(x)* (we may use the unchanged English items to indicate the original, Proto-Germanic sounds).

E. pool : G. Pfuhl   E. shape : G. schöpfen
E. tongue : G. Zunge   E. sit : G. sitzen
E. cow : G. Kuh, but   E. wake : G. wecken, but
   Swiss kxū   Swiss wekxen

2. Late Proto-Germanic *-p- -t- -k- -p -t -k* > Old High German *-f (f) -s(s) -x(x)*.

E. hope : G. hoffen   E. up : G. auf
E. water : G. Wasser   E. it : es
E. cake : G. Kuchen   E. book : G. Buch

According to the principles of sound change formulated by the neo-grammarians, we should expect to find that all late Proto-Germanic *-k- -k* become *x* (ch) over the entire High German territory. For sounds in the same environment were assumed to change consistently, without exception, throughout a dialect area. When, however, the data assembled by Wenker's questionnaire were examined, different isoglosses were found for words similar in structure, such as German *machen* 'make,' *ich* 'I.' (See Map 2.) Although the isoglosses for these two words are virtually identical from the eastern extent of German speech to the neighborhood of the Rhine, at that point they separate. The isogloss for *machen* crosses the Rhine near Benrath, somewhat south of Ürdingen, the point at which that for *ich* crosses the river. The two isoglosses are labeled after the villages the

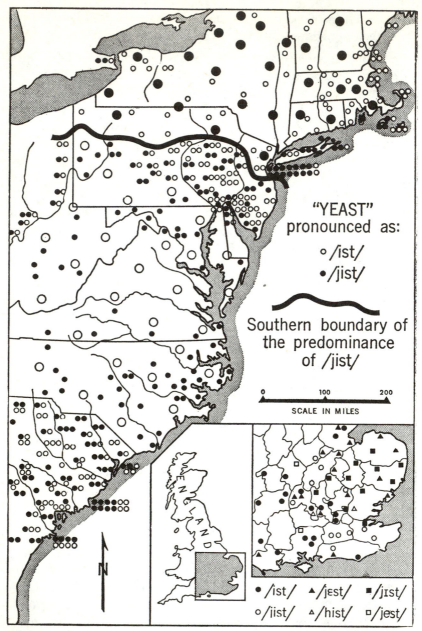

Map 1.   The pronunciation of *yeast* in the Atlantic States. Note the precision used in providing the information, and the insert map giving the distribution of pronunciation in southern England, by which the sources of American dialect forms can be explored. Taken from *Pronunciation of English in the Atlantic States* by Hans Kurath and Raven I. McDavid. (Ann Arbor, The University of Michigan Press, 1961). Included with the permission of Hans Kurath.

Benrath line and the **Ürdingen line**. Their divergence near the Rhine plus that of other isoglosses, which fan out at this point, led to the label the **Rhenish fan** and require an explanation.

The explanation can be furnished from cultural history. The Benrath line corresponds to the extent of Cologne's influence from the thirteenth

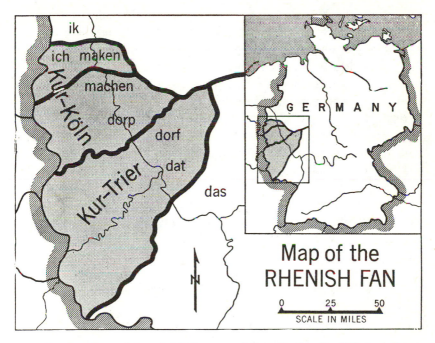

Map 2. One of the classical areas of investigation in dialect study shows the extent of spread of the change $k > x$ in Germany, and the enclave in which PGmc. t is unshifted in *dat. wat, it, allet*. Shadings indicate the Rhenish fan and the enclave.

century; the Ürdingen line, to its influence from the fourteenth to the sixteenth centuries (see Bach, *Deutsche Mundartforschung*, 133–34.) The forms for 'make' were fixed at the early time; those for 'I' later. One can account for the different isoglosses by assuming that a sound change, $k > x$, had taken place in southern Germany and that its effects were gradually extended northward. The extent of spread of innovation in any word is determined by the cultural prestige of speakers who use it. Findings like those for German *machen* and *ich*, repeated many times over in various dialect studies, led to a more accurate understanding of language change and to greater concern with cultural patterns of communities in which a given language is spoken.

As indicated above, the three voiceless tense stops p t k of Upper

German were shifted. When medial and final, they became fricatives $f \; \theta \; \chi$, in accordance with the following rule:

$$\text{Rule 1.} \quad \begin{bmatrix} +\text{cns} \\ +\text{tense} \end{bmatrix} \rightarrow +\text{cont} \Big/ [+\text{voc}] - \left\{ \begin{matrix} [+\text{voc}] \\ \# \end{matrix} \right\}$$

That is, tense consonants became fricatives in the environment after vowels and before vowels or pauses. The results of the change were extended northward and adopted in varying degrees in accordance with the extent of prestige of the southern-German dialects; the absolute limits of adoption may be indicated by a line extending across German-speaking territory from approximately Cologne eastward, just south of Berlin. Subsequently, German dialects have been differentiated largely by the extent to which they employed this rule for each of the voiceless, tense, or fortis stops in the stated environments. In Low Franconian and Low German the rule was not practiced at all, leading to a differentiation of the continental West Germanic area into two major subgroups, as Chart 1 indicates.

By a second rule, initial voiceless tense stops *p t k* (and intervocalic long *pp tt kk*, which apparently were similarly articulated) became affricates: *pf ts kx*:

$$\text{Rule 2.} \quad \begin{bmatrix} +\text{cns} \\ +\text{tense} \end{bmatrix} \rightarrow [+\text{delayed release}] \Big/ \left\{ \begin{matrix} [\#\text{---}+\text{voc}] \\ [\underline{+\text{gemination}}] \end{matrix} \right\}$$

That is, tense consonants became affricates in the environments initially before vowel and when geminated. This rule was not extended as far to the north as was the first rule, leading to subdivisions of the High German territory, as Chart 1 indicates. The dialects in which this rule was adopted are known as Upper German, in contrast with the Middle German dialects, in which Rule 1 was adopted, and Low German, in which neither rule was adopted.

The distinction between Upper German and Middle German was reinforced by the devoicing of *b d g* in Upper German. The effect of these changes in the continental Germanic languages may illustrate the bases for the differentiation of dialects. A comprehensive series of changes, adopted in part by contiguous areas, leads to subdivisions of a given linguistic area in accordance with the extent of social groupings.

Even in such large-scale shifts, the rules may not be applied to all words, as we may illustrate by the unshifted *t* in *dat it wat*, the German forms for *that it what* in the Mosel Franconian area. Here *-t* shows up as *-s* in words like *great*, G. *gross*, but not in the words cited or the *-et*

CHART 1

1. The Germanic Voiced Spirants (Intermediate Period)

ð>d, b>b ▢

-b->b, γ->g ▤

-γ->g ▥

-γ>k ▨

2. The H.G. Shift of Voiceless Stops

p¹t¹k¹>ff, ʒʒ, xx ⎱ ▤
t²>ts

p²>pf ▦

k²>kx ▨

3. The H.G. Shift of Voiced Stops

d>t ▤

b>p, g>k ▥

	West-Germanic	Middle-Franconian	Rhenish-Franconian	East-Franconian	Alemannian	Bavarian	New High German Examples
1.	t¹	ʒʒ	ʒʒ	ʒʒ	ʒʒ	ʒʒ	Wasser (M.F. dat)
2.	p¹	ff	ff	ff	ff	ff	offen (M.F. up)
3.	k¹	xx	xx	xx	xx	xx	machen
4.	t²	ts	ts	ts	ts	ts	zwei
5.	p²	—	ff, rf	pf	pf	pf	Pflug
6.	k²	—	—	—	(kx)	(kx)	kalt
7.	d	d̥	d̥	d(t)	d(t)	(d)t	tun (Wind)
8.	b-	b̥	b̥	b̥	b(p)	b(p)	Berg (Passau)
9.	-b-	v	b>v	b>v	b(p)	b>v	Weiber (Rippe)
10.	γ-	—	g̊	g̊	g̊(k)	g̊(k)	geben
11.	-γ-	—	—	—	g̊(k)	g̊(k)	Auge (Rücken)
12.	-γ				-k	(k)	Tag
	þ	d̥	d̥	d̥	d̥	d̥	der

Chart 1 is taken from Eduard Prokosch, *The Sounds and History of the German Language* (New York: Holt, 1916, p. 130).

ending of the adjective, for example, *allet* rather than standard German *alles*, nom. sg. nt. 'all.' Although scholars are not agreed in their explanations for these unshifted forms, they may be ascribed to difference in syntactic environment. We may assume that the unshifted *dat it wat allet* were adopted from weakly stressed sentence positions, in which the change *t > s* was not carried through. Again, information concerning the use of forms required broadening to include their precise environments not only within words, but within sentences.

8.4   Classification of dialects

Such problems encountered in dialect geography studies led to a questioning of former views concerning (1) the regularity of sound change and (2) the usefulness of setting up dialects. Extreme rebellion against the tidy view of language ascribed to the neogrammarians may be illustrated by the slogan: *every word has its own history* and by Gaston Paris' statement on the virtually imperceptible gradations from dialect to dialect in French, even into Italian.

No one can deny that every word, like every social convention or every artifact, has its own history. But the statement is as misleading as is the slogan: *sound change takes place according to laws that admit no exception.* A word is a composite of morphemes and phonemes. Since the allophones of the phonemes vary with their environment, every word will have undergone changes different from all other words. To conclude that one should describe every word separately indicates a poor understanding of the social functioning of language. Even worse are the linguistic studies that deal with the history of individual sounds from proto-languages to the present. Studies based on such methods resemble lists rather than descriptions. Neither phonemes nor morphemes are independent entities in language; rather, they pattern with other sets and subsets of phonemes and morphemes. Fortunately, dialect geographers, like historical linguists who learned much from the neogrammarians, have come to understand the disadvantage of basing methodology on slogans.

The usefulness of positing dialects was graphically questioned by Gaston Paris in his story of the traveler who proceeds slowly from Paris to Italy. Traveling a few miles at a stretch, and adapting his speech constantly to each local dialect, he would scarcely notice differences in speech in the French area; he might not even notice when he crossed the supposedly greater boundary from France to Italy. For even here he would not find an abrupt speech cleavage such as he might encounter if he crossed into Germanic territory.

In spite of the absence of sharp dialect, or language, boundaries, dialect geographers have not abandoned subclassification of languages. For dialect classification they have progressed from a reliance on isoglosses for important linguistic features, such as the *machen* isogloss, through **bundles of isoglosses** to correlation methods. Contemporary investigators seek to learn whether a list of features is present at given points. They then correlate their results and connect points with similar correlation coefficients with lines known as **isopleths** or **isogrades**. These may represent not only various isoglosses but also folk customs, such as tales, superstitions, and agricultural practices. Further, they may reflect earlier political boundaries, which in turn were probably determined by geographical features (Weinreich, *Word*, 10.397–98). Isopleths, accordingly, circumscribe areas of culture that have exerted a uniform effect on language. These for linguistic purposes are called language, or dialect, areas.

8.5   Characteristics of dialect areas

Although given a common label, speech within a language area is not uniform. Language areas generally center about a point that is touched by relatively few isoglosses. Such points, which other speakers regard as areas of prestige, are known as **focal areas**. Innovations transmitted from them are accepted by surrounding areas as far as the prestige of the focal area extends. As an example we may cite the distribution of *tonic* (a soft drink) in New England. Its general use around Boston indicates the extent of influence exerted by the speakers in the Boston area. Outside the area, *tonic* has not succeeded in replacing older forms.

At the limits of well-defined speech areas, we find **transition areas**. These may show characteristics of two neighboring focal areas, as do western New Hampshire, central Massachusetts, and Rhode Island in their terms for a soft drink.

Further characteristic types of area, known as **relic areas**, lie beyond the extent of expanding isoglosses. Relic areas are generally found in locations that are difficult of access for cultural, political, or geographic reasons. They may be discontinuous, as are the relic areas on Map 3 in which final *r* is preserved.

The status of preconsonantal and final *r* in New England, as in *hard*, *far*, may illustrate the various types of area. Around Boston there is little evidence for this *r*; isoglosses would be remote from the city. We conclude, as from the word "tonic." that Boston is a focal area. In western Massachusetts and elsewhere along the Connecticut River, usage is divided, with some speakers pronouncing, others dropping, *r*. This is a transition area between the *r*-speech of the Hudson Valley and the *r*-less speech of Boston. In addition, we find the *r* of this environment maintained on Martha's Vineyard, Marblehead, and Cape Ann, which are relic areas.

Since the time of the German and French dialect projects, which established much of the methodology of dialect geography, many studies have been made of speech communities and their subdivisions.

A notable study by G. G. Kloeke interpreted the distribution of varying forms of the words for 'house' and 'mouse' in the Netherlands by investigating the social uses of these words. The earlier forms were like those recorded in Old English, *hūs* and *mūs*. They have undergone a variety of

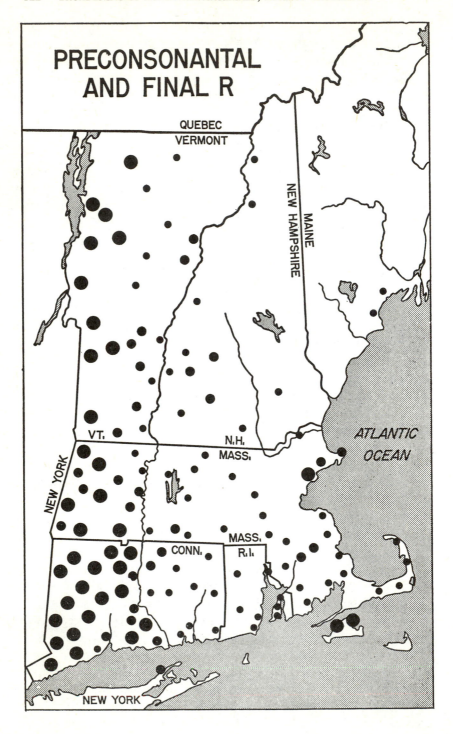

PRECONSONANTAL
AND FINAL R

changes in Dutch-speaking territory. Kloeke demonstrated that the spread of the changes may be attributed to different social dialects, as well as to different geographical dialects. In the word for 'house.' more likely than that for 'mouse' to be included in formal conversation, an innovating pronunciation of a focal area has also been disseminated more widely. Successive innovations for both words spread from the cities of Antwerp and, later, Amsterdam, which were focal areas, leaving relic areas on the periphery of the country. Moreover, on the borders between Low German and Dutch speech, we find a transition area in which the spread of innovations was checked.

8.6   Implications of dialect study for language classification

Such studies of dialect distribution within various languages have led to better understanding of speech communities and of the distribution of linguistic features. From the findings of dialect geography in contemporary speech communities, attempts have been made to explain the linguistic situation of past periods, as in the Proto-Indo-European community.

Among the Indo-European languages, verb endings with a characteristic *r* to mark the middle voice are limited to Celtic, Italic, Hittite, and Tocharian. Celtic and Italic were at the western periphery of the Indo-

---

Map 3.   Shows the distribution of preconsonantal and final *r*, illustrating the influence of the focal area Boston, transitions to other dialect areas, and relic areas.

An *r* preceding a vowel, as in *road, borrow, far out*, is pronounced in all parts of New England. But before consonants and finally, as in *hard, how far?*, usage is regional: in western New England and in New Brunswick the *r* is regularly pronounced, in most of eastern New England it is dropped, while the Connecticut Valley is mixed and unstable in practice.

Martha's Vineyard, Marblehead, and Cape Ann, all secluded communities, appear as "*r* islands" in eastern New England, where this *r* is still losing ground. On the other hand, the *r* is gaining ground in the Connecticut Valley.

The largest circles indicate regular use of this *r*; the smallest ones, sporadic use; and the remainder, rather evenly divided usage.

Taken from *Handbook of the Linguistic Geography of New England* by Hans Kurath in collaboration with Marcus L. Hansen, Julia Bloch, and Bernard Bloch. Providence, R. I.: Brown University, 1939. Copyright, 1939, by The American Council of Learned Societies. Included with the permission of Hans Kurath.

European area; the two other subgroups were probably located elsewhere on its periphery. We may therefore account for the *r*-middles as relic forms that survived in the peripheral areas of the Indo-European community. Germanic, Greek, Baltic, Slavic, Albanian, Armenian and Indo-Iranian, make up the central dialects. Innovations in the middle voice, patterned on endings for the active voice, were spread through this central area but did not eliminate the *r*-endings on the periphery.

Another innovation that spread through a part of the central area is the change of some *k*'s to sibilants, as in the word for 'hundred' (see Chapter 2, pages 27–28). The languages with the innovation are Indo-Iranian, Armenian, Albanian, and, imperfectly, Slavic and Baltic. Applying the findings of contemporary dialect geography in this way to ancient speech areas has given us a much more flexible, and realistic, view of their interrelationships.

Linguistic study may also lead to an understanding of earlier cultural relationships. For example, if we had only linguistic information about prior settlement patterns in Louisiana and Texas, we could still determine from the distribution of words for 'small bonus' the predominant influence of French and of Spanish settlers (see Map 4). After millennia have elasped, such distribution may become clouded, and its interpretation require intricate analysis. Nevertheless, interpretations of this sort have been attempted for areas of present-day Romance languages, with the aim of determining prior language groups. But, since no data survive from these, the conclusions must be viewed with reserve.

8.7   Implications of dialect study for the history of individual words

The history of individual words has also been clarified by dialect geographers, especially by Gilliéron. He was greatly interested in the relationships of homophones to each other, assuming that in the course of time one of them would be eliminated. This process is referred to as **loss by collision**. In the French collections he found good material in support of his thesis. The word *viande* 'food,' from Lat. *vivenda* nt. pl. of the quasi gerundive of *vivere* 'live,' replaced *char* < *carne* 'food, meat' in the focal area of Paris, where *char* came to be homophonous with the Old French form of *chère* 'dear' < Lat. *cara*. In this way he provided one explanation for some losses in language, although his successors suggest that he exaggerated the extent of loss by collision. Yet the examples they provide are from different subsystems of the language, such as the noun *bear* and the verb *bear*, or *two*, *too*, and *to*. When sound changes lead to homonymity

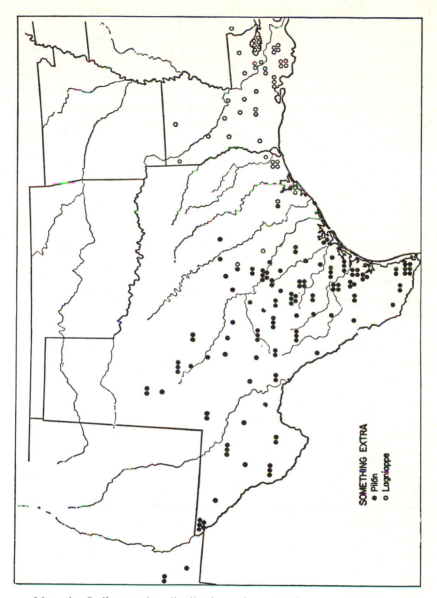

Map 4. Indicates the distribution of words for a small bonus, *lagniappe* and *pilon*, in the Texas area. The extent of French influence is clearly demarcated from that of Spanish. Taken by permission from *The Regional Vocabulary of Texas* by E. Bagby Atwood. Austin: The University of Texas Press, 1962.

for items used in similar environments such as *char*, or *gat*, for 'cat' and 'rooster' in southwestern France, the likelihood of substitutes for one of the homonyms is great. In one of his classical studies, Gilliéron demonstrated how the words for 'pheasant' and 'vicar' were substituted for the old word for 'rooster' in precisely the area where it coincided with the word for 'cat.'

Another phenomenon accounted for by dialect geography studies is the occurrence of **blends**. These occur in various formations. In western Germany two words for 'potato,' *Erdapfel* and *Grundbirne*, gave rise to *Erdbirne*. In the western Taunus area two words for 'brake,' the native *Hemme* and *Meckenick*, from Fr. *mécanique*, have given rise to *Hemmenick* (see Bach, *Deutsche Mundartforschung*, 158ff. for these and others). Such blends are found particularly in transition areas.

8.8   Extension of dialect study

Because dialect studies have been especially successful in explaining individual forms, dialect geographers have concerned themselves primarily with single items rather than with structures or substructures of language. This concern may have been further magnified by the necessity of constructing isoglosses for individual items rather than for segments of a substructure. Besides treating linguistic facts individually, dialect geographers have even questioned whether their study can be structural (e.g., U. Weinreich, "Is a Structural Dialectology Possible?" *Word*, 10.388–400, 1954).

The question was already answered by Bloomfield, when in *Language*, 323, he demanded of a dialect dictionary that it "give a phonemic scheme for each local type of speech. . . ." Yet dialect geographers, other than a few like Weinreich, have disregarded this demand, possibly because of the complexity of their subject. Any dialect geographer with a sizable questionnaire collects enough material from one informant to produce a skeletal grammar. Pressed for time, however, he proceeds to a further speaker without actually producing such a grammar. Instead, he deposits the materials in an archive for further study. Subsequent scholars using the archive are generally interested primarily in noting common linguistic features. They can determine these from unprocessed questionnaires, and, thus, structural statements rarely result. A possible solution lies in the application of data-processing techniques for listing the collected data; material can then be retrieved in accordance with specified instructions.

One of the contributions of dialect geography to the present lies in making us aware of the great variety in language. Through the diversity and wealth of forms it has disclosed, dialect geography has broadened greatly our views of language. Historical grammars no longer treat languages as single strata, but rather as complexes composed of numerous strata. A given speaker masters some of these. But the complete language is discernible only as one collects material from a variety of speakers.

The linguists at the beginning of the nineteenth century were concerned essentially with the standard language. Some linguists of today maintain such a restricted concern; a notable example is Noam Chomsky, whose "linguistic theory is concerned primarily with an ideal speaker-listener, in a completely homogeneous speech-community" (*Aspects*, page 3). But even the early dialect geographers went on to explore the geographically varying strata of language. Subsequent study aroused concern for strata determined also by social, functional, and occupational differences. In this way a view of language more complex than that of the founders of historical linguistics has been contributed to historical linguistics by the study of dialect geography. Contemporary study of language variation according to geographical, occupational, and social groups is carried out in the field of sociolinguistics.

8.9   Contributions of sociolinguistics to our understanding of change in language

Historical linguists have long held that dialects may influence one another, leading to linguistic changes. In recent investigations the interrelationships between dialects, and the effects of such interrelationships, have been examined in detail. Further studies have even attempted to account for language change in general, on the basis of dialect relationships.

A notable study of the effects of dialect interrelationships was carried out by William Labov in New York City. In a modern metropolis, speakers are in contact with a variety of dialects, dialects determined by the age of speakers, by ethnic backgrounds, by social and economic classes. Among the characteristics in which New York City speakers differ is the use of final and preconsonantal /r/, for example, in *car* and *card*. Labov found that /r/ was a prestige feature. Speakers who did not normally use it were careful to introduce it when they wished to impress others. Moreover, they extended features of prestige to environments beyond their normal range. In this way, according to Labov, the results of changes may be introduced to new linguistic environments. As changes are transmitted, their impact on language may accordingly be increased. For example, if a change like that of early Old High German $p\ t\ k$ to $f\ \theta\ \chi$ occurred originally in one area, it might have been expanded in scope when it was adopted by speakers in neighboring areas. Such observations may help clarify the spread of linguistic changes in the past. Labov's study also illustrates the linguistic situation in a contemporary society. In earlier dialect study, focal areas of prestige were identified geographically; the capital of a political unit like Paris or Boston might provide patterns for neighboring speakers. If changes were introduced into such prestige dialects, they might be adopted by speakers in neighboring areas, as we observed earlier in this chapter. Labov's study has made it clear that changes may not only emanate from specific geographical areas but also from specific social or economic groups. For understanding language change, the dialects of such groups must be investigated as have the geographical dialects of the past.

Besides expanding the scope of dialect investigation, linguists have also been formulating the findings of dialect study more precisely. Characteristic features of dialects are being stated in ordered rules. Differences between dialects may then consist not solely of differing linguistic characteristics expressed by means of differing rules but also of differing orders of rules. S. J. Keyser proposed to account in this way for variations in eastern American English dialects (*Language* 39. 303–316, 1963). This situation in language may be illustrated by a German example.

In the twelfth century, $\bar{\imath} > ei$ in Austria and South Germany, as in NHG *Seite* < MHG *sīte*. The change was extended northward, and reached the Mosel area in the sixteenth century. Middle High German also had an *ie* diphthong, pronounced [iə]. This *ie* changed to $\bar{\imath}$ in the eleventh and twelfth centuries in Central Germany, as in NHG *ließ* 'permitted,' and the change was extended southward. In the dialect of Wetterau, the $\bar{\imath} < iə$ was adopted before the influence of the change $\bar{\imath} > ei$ was transmitted from the south; as a result the vowel of *ließ* and other words with earlier *iə* also was changed to *ei* when the $\bar{\imath} > ei$ change reached the Wetterau dialect. Grammars of the German dialects would therefore have different rule orders. In a grammar of dialects to the south, the $\bar{\imath} > ei$ rule would be ordered before that of *ie* > $\bar{\imath}$; in a grammar of dialects to the north, the *ie* > $\bar{\imath}$ rule would have an earlier order. The relationships between these dialects with regard to these characteristics would therefore be indicated in the order of rules that indicate the results of previous sound changes.

Studies like those of Labov and Keyser have helped clarify the relationships found in languages after sound changes have taken place, but they have not indicated the reasons why changes take place. Other scholars, however, have proposed that the very existence of dialects in language may account for some changes. Alf Sommerfelt, cited such an explanation for a sound change in a Norwegian dialect (*Diachronic and Synchronic Aspects of Language* (The Hague: 1962, page 222). According to an investigator of this dialect, A. B. Larsen, the speakers introduced a change of *ei* to *ai* to provide a greater contrast with a neighboring dialect. If this explanation is correct, we would have to assume that in at least some changes the speakers consciously introduce the innovations. Whether such deliberate innovations can be demonstrated, differentiation of language in relation to social situations has received remarkable support from a study of bird songs.

Observation of bird songs has disclosed that some birds have developed dialects, among them sparrows (see Fernando Nottebohm, "Ontogeny of Bird Song," *Science* 167.950–56, 1970). Two dialects of sparrows in Argentina are associated with the territory in which the birds nest. Nottebohm concludes that the dialects play a part in the mating systems of the two groups of sparrows, and that as a result they "encourage the emergence of locally adaptive traits" (954). If we apply this observation to human communities, we would propose that distinct dialects may have emerged in an attempt to delimit specific social groups.

This suggestion is at variance with many views concerning language. For linguists and other observers have generally assumed that the dominant aim in communication is to break down barriers between groups. Apparently, however, the formation of differing dialects, and eventually separate languages, provides advantages to social groups. For this reason, linguistic change may be fostered, and even inaugurated. Such a conclusion helps to account for the huge number of languages that developed in the Americas over a relatively short period, and also for the huge number in a small area like New Guinea.

This conclusion also points to the importance of determining the attitudes of speakers in attempting to account for linguistic change, whether the attitudes favor or oppose change. The most difficult problem in accounting for change concerns its occurrence in a given language at a given time. As we noted in Chapter 1, various reasons have been proposed for change in language: the effect of one language on another; the effect of children learning their language; the effect of the system of a language. These potential influences are always present among any groups of speakers. Few languages are spoken in total isolation. Year after year, babies are learning a language and other social conventions. Languages are never in complete balance. Yet change is not constant, nor parallel among the groups who speak different languages. The Germanic consonant system underwent a large-scale change in the centuries before the beginning of our era. The English vowel system underwent a major change in the fifteenth and sixteenth centuries. The syntactic system of Latin underwent major changes as the Romance languages developed. But comparable languages, for example Baltic and Slavic, did not undergo comparable changes. We may conclude that for understanding change, we must know the social conditions in which languages are spoken and the attitudes of speakers. These matters will be discussed again in Chapter 12:7.5, after we examine the processes involved in phonological, syntactic, and semantic change.

Selected Further Readings

During this century there has probably been more study and publication in dialect geography than in any other field of linguistics. To master its principles, one may best find from Sever Pop's *La Dialectologie* and, after 1950, from the *Linguistic Bibliography*, the primary publications in one's special field of interest —Italian, Swiss, Finnish, and so on—and deal with the data themselves.

Besides the publications providing such data, there are handbooks that are standard for each area. For American English, one should consult H. Kurath, *Handbook of the Linguistic Geography of New England*, for general principles as well as a statement on the work carried out in New England. The summary by R. I. McDavid in W. N. Francis' *The Structure of American English* brings this up to date for American English. For British English, one should consult the *Survey of English Dialects*, ed. H. Orton and E. Dieth. For German, consult A. Bach, *Deutsche Mundartforschung*; for French, A. Dauzat, *La géographie linguistique*; for Dutch, G. G. Kloeke, *De Hollandsche expansie*.

Individual studies that illustrate the application of the principles of dialect geography to restricted fields are E. B. Atwood's *A Survey of Verb Forms in the Eastern United States* and H. Kurath and R. I. McDavid, *The Pronunciation of English in the Atlantic States*. For a study of social dialects in their inter-relationships with one another see William Labov, *The Social Stratification of English in New York City*. A theoretical statement relating the findings of dialect geography with change is 'Empirical Foundations for a Theory of Language Change" by U. Weinreich, W. Labov, and M. I. Herzog, pp. 95–195 of *Directions for Historical Linguistics*, edited by W. P. Lehmann and Yakov Malkiel (Austin: 1968).

Chart I is taken from E. Prokosch, *The Sounds and History of the German Language* (New York, 1916) pages 130–31.

CHAPTER 9

Models of language and of linguistic communities with reference to change

9.1 Views of language in the nineteenth century

Historical linguists in the nineteenth and early twentieth centuries held views on language that were based on a long tradition going back to the Greeks. A short sketch can scarcely give an adequate account of these views. It may not be unjust, however, to state that linguists dealt with the sound system, the system of forms and their order, and the lexicon of languages without interrelating these three components of language. Moreover, since students of language were especially concerned with dead languages, notably Latin and Greek, grammars gave most attention to the problems faced in dealing with these languages. Since both Latin and Greek have many inflections, historical grammars emphasized morphology. Further, since scholars dealing with language were concerned with the meanings of the texts, as in interpreting Greek and Latin literature, they were less interested in the sound system than is anyone dealing with a living language. Latin, for example, was pronounced in accordance with the speaker's native language, like Italian in Italy, like German in Germany, and so on. However unjust this characterization may be to some linguistic works of the nineteenth and early twentieth centuries, linguists of the time did not propose a theory or model of language but instead used Latin grammar as a pattern for describing other languages.

In making one's views precise on phenomena as complex as languages and language groups, it is useful to state them in terms of a model, for models provide a convenient way of confirming a system of general conclusions. If they accurately represent the data, they assist in clarifying views, in posing and solving problems. Currently many linguistic analyses are so closely associated with specific models that they can only be understood if one knows the model as well as the data.

A further aim in formulating models is to develop procedures that might apply to all languages and to determine universal principles that govern language. Such procedures were first developed in phonology. The great phoneticians H. Sweet, E. Sievers, O. Jespersen, and others came to recognize that the phonological system of a language is not made up of the sounds alone but of classes of sounds determined by their use in any language. Furthermore, they recognized that these classes can be described by means of a few distinctive characteristics. For example, they noted that English *t* is characterized by complete closure, by closure at the alveolar ridge, and so on; and that when initial, it is aspirated, as in *top*, but when after *s* as in *stop*, it is unaspirated. Since speakers of Chinese make different use of these characteristics, in Chinese *t* and *tʰ* belong to different classes; for speakers of English, they belong to the same class. In Chinese they are used to distinguish words; in English, on the other hand, they do not distinguish words. **Phoneme**, the term introduced for such classes of sounds, was first proposed by M. Kruszewski. It has been widely discussed and variously defined. What was most important for linguistic study was the realization that language is not an aggregation of physical phenomena, but rather a set of abstractions making up a system. Determining the entities of such systems and how they are interrelated has been one of the major concerns of linguistics.

Views of language have become increasingly abstract, and grammars increasingly formalized. For example, the syntactic structure of languages is now represented in abstract formulas, somewhat as sound systems have been. Such formalization is carried out to facilitate the interpretation of linguistic phenomena. Accordingly, in the course of linguistic study, grammars have become increasingly technical. Although such grammars are difficult for introductory students, they are designed both to permit verification by general principles and to account concisely for the data of the languages under discussion. A model accounting for the various elements of language is sketched in Chapter 9:5.

As each new model is proposed, it may seem that earlier publications have become obsolete. Many have not, whose authors understood the data. For example, Grimm's formulation of the consonant changes between

Proto-Indo-European and Proto-Germanic is still largely valid. As was indicated in Chapter 5, Grimm's terminology must be brought up to date. Moreover, many attempts have been made to determine more precisely the data involved in the series of changes and to provide a more detailed statement of the processes of the changes. But the three major rules formulated by Grimm accounted for the bulk of the data.

The reasons for Jacob Grimm's accurate insights would require lengthy discussion. One reason is that his views of language, and the views of Western grammatical tradition, were not as naïve as they may appear to one who interprets their terminology superficially. Although Grimm, like previous students of language, referred to sounds as "letters," Western grammarians had long distinguished between letters as symbols for sounds, and their *potestas*, that is, their value as sounds or classes of sounds. When one examines Grimm's formulation, it becomes clear that although he used the word for "letter," he was dealing with classes of sounds, not with symbols of the writing system. Hence the validity of his formulation.

Historical linguistic study in the nineteenth and early twentieth centuries resulted in contributions one would expect of an expanding area of study. More and more information about languages and their history was assembled. This increasing information in turn provided increasing understanding of language, and also led to attempts to formulate more useful theories or models of language.

9.2   Some theoretical contributions of Saussure

Some of the most important theoretical contributions to our understanding of language were made by Ferdinand de Saussure (1857–1913). Trained in Leipzig, the center of the neogrammarians, Saussure was thoroughly acquainted with earlier linguistic theory and built on it. His theoretical formulations were published from lecture notes of his students and were increasingly influential on linguists. Among the most influential are the following.

Language for Saussure was a system in which all parts are interrelated. In the words of his successor in Paris, Antoine Meillet, language is *une système où tout se tient* 'a system where everything is interrelated.' This conception of language entails relating all segments of a language to one another. Any entity, such as *t* or a case form like the genitive, must be treated together with all other entities; for example, English *t* must be treated in conjunction with *p k b d g*, the Latin genitive in conjunction with the nominative, dative, accusative, and ablative. By a further extension of this view, the phonology of a language cannot be treated independently of the syntax or the lexicon. With such a view of language, treating any segment of language requires detailed investigation. One should not, for example, deal with the development of PIE *t* to Germanic without dealing with the development of PIE *d* and *dh*; nor even without dealing with the development of the other consonants, the vowels, the accent system, the syntactic system, and so on.

A second important view of Saussure's distinguished between language as a system and language as used by the individual. Language as a system he called **langue**; language in use, **parole**. Historical linguists have dealt primarily with *langue*. The phonological entities in our handbooks, for example PIE *p t k k^w*, are entities of the system; whether so identified or not, they must be viewed as phonemes. In many recent theoretical studies dealing with language, the conception of *langue* is comparable to the term **theory of competence**, that of *parole* to a **theory of performance**. Since historical studies deal with *langue*, they must be interpreted from the point of view of a theory of competence.

The historical grammars that have been produced for various languages have certain shortcomings. Few are explicit about the model of language proposed by the author; and most authors have tacitly assumed that the user would have a view of language based roughly on Latin. Moreover, few have dealt comprehensively with syntax; B. Delbrück's works are an exception. Further, the restricted presentation required by any handbook may have caused the author to eliminate data we would like to see included. But replacements for these grammars have been slow to emerge. When further grammars have been published, many of the general conclusions of previous grammars have been little modified, particularly their conclusions on the interrelationships of languages. Historical grammars of the past will therefore continue to be used; and students must interpret them in accordance with the theoretical positions held by their authors.

9.3   The family, family tree, and wave models of linguistic communities

In addition to providing an explicit model of language, historical linguists must also provide a model for language groups in the course of change. As languages change, they maintain some points of similarity but come to differ in others. Historical linguists have attempted to visualize these on the one hand in accordance with interrelationships that can be established between languages and, on the other, with the processes involved in linguistic change. These efforts have led to the classification of languages presented in Chapter 2, and also to the terminology for referring to such groupings.

The first model widely used for depicting linguistic relationships was the family. After Sir William Jones called attention to the connections between Sanskrit, Greek, Latin, and Germanic, linguists set out to determine and represent the relationships between these languages. They did so by likening various languages to members of a family, and in this way created terminology that we may deplore in its literal sense but that we in great part maintain.

We speak of the Indo-European group and other such groups as a **language family**. Greek and Latin, and other Indo-European languages, may be called **sister languages**. And we may speak of the **parent language**, Proto-Indo-European. We also say that Greek is **descended** from Proto-Indo-European. The languages in a family we call **related**; words or other linguistic entities that we can trace to a common source we call **cognates**.

The family model was useful in working out the interrelationships of languages. The Germanic languages had obviously undergone changes different from those of Greek or Latin; we indicate the subsequent independence by labeling them **sister languages**. After some thought, however, shortcomings of the family model are obvious, for modern Germanic languages like English and German are related to modern Greek not as sisters, but rather as distant cousins. When viewed over a great expanse of time, a language family behaves differently from a natural family, for its members may grow old without dying, and may develop new interrelationships that are hard to label with relationship terms that are not cumbersome. Shortly after the middle of the nineteenth century, a new model was proposed that solved some of these problems, continued others, and raised still others—the **family tree**.

The suggestion that the relationship between subgroups of a language is similar to that between branches of a tree was propounded by August Schleicher, who was strongly influenced by views on evolution. His model is more sophisticated than that of the family, permitting a clear view of languages and also their various further developments—from original branches through smaller and smaller sub-branches, which show relationships in both time and space.

As with the family model, we use terminology today that is based on the view of a language group as a tree. We say that English **branched off** from Germanic, which in turn is a branch of Indo-European, and so on. But, very early, dangers in this model became apparent.

One shortcoming the family-tree model shares with the family model is its depiction of a language as a biological organism. Languages, unlike

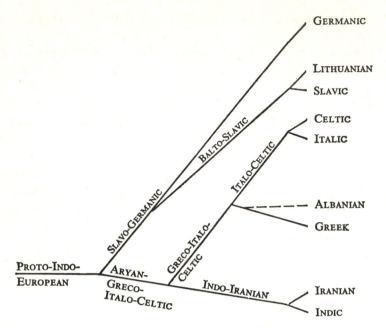

Schleicher's Indo-European family tree.

animals or trees, do not have an independent existence. They are sets of conventions, like conventions of fashion, games, and other human behavior. Changes are introduced in them by their speakers, not spontaneously by the language itself.

The shortcoming that caused replacement of the family-tree model, however, is the view of language change it requires. If English is really a distinct branch of the Indo-European tree, it should permit no modification by another branch or subbranch that separated from the stem earlier, such as French or Sanskrit. Yet we know that many French words, and also Sanskrit words, have been taken into English. Even more troublesome, we find common changes taking place in neighboring languages that long before had separately branched off from the parent language.

Yet because of its simplicity and partial appositeness, the family-tree model still influences views and provides terminology. Virtually all genealogical relationships have been based on it. But a troublesome misconception results from names of successive stages of a language, like Old English, Middle English, New English. These terms suggest that we view New English as a direct descendant of Old English. We know, however, that modern standard English developed from the London dialect, a Midland form of speech, while our chief Old English materials have come down to us in a West Saxon form. To try to trace modern standard English

directly to the language of the *Beowulf* or of Alfred's works causes diffi-
culties. Similarly New High German is not a direct descendant of the
Middle High German found in important medieval literature. New High
German is essentially a central German dialect, while Middle High
German was a southern German dialect. In using the family-tree model,
these important facts of linguistic history are concealed.

Primarily because of the inadequacy of the family-tree theory in
accounting for linguistic change, the **wave theory** was proposed. In accordance with it, languages are spoken side by side over a given area and
influenced by changes introduced at one point; these then spread like the
waves on a pond that are caused by an object hitting the surface of the
water. With this theory, proposed in 1872 by J. Schmidt, the Indo-
European languages may be depicted as follows:

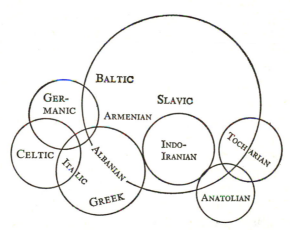

A revised form of Schmidt's representation of the distribution of the
Indo-European languages.

In permitting us to show flexibly interrelationships between languages,
and changes affecting them, the wave theory is preferable to the family-tree
theory. Both however view language far too simply.

If languages were relatively homogeneous, either theory would be
acceptable. For "sound change could take place according to laws that
admit no exception" either along the branches of a tree, or over an expanse
in which languages existed side by side. When, however, studies carried out
by dialect geographers showed that a language is subdivided in area into
dialects—and by different social and occupational groupings—any
bidimensional model, even when supplemented by the third dimension of
time, became inadequate. We now view language as a set of social

conventions so complex that a simple biological or geometrical model is totally inadequate.

9.4   Varieties of language in relation to change

Dialect geography studies have demonstrated that though a language has common structural features and vocabulary, it also shows variations from one group of speakers to another. In any language there are subsets or dialects of various types: geographical, social, functional, and occupational. All these must be studied and described individually for each language.

Geographical differences in a language are determined by the extent of its use, the cultural interrelationships of its speakers, the duration of settlement of its speakers, and so on.

Social differences are determined almost completely by cultural interrelationships. In general we may expect even in nonliterate groups at least three forms of speech: a cultivated, a common or standard, and a nonstandard—in modern societies, an uneducated. The standard form of speech is rarely used as such in literary, religious, prophetic, or even political utterances. Nonstandard forms may be found among antisocial groups, such as criminals, or a rebellious younger generation, or among rustics.

Functional differences again reflect cultural interrelationships. Although their variety differs from language to language, we may speak of at least two styles, formal versus informal; in many languages, there are more. Until recently Japanese included, besides a formal and an informal, an epistolary style for use in formal letters; further, there was a style used only to and by dignitaries. Only the Japanese emperor may use *chin* 'I.' A reflection of this style was applied with humorous effect in the *Mikado*; the word means 'honorable gate' and was used for the emperor in somewhat the same way as the 'Sublime Porte' was used for the former Turkish government.

Such geographical, social, and functional varieties of language are imposed on each other. There may be, for example, formal and informal varieties of nonstandard, standard, and cultivated speech. Somewhat different are occupational subsets. Specialists of various kinds: engineers, jockeys, biochemists, linguists, have developed their own jargons, which consist largely of special vocabularies. These may be applied in any of the subsets mentioned above.

We have been discussing language as a complex set of conventions used by a group of speakers. Subsets are also found within an **idiolect**, the language of a single speaker. A speaker may change his place of living, his social status, his relations to his associates, his occupation, and by these changes virtually be forced to introduce changes in his language. If we constructed a model for a language or a language family, we would have to include in it such multistrata units for each idiolect.

These subsets of a language provide the possibility of additions, changes, losses. For example, as technological features are introduced, modified, or retired, language referring to them also changes. In this way variety in language virtually provides built-in mechanisms for change. Some linguists ascribe change in language primarily to the interplay of dialects.

In sketching the complexity of language to this point, we have been viewing the language used by a single generation of speakers. As children acquire their language, further possibilities are provided for the introduction of change. Some linguists assume that language acquisition is the basic cause of change in language.

Since change in language is the prime concern of historical linguistics, we must view the modifications of the various components of language in the dimension of time. We may arbitrarily select any two points of time for such study. Our results are more useful, however, if we compare the varying language of two or more periods that have been differentiated by considerable changes in structure (see Chapter 10:1).

Such changes may be introduced in the interplay of geographical dialects. They may also be introduced from without, from other languages. Upon introduction, they may be imposed from speaker to speaker, along lines of communication. If so we may find wedge-shaped isoglosses along basic routes of travel, such as the Rhine. Changes may, on the other hand, be transmitted from center to center. H. Kurath points out that all the chief colonial centers in America except Philadelphia lost preconsonantal *r*; apparently Philadelphia—the second largest city in the British Empire in the eighteenth century—alone withstood spread of this change from across the Atlantic.

Any group of speakers with distinct patterns of usage, such as students, linguists, or specialists in space research, may introduce new forms and usages. If such groups are influential, these innovations may affect the language of others.

Among studies of the effect of social dialects on a language is Friedrich Kluge's investigation of the German student language, published in 1895. In this study he indicated especially the sources of various German words. One example is the word *flott* 'excellent, beautiful,' which students borrowed from nautical language, where it meant 'afloat, swimming,' and the like. Studies of the social dialects of other languages have disclosed similar innovations.

Other such studies have been concerned with the spread of changes.

Recent investigations by William Labov have disclosed how speakers in New York may favor specific pronunciations in certain social situations. For example, speakers who do not normally use *r* in words like *third* are very careful to use it when they find themselves in an elevated social situation.

Accordingly, the recognition that language is composed of geographical, social, functional, and occupational dialects, and dialects varying with the age of speakers, illuminates the ways in which languages have been changed and changes have been extended. Such dialects are parts of the system that individual speakers learn as they master a language.

9.5   Treatment of change in transformational models of language

In depicting language as a system, a widely used model is that proposed by Chomsky in 1965. In accordance with it, a grammar consists of three components: a phonological, a syntactic, and a semantic. The syntactic component is central. Consisting of a lexicon and rules governing their relationships, it generates a deep structure and a surface structure. The deep and surface structures are related by means of transformational rules.

In this model the semantic component is associated primarily with the deep structure, yielding semantic interpretations of it. In a variant model the semantic component yields the deep structures.

The phonological component is associated primarily with the surface structure, yielding phonetic representations.

This model may be represented as follows:

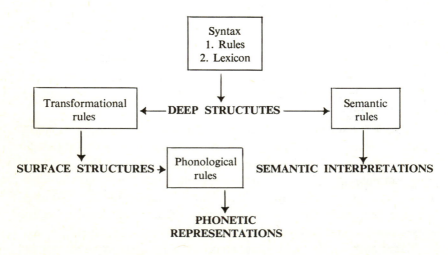

Grammars based on these models depict language as a set of entities governed by ordered rules. Change is identified as modification of rules.

In all components the entities are represented as feature bundles; For example, the Proto-Germanic phonological entity /f/ is labeled +consonantal, −vocalic, +continuant, and so on. Such features correspond to the distinctive characteristics of sound classes found in historical linguistic handbooks of the past; but the features are now more precisely identified. Accordingly, contemporary linguistic studies set out to specify linguistic data in greater detail than do the handbooks of our predecessors; in this way they should lead to a more thorough understanding of linguistic change.

For example, Grimm depicted the Germanic consonant changes as a series of ordered rules. Yet, as we have noted, his identification of the entities involved was not accurate. Moreover, he and his successors used ordering only for major changes in a language.

Contemporary linguists also propose to describe an entire language, for example its entire phonological system, by means of grammars consisting of ordered rules. If, then, a segment of a phonological system is changed, the process may be indicated with reference to rules. Rules may be added; they may be lost; they may be extended or diminished in scope. Or, specific rules may be reordered. For example, the rules formulated by Grimm are examples of rule addition. The change of PIE p t k k^w to PGmc $f\,\theta\,\chi\,\chi^w$ may be stated as the addition of a rule specifying the change of tense voiceless consonants to continuant articulation.

$$\begin{bmatrix} +\text{consonant} \\ +\text{tense} \\ -\text{voice} \end{bmatrix} \rightarrow [+\text{continuant}]$$

Details on the formulation of such rules may be noted in the workbook. In general, phonological rules would have to be more explicit than is the rule given here. This rule implies that every PIE p t k k^w became PGmc $f\,\theta\,\chi\,\chi^w$. Since the change did not take place when these phonemes followed Proto-Germanic f s χ, the rule in a Germanic grammar would need to be more elaborate.

For well-described languages, such rules are reformulations of statements in handbooks. Many reformulations represent no noteworthy modifications of traditional historical linguistics.

A modification however has been introduced by linguists who view phonology solely in terms of surface syntactic structures, the so-called generative phonologists. The phonological classes proposed by them, known as **systematic phonemes**, are based on syntactic considerations. By contrast, the phonological classes of most earlier historical linguistic study, now often called **autonomous phonemes**, are based solely on phonological considerations; the morphophonemes of earlier treatments are comparable to systematic phonemes. The assumption of systematic phonemes at times leads to strikingly different phonological descriptions of language, which may entail strikingly different historical treatments.

For example, Chomsky and Halle, *The Sound Pattern of English* 233–234, propose labiovelar phonemes $|k^w \ g^w \ x^w|$ for current English, as well as $|x|$. $|x|$ is assumed in a lexical item like *right* so that general phonological rules may be applied in the derivation of forms like *righteous*. Such a presentation of contemporary English does not commit one to a modification of traditional accounts of historical English grammars, which generally hold that $/x/$ was lost from the sound system of Standard English in the sixteenth century. Students using the phonological analyses of Chomsky and Halle, and of others with similar views, must take into account the theoretical assumptions underlying their analyses.

Whatever model of language a historical linguist proposes, language must be depicted as a complex of various strata, in each of which individuals employ composites of the extant possibilities. The variety of these allow many possibilities of change. On the other hand, the pressures toward accuracy of understanding, which are highly exacting, work against the introduction of change. For example, educational systems and communication networks tend to maintain patterns. As we noted in Chapter 8, the attitudes of speakers are important in determining when changes occur in language.

9.6 Determination of change in systems

When changes have occurred, historical linguists determine them, and earlier forms of language, by use of the comparative method and the method of internal reconstruction. They determine variation in language by the methods developed in dialect geography and subsequently elaborated in sociolinguistics. Through detailed field work, it has become clear that no idiolect or language is perfectly systematic; we find variation and imbalance in all languages, especially in areas of cultural change. In such areas innovations and changes are likely. If a new cultural fashion such as interest in highly rhythmic music becomes popular, jive talk (technical language associated with it) may fill out areas inadequate for discussion of it in the previous language. New technological developments, such as electricity, medicine, machines, also bring about innovations in language. Space exploration disclosed a need for new technical terminology. The

Russian term *sputnik*, literally 'fellow-traveler,' filled one of the gaps; many other terms, such as *astronaut*, have filled others.

Imbalance in the phonological system of a language is more difficult to deal with than is that of vocabulary, as we may illustrate by means of oral stops and nasals in English.

The English voiceless and voiced stops, and nasals, provide a systematic scheme:

p	t	k
b	d	g
m	n	ŋ

As presented here, this subset of the English phonological system seems to be systematic and balanced. In distribution, however, the balance is incomplete; /ŋ/ is not used initially. When we proceed to the fricatives, we find even less of a system: /f/ is labiodental, not bilabial; /θ/ is interdental, not alveolar, /s š/ do not balance /k/. If we go on to examine clusters of the stop, fricative and nasal phonemes preceded by /s/, we find further lack of symmetry, and imbalance: /sp st sk sf sm sn/ occur, but not */sb sd sg sŋ sθ ss sš/.

Change often is introduced in such unbalanced patterns of the phonological, morphological, and syntactic systems, as in deficient segments of the vocabulary. From these patterns it may be extended to other segments of the system.

Innovations may also be introduced for reasons we cannot determine. These innovations may have a pervasive effect on language. For example, an initial stress accent was introduced into Proto-Germanic, as we know from the effects of Verner's law. Subsequently, unstressed medial and final syllables came to be lost. These losses occurred relatively quickly; the name *HlewagastiR*, attested on the Gallehus horn about 350 A.D., is reduced to the bisyllabic *Hlégestr* of Old Norse in less than a millennium. Eventually most final syllables were lost, including those that marked morphological categories. Modern English, Modern Norwegian, and Modern German dialects have maintained very few final syllables and accordingly few inflectional markers.

In this way the innovation of initial stress had a profound effect on the morphological and syntactic system of the Germanic languages, not only on its phonological system. Syntactic relationships came to be indicated by order and by function words, such as articles, auxiliaries, and prepositions.

During this early Germanic period other changes were being introduced, such as the change from the Object Verb order of the Gallehus inscription to a Verb Object order. In the course of time, the Germanic languages have become largely VO in structure. Furthermore, many new words were introduced especially from Celtic and Latin. Celtic terms for government were introduced, such as Goth. *reiks*, ON *rīkr*, OE *rīhhi* 'powerful,' OE *rica* 'ruler'; Latin terms for products of civilization were introduced, such as Goth. *wein*, ON *vīn*, OE *wīn*, OHG *wīn* 'wine'. These changes also affected the phonological system, for example, the introduction of long *ā* in borrowings from Latin, such as Goth. *aurali* < Lat. *ōrārium* 'face cloth.' In this way changes are introduced into the phonological and syntactic systems, and into the lexicon, with possible far-ranging effects on the language. The next chapters will deal with the phenomena, mechanisms, and to some extent the causes of such changes.

Selected Further Readings

For application of the family-tree and wave models to the Indo-European languages, see H. Pedersen, *Linguistic Science in the Nineteenth Century*, 311–18, and L. Bloomfield, *Language*, 311–18. Pedersen gives further data on the proponents of these models. A general sketch of linguistic study may be found in R. H. Robins, *A Short History of Linguistics*.

A. Martinet, *Éléments de linguistique générale*, is particularly concerned with the developments found in systems. He introduced terms like "push chains" and "drag chains" to characterize changes induced by gaps in the system. P. Kiparsky has discussed the analysis of change in language by means of grammars composed in rules, as in his article "Linguistic Universals and Language Change," *Universals in Linguistic Theory*, edited by E. Bach and R. T. Harms (New York, 1968), pages 171–202, and in his article "Historical Linguistics," *A Survey of Linguistic Science*, edited by William Orr Dingwall (College Park, Maryland, 1971), pages 577–642.

Earlier linguistic study has been so consistently criticized for lack of concern with syntax that special reference is made here to the work of B. Delbrück, notably the three last volumes of Brugmann-Delbrück, *Grundriss der vergleichenden Grammatik der indogermanischen Sprachen*.

For German student language at the turn of the century, see Friedrich Kluge, *Deutsche Studentensprache*. (Strassburg, 1895). For a discussion of the "social stratification of (r) in New York City department stores," see pages 63–89 of William Labov, *The Social Stratification of English in New York City*. (Washington, 1966).

For the format of the model on page 140 and comments on the chapter, I am grateful to Rolf Stachowitz.

CHAPTER 10

Sound change—change in phonological systems

10.1 Modification and change

What do we mean by sound change? When languages are compared at various periods, we find correspondences between their elements. In comparing Middle English with Modern English, for example, we observe obvious correspondences between ME *set*, NE *set*, somewhat less obvious between ME *wīf*, NE *wife*; ME *hūs*, NE *house*. We conclude that NE *set*, *wife*, *house* are the contemporary forms of ME *set*, *wīf*, *hūs*, and we label these Modern English forms **replacements** for the Middle English. The replacements [wayf] for ME [wiːf] and [haws] for ME [huːs] have resulted from modifications in the language. Modifications that lead to the introduction of new phonological elements in a language, to loss, or to realignments of old elements, we refer to as **sound change**. This term is used only for events that result in disruption of the phonological system.

The investigation of sound change is one of the chief concerns of historical linguistics. In this chapter we will examine correspondences between phonological elements at two or more stages of a language, and discuss the processes, patterns, and spread of change in phonological systems. Finally, we will examine proposed explanations for modifications and sound change.

Between the English of Chaucer (†1400) and that spoken today, probably all elements in the phonological system have been modified. Some of the modifications were very minor; Chaucer's pronunciation of ME *set* would probably be understood by us today, though in details it might seem peculiar. Other pronunciations of his, we might not understand at all, such as his ME *see* /se:/ versus our NE *see* /siy/, ME *tōth* /to:θ/ versus our NE *tooth* /tuwθ). Historical grammars concern themselves largely with such striking changes. Yet to understand the process of change in language, we will first examine briefly replacements that do not disrupt the system and that therefore seem minor or not worth notice in general historical surveys of a language, but that may eventually lead to changes.

One feature of Chaucer's pronunciation of *set* that may have differed only slightly from ours is his articulation of /t/; it would probably remind us of the *t* used by a Spanish speaker. Since we have no descriptions of Chaucer's pronunciation, we cannot be sure of this conclusion, but we can assume that at one time English /t d n/ were dentals. Over the past centuries their articulation has been progressively retracted, so that they are now alveolars. As this retraction took place, it did not bring about changes in the syntactic or semantic systems of the language. Nor was the system of phonemic contrasts affected; NE /t/ contrasts with NE /p k/, etc., just as did ME /t/ with ME /p k/, etc. This modification of /t/ has accordingly not led to a sound change.

Another modification that must have been introduced in the course of the history of English is the aspiration of voiceless stops before stressed vowels when not preceded by /s/, as in *pool* [p^{h}uwl] versus spool [sp$^=$uwl], *tool* [t^{h}uwl] and cool [k^{h}uwl]. We assume that Germanic /p t k/ in such words were unaspirated because they developed from /b d g/. At some time between the changes described in Grimm's law and the present, aspiration must have been added in words like *pool, tool, cool*. But like the alveolar pronunciation of NE /t d n/, this modification has had no effect on the phonological system of English. For the aspirates are automatic variants, or allophones of /p t k/ in specific environments.

In time, such modifications may lead to disruptions of the phonological system, that is, to sound change. Most linguists assume, for example, that PIE /p t k/ first became aspirates [p^h t^h k^h] before they were changed to fricatives in the Proto-Germanic etyma of words like NE *five, three, right*. But since the phonological system of contemporary English has not been changed by the introduction of [p^h t^h k^h], the altered pronunciations are simply modifications, not sound changes.

While such modifications are apparently going on constantly in language, we have little information about them in languages of the past.

Speakers, including scribes, take account only of changes in phonological systems, not of modifications. Scribes may introduce new spellings after sound changes take place, or they may betray changes by inconsistencies or errors of spelling. With a long series of texts, we can therefore document changes that have taken place in individual languages.

Historical English linguists are fortunate in having many texts by means of which they can study change. As illustration we will examine the beginning of Chaucer's Prologue to the *Canterbury Tales*. The lines are given first in conventional Middle English spelling, accompanied by a literal translation, then in phonemic transcription, accompanied by a contemporary English phonemic transcription. Middle English patterns of morphology and syntax have been maintained so that the phonological changes would be better illustrated.

Middle English:

1. Whan that Aprille with his schoures swoote
2. the drought of March hath perced to the roote
3. and bathed evry veyn in swich licour,
4. of which vertu engendred is the flour;
5. whan Zephirus eek with his swete breeth
6. inspired hath in evry holt and heeth
7. the tendre croppes, and the yonge sonne
8. hath in the Ram his halve cours yronne,
9. and smale fowles maken melodye,
10. that slepen al the nyght with open ye—
11. so priketh hem nature in her corages—
12. than longen folk to goon on pilgrimages.

Translation:

1. When (that) April with its sweet showers,
2. has pierced the drought of March to the root,
3. and bathed every vein in such moisture (liquor),
4. from whose effects (virtue) flowers are produced;
5. When Zephirus also with his sweet breath,
6. has inspired in every wood and heath,
7. the tender crops, and (when) the young sun
8. has run half of his course through Aries,
9. and (when) the small birds (fowls) make (their) melodies,
10. which sleep all the night with open eyes—
11. thus nature inspires them in their spirits—
12. at that time people want to go on pilgrimages.

Middle English phonemic representation

1. hwan θat āpril wiθ his šūres swōte
2. θe druχt of marč haθ pērsed tō θe rōte
3. and bāðed evri vein in swič likūr
4. of hwič verteu enǰendred is θe flūr
5. hwan zefirus ēk wiθ his swēte brē̄θ
6. inspīred haθ in evri holt and hē̄θ
7. θe tendre kroppes and θe yunge sunne
8. haθ in θe ram his halve kūrs irunne
9. and smale fūles māken melodīe
10. θat slēpen al θe niχt wiθ ɔ̄pen īe
11. sɔ̄ prikeθ hem nateur in her kurāǰes
12. θan longen folk tō gɔ̄n on pilgrimāǰes

New English phonemic representation

1. hwen (ðæt) eypril wið hiz šawərz swiyt
2. ðə drawt əv marč hæz pirst tuw ðə ruwt
3. ænd beyðd evriy veyn in səč likər
4. əv hwič vərčuw enǰendərd iz ðə flawr
5. hwen zefərəs iyk wið his swiyt breθ
6. inspayrd hæz in evriy holt ænd hiyθ
7. ðə tendər kraps ænd ðe yəŋ sən
8. hæz in ðə ræm hiz hæf kɔrs rən
9. ænd smɔl fawlz meyk melədiy
10. ðæt sliyp ɔl ðə nayt wið owpən ay
11. sow priks ðem neyčər in ðer kərəǰəz
12. ðen lɔŋ fowk tə gow on pilgriməǰəz

Comparing the Middle English and the New English texts, we note that the vowels have changed considerably, notably the long vowels. Further, many unstressed syllables have been lost, leading to consonant clusters in New English, as in /pirst beyðd kraps/, and to syllables ending in consonants rather than vowels, as in /swiyt ruwt sən/. Furthermore, the accent of the words which were borrowed from French has generally been moved toward the beginning of words, in keeping with the Germanic accent position, as in /líkər mélədiy kə́rəǰ/; in accordance with such accent placement, the vowels of formerly stressed syllables have been shortened, as in the second syllable of *liquor*. These changes brought about great differences between Middle English and New English.

The most notable changes affected the Middle English long vowels, all of which underwent change, as we see from the following examples. ME /ī/, as in /inspīred/, line 6, and /eī/, line 10, has changed to NE /ay/.

ME /ū/, as in /šūres/, line 1, and /flūr/, line 4, has changed to NE /aw/. ME /ē/, as in /ēk/, line 5, has changed to NE /iy/, as has ME /ɛ̄/, as in /hɛ̄θ/, line 6. Moreover, ME /ā/, as in /āpril/, line 1, has changed to NE /ey/. Further, ME /ō/, as in /rōte/, line 2, has changed to NE /uw/, and ME /ɔ̄/, as in /ɔ̄pen/, line 10, has changed to NE /ow/. We will examine these changes again below. They are cited here as examples of the kind of sound change with which historical treatments of phonology are particularly concerned.

By means of other words in these twelve lines we also note that not every Middle English long vowel is replaced by one of the New English elements given above. For example, *breath*, the modern form of ME /brɛ̄θ/, line 5, no longer rhymes with *heath*. Its vowel was shortened, as were the vowels of other words ending in dental consonants, such as *dead*, *red*, *bread*, and *thread*; thus, they did not undergo the change of ME /ɛ̄/ to NE /iy/. A different type of disruption is found for /swōte/; like *root* from /rōte/, its modern form should have the element /uw/. Instead, the form found in line 5, /swēte/ > /swiyt/ has been generalized, ousting a potential /swuwt/. As this discussion may indicate, when we write the history of a language, we first determine the regular correspondences of its phonemes, including its major sound changes; and then we account for exceptions. To illustrate this procedure, we will examine the principal correspondences between the sound systems of Middle English and New English.

10.2 The Middle English and New English phonological systems as examples of phonological change

In dealing with sound change, we require that grammars not only discuss individual changes but also that they present them within the systems of two successive stages of a language. For as we have noted above, sound change always involves alterations in a system. Unless we know the systems concerned, we cannot interpret the changes. In studying the changes of Middle English then, we examine the consonant and vowel systems of New English as well as Middle English.

Comparing the Middle and New English consonant systems, we find little difference between them in number of phonemes.

Middle English						New English				
p	t	č	k			p	t	č	k	
b	d	ǰ	g			b	d	ǰ	g	
f	θ	s	š	x	h	f	θ	s	š	
v	ð	z				v	ð	z	ž	
m	n					m	n		ŋ	
w	l	r	y			w	l	r	y	h

One Middle English consonant phoneme /x/ has been lost, as in *light*; compare NHG *Licht* [lixt]. (If however ME *x* is interpreted as an allophone of *h*, this is merely an allophonic change.)

Two new consonant phonemes have been added: /ž/, which developed from the cluster /zy/ as in *vision*, and was carried over in French loanwords such as *rouge*, and /ŋ/. In Middle English we do not posit a phoneme /ŋ/. Earlier, [ŋ] was an allophone of /n/ before velars. Modern Italian still has such variation for the phoneme /n/, with the allophone [ŋ] occurring only before [k] and [g]. Middle English [ŋ] became a separate phoneme when voiced stops after nasals were lost in late Middle English, as in *climb*, *lawn* (cf. OFr. *launde*) and *long*. Through the loss of -*g*, the [ŋ] allophone was split from the phoneme /n/, becoming a separate phoneme as in NE /lɔŋ/ vs. /lɔn/. Apart from the loss of /x/ and the addition of two phonemes, the consonant systems of the two successive stages are similar in structure and number of members.

While the consonant systems differ little, the vowel systems are strikingly different. We give first the Middle English system, using a notation similar to Middle English orthography.

Short Vowels		Long Vowels		Diphthongs			
i	u	ī	ū				
e	o	ē	ō	ei eu		oi ou	
a		ḕ ā ɔ̄		ai au			

Apart from rearrangements, the principal allophones of vowels of the Middle English short-vowel system underwent few modifications, as we may illustrate:

ME ship   NE ship   ME busch   NE bush
    ME set   NE set   ME lock : NE (Brit.) lock
    ME bak (OE bæk)   NE back

In the environments given here, the pronunciation of the Middle English short vowels and that of New English short vowels agree, though ME /a/ was probably articulated farther back than is NE /æ/. Simply listing these correspondences, however, gives an inadequate view of the relationships between the two systems. For between Middle English and New English, the characterization of vowels and consonants by quantity was abandoned, leading to a New English system like the Middle English long-vowel system in configuration, but with additional phonemes. Moreover, ME [ə], an unstressed allophone of ME /e/, has become a New English phoneme, with additions from ME /u/, which became NE /ə/, as in *cut, tusk, hull*, except after labials, as in *put, bush, full, wolf*.

To illustrate the quantity distinction between long and short consonants in Middle English, we may cite *sunne* 'sun' and *sune* 'son.' Because of the difference in length of *n*, these words did not rhyme in Middle English. With the loss of long consonants, however, they became homophones in New English. Similarly Middle English vowels that were distinguished by length (somewhat like the vowels in NHG *Stadt* [štat] 'city' and *Staat* [šta:t] 'state') lost the distinction. ME *shamle* 'shamble' had short *a* before two consonants, but ME *sādel* 'saddle' had a long *ā* before consonant plus vowel. When the final syllables of both words came to be pronounced alike, the stem vowels became *æ* as in their New English forms. On the other hand, long vowels maintained until the time of the Great English Vowel Shift, as in *crādel* 'cradle,' underwent the shift described in the following paragraph. In Middle English the vowels were distinguished by quantity as well as by quality, whereas in New English the primary distinction is by quality. The loss of the quantity distinction has resulted in a totally different vowel system.

The change of long vowels between Middle English and the present is known as the Great English Vowel Shift, often abbreviated GVS in historical grammars of English. This change is remarkable, for all the Middle English vowels are modified similarly, by raising; /ī ū/, however, were already high vowels and could be raised no further. Their counterparts in Modern English are the diphthongs /ay/ and /aw/. ME /ē/ and /ɛ̄/ have fallen together to yield NE /iy/; ME /ā/ was fronted and raised to NE /ey/; ME /ō/ was raised to NE /uw/; ME /ɔ̄/ was raised to NE /ow/. Examples are:

ME	NE	ME	NE	ME	NE
wīf /wi:f/	wife /wáyf/			hous /hu:s/	house /háws/
seen /se:n/	seen /síyn/			spon /spo:n/	spoon /spúwn/
see /sɛ:/	sea /síy/			ham /hɔ:m/	home /hówm/
		name /na:me/	name /néym/		

These changes alone would have resulted in a totally different vowel system, but the Middle English symmetrical system of diphthongs (the three low short vowels followed by the two high) was also changed.

Middle English /ei ai/, which had probably fallen together by the time of Chaucer, merged with the reflex of ME /ā/, e.g., ME *vein*, NE *vein* /véyn/, ME *day, dai* /dai/ > NE *day* /déy/. ME /oi/ remained unchanged, e.g., ME *boi, boy* /boi/ > NE *boy* /bɔ́y/.

ME /eu/ merged with /uw/ from ME /ō/, e.g., ME *fruit* /freut/, NE *fruit* /frúwt/, ME *virteu*, NE /vә́rčuw/ (also in New English forms with /yuw/, e.g., *pure*). ME /ou/ merged with /ow/ from ME /ā/, e.g.,

ME *boue* /boue/ > NE *bow* /bów/. ME /au/ became a low, back vowel, e.g., ME *cause* /kauze/ > NE *cause* /kɔ́z/.

It is clear from these examples that the Middle English vowel system was modified so greatly that it is difficult to plot the Modern English system beside it, as we have done for the consonants. In accordance with the diphthongal analysis proposed by Sweet, Wyld, Bloomfield, Bloch, Trager, and others, the Modern English vowel system characteristic of Midland American English speakers may be presented as follows:

i ship		u bush	iy see	uw spoon
e set	ə some		ey say	ow bow
æ back	a lock	ɔ cause	ay wife ɔy boy aw house	

In the vowel system proposed for educated British English, these words are arranged as follows (see my *Descriptive Linguistics*, p. 48):

Simple	Complex	
i ship	i^i see	
e set	e^i say	
a back	a^i wife	a^u house
ə some		ə^u bow
o cause/lock	o^i boy	
u bush		u^u spoon

In addition, the six simple vowels of British English, and the vowels of *tie* and *town*, may be followed by ə, as in *tear*, *tire*, *tower*; in the Midland dialect of American English, the corresponding sound is *r*. Except for these combinations with ə, the British and American systems differ primarily in the low short vowels. In both of these systems, however, the set of Middle English vowels has been completely changed. The conservatism of the consonants, side by side with the innovations in the vowel system and in syllabic structure, may illustrate how languages change in some of their segments while undergoing little change in others.

10.3   The processes involved in sound change

From the changes between the Middle English and the New English phonological systems, we may illustrate the essentials necessary for a general understanding of sound change. As may be observed from English, sound changes take place by modifications of sounds to similarly articulated sounds. For example, ME [ē] became NE [iy] rather than the totally different [uw] or [s]. Moreover, allophones of phonemes often differ in accordance with their environment; when sound changes take place, the direction may be a result of the phonetic surroundings of the sounds concerned. For example, we might expect a rounded vowel like [u] to be maintained in the neighborhood of labial consonants, as was ME [u] in words like *put, bull, full*, when in other environments it became a central vowel, as in *tuck, duck, cut*. A thorough knowledge of articulatory phonetics is thus essential for understanding the processes of change.

Understanding the processes of sound change also involves a knowledge of the kinds of changes that sound systems can undergo. In setting up correspondences between Middle and New English, grammars often list only the most frequent correspondences, as if all Middle English phonemes had merely one reflex in New English, for example, as if all ME /u/ had become NE /u/. Furthermore, accounts of the GVS suggest that all ME /ī/ > NE /ay/. Yet, as we see in the few lines cited from Chaucer above, ME /ī/ also underwent other changes, as in *melodīe*, where it was shortened when the accent was placed on the first syllable. Simple treatments of sound systems are accordingly unrealistic, justifiable only for pedagogical reasons. Sound change of the type we have been considering takes place by subclasses of phonemes, labeled allophones. ME /u/, for instance, became NE /u/ only after labials, as noted in the preceding paragraph; elsewhere it became /ə/. The Middle English long vowels underwent the GVS only when they had primary accent. As with the addition of NE /ŋ/, the differing developments correlate with differing allophones in Middle English. The changes we have been discussing, we therefore label **change by allophones**.

10.3.1 *Conditioned versus unconditioned change*   Allophones of phonemes are restricted to certain environments in which they are conditioned by their surroundings. For example, ME /n/ was conditioned to velar articulation [ŋ] by a following velar consonant. When such allophones undergo a change, we speak of a **conditioned**, or a **combinatory, change**. Other examples are PGmc. /f θ s χ/ to PGmc. /b ð z g/ when not preceded by the chief stress, as in the words accounted for by Verner's law.

Much more rarely, all members of a phoneme change, and we speak of an **unconditioned change**. Examples are: PIE /o/ to PGmc. /a/, as in Goth. *asts* 'branch' < PIE /ósdos/ (with loss in Germanic of the second vowel); PGmc. /z/ to OE /r/, as in OE *wæron* 'were.' It should be noted, however, that when handbooks speak of unconditioned change, they do not take into account losses of certain members of the earlier phoneme. Thus the change of PIE /o/ to PGmc. /a/ is called unconditioned, even though the *o* of unstressed syllables was lost, as in the second syllable of PIE /ósdos/. Moreover some PGmc. /z/ were lost, as in OE *mēd* 'meed.' Accordingly it may be true that no change affects all occurrences of a phoneme. Completely unconditioned changes may then be impossible to document in languages.

10.3.2 Phonetic processes involved in change
When changes take place, they usually involve modification of one or more distinctive features of a phoneme. NE /t/, for example, is a stop produced by alveolar closure while the velum is raised and the glottis is open. Some of its allophones are also characterized by aspiration, such as its allophone before stressed vowel, as in *top*; that after /s/, as in *stop*, is unaspirated. The allophone of /t/ after stressed vowels and before unstressed, as in *butting*, *butter*, *bottom*, etc., came to be unaspirated and very short for many speakers of American English; articulated in this way, it became voiced between voiced sounds, so that *butting* and *budding*, *latter* and *ladder*, and so on, became homophones. For such speakers the short *t* between vowels became voiced, that is, instead of the distinctive feature [−voice], the distinctive feature [+voice] was introduced. In accounts of changes, we accordingly identify the distinctive features of phonemes and allophones, for through their modification sound changes take place.

From the time of J. Grimm, historical linguists have indicated sound changes by means of rules. Handbooks of the past state rules of sound change by means of classes of sounds or phonemes, specifying when necessary the environments concerned. Many current analyses state them by means of distinctive features. In the examples given below, rules of both types will be illustrated. Since these rules deal primarily with changes between Late Proto-Indo-European and the early dialects, you may consult the charts of the Late Proto-Indo-European phonemes and the Late Proto-Germanic phonemes, and their distinctive features, given in Chapter 3:4.

A change may occur in **place of articulation**: labials may become labiodentals, dentals may become alveolars, velars may become palatals, and so on. A change from dental to alveolar occurred when PGmc. /t/ became OHG /s/; cf. Eng. *hate* = Germ. *hassen*. A change of velar to palatal occurred when PIE /k/ under certain conditions became [š] in some of the dialects; cf. Lat. *centum* = Skt. *śatam* 'hundred.'

This last change is stated as follows in terms of phonemes:

Rule 1a.   PIE k g gh > PIndic š ž

In terms of distinctive features, it is stated:

Rule 1b. $\begin{bmatrix} +\text{cns} \\ +\text{high} \\ -\text{ant} \end{bmatrix} \rightarrow \begin{bmatrix} -\text{back} \\ +\text{std} \end{bmatrix}$

This rule indicates that PIE consonants, which had the further distinctive features of height and -anterior, or back, articulation, became strident and palatal.

The rule in both forms indicates that the change is unconditional, that is, that all PIE /k g gh/ became Proto-Indic /š ž/. Yet this change is not found in all words with PIE *k g gh*. For a precise statement of the changes, to the extent they can be determined, one would have to consult a specialized handbook or article; yet even these have been inadequately precise. Complete and accurate descriptions of phonological changes remain to be provided for all languages.

A change may occur in **manner of articulation**; stops may become fricatives or affricates, obstruents may become semivowels or vice versa, and so on. A change from stop to fricative occurred when PIE /p/ became PGmc. /f/; cf. Lat. *pater* = Goth. *fadar*. A change from stop to affricate, when PGmc. /p/ became OHG /pf/; cf. Eng. *pool* = Germ. *Pfuhl*. A change from semivowel to stop occurred when PGmc. *ww* > NEGmc. *ggw*, as in Goth. *triggws*, ON *tryggr* = OHG *triuwi* 'true, faithful'; the two *g*'s indicate that the sound in question was a stop, not a fricative.

The last change is stated as follows in terms of phonemes:

Rule 2a.   PGmc. ww > NEGmc gw (spelled ggw)

In terms of distinctive features, it is stated:

Rule 2b.
$$\begin{bmatrix} +\text{cns} \\ +\text{back} \\ +\text{vd} \end{bmatrix} \rightarrow -\text{rd} \ \Big/ \ \underline{\quad} \begin{bmatrix} +\text{cns} \\ +\text{back} \\ +\text{rd} \end{bmatrix}$$

This rule indicates a conditioned change, that is, that PGmc. *w* became NEGmc. [g] only in the environment preceding *w*. For the interpretation of this rule, the omission of the feature [tense] is significant; the change did not take place before PGmc. *g^w*, which was distinguished from PGmc. *w* by tenseness.

A change may occur in the **position of the velum**; nasal sounds may become denasalized, non-nasals may become nasals. OIcel. *ellefo* 'eleven' corresponds to Goth. *ainlif*; OIcel. *annar* 'other,' on the other hand, corresponds to Goth *anþar*. Nasal consonants were lost in Old English, with lengthening of the preceding vowel, when they occurred before voiceless fricatives; cf. Eng. *five* = Germ. *fünf*, Eng. *goose* = Germ. *Gans*. Nasal articulation may not be lost completely but may affect neighboring vowels, as in Fr. *vin* [vɛ̃] < Lat. *vinum* 'wine.'

The change of short vowels to long vowels in pre-Old English, with loss of following nasal, is stated as follows in terms of phonemes:

Rule 3a.   pre OE $\breve{V}$ + m/n + f/þ/s > OE $\bar{V}$ + f/þ/s

In terms of distinctive features, it is stated:

Rule 3b.

$$[-\text{cns}]\ [+\text{nas}] \rightarrow [+\text{tense}]\ \text{ø}\ \Bigg/ \ — \begin{bmatrix} -\text{res} \\ +\text{cnt} \\ -\text{voice} \end{bmatrix}$$

That is, vowels that preceded nasals came to be lengthened, and the nasal was lost in the environment preceding voiceless fricatives.

A change may take place in **glottal articulation**; voiced sounds may be devoiced, voiceless sounds may be voiced. An example of voiced sounds becoming devoiced is PIE /b d g/ becoming PGmc. /p t k/; cf. Lat. *duo* = Eng. *two*. An example of voiceless sounds becoming voiced, PGmc. /f θ s χ/, without chief accent on the preceding syllable becoming PGmc. /b ð z g/, as in PGmc. *tuχún-* > PGmc. /tugun/, OE *tugon* 'pulled.'

The last change is stated as follows in terms of phonemes:

Rule 4a.   PGmc. f θ s χ χ^w > b ð z g g^w when not preceded by the
chief accent.

In terms of distinctive features, it is stated:

Rule 4b. $\begin{bmatrix} -\text{res} \\ -\text{tense} \\ +\text{cnt} \end{bmatrix} \rightarrow +\text{vce}\ \Bigg/\ \begin{bmatrix} +\text{res} \\ -\text{act} \end{bmatrix} — [+\text{res}]$

That is, all lax continuants that were not resonants came to be voiced in the environment between unstressed vowel and vowel.

A change may involve **loss**. OE /h/ before /l n r/ was lost, as in *loud* < OE /hlu:d/, *nut* < OE /hnutu/, *ring* < OE /hring/. ME /g/ was lost after [ŋ], as in *long*. Final, weakly stressed vowels were lost in early New English, as in /persed/ > /pirst/ *pierced*, roote > *root*, and so on. As in these examples, losses may be complete, though they may also have an effect on a neighboring element. When for example [χ] was lost in *light*, *thought*, *fight* (cf. Germ. *Licht*, *dachte*, *fechten*), and so on, in early Modern English, the preceding vowel was lengthened. This phenomenon is known as **compensatory lengthening**. Other examples are OE *gōs* < pre-OE **gans*, cf. Germ. *Gans* 'goose,' OE *ūs* < pre-OE **uns*, 'us,' in which nasals were lost before voiceless fricatives, with compensatory lengthening of the preceding vowel, as indicated in Rule 3 above. The same change occurred earlier in OE *brōhte* < PGmc. /branχta/ 'brought' and OE *þōhte* < PGmc. /þanχta/ 'thought.'

Changes may also take place in the characteristic features of vowels, as in the degree of vowel opening. Open vowels may become more closed;

closed vowels, more open. In Middle English, /ɛ̄/, as in *sea*, became more closed, so that we now rhyme its vowel with that of *see*. The closed vowels /ī/ and /ū/ of *wife* and *house*, on the other hand, came to be more open.

The change of ME /ɛ̄/ to NE /iy/ is stated as follows in terms of phonemes:

Rule 5a.   ME ɛ̄ > NE iy

In terms of distinctive features, it is stated:

Rule 5b. $\begin{bmatrix} +\text{voc} \\ +\text{tense} \\ +\text{ant} \end{bmatrix} \rightarrow [+\text{high}]$

That is, the low tense vowel ɛ: became raised to /iy/.

Changes may take place in the degree of fronting. Back vowels may become front vowels, and vice versa. When umlaut was carried through in pre-Old English, when for example /ū/ became /ǖ/, as in /mǖs/ the plural of /mūs/ 'mouse,' back vowels were fronted.

The change of pre-OE long and short *o* and *u* to front rounded vowels is stated as follows in terms of phonemes:

Rule 6a.   pre-OE ŏ ŭ > early OE ȫ ǖ before *i ī j*

In terms of distinctive features, it is stated:

Rule 6b. $\begin{bmatrix} +\text{voc} \\ +\text{round} \end{bmatrix} > [-\text{back}] \Big/ \!-\!(C_o) \begin{bmatrix} +\text{high} \\ -\text{back} \end{bmatrix}$

That is, all rounded vowels, whether long or short, became fronted when they stood before a high front vowel or *j*, regardless of the type of intervening consonants.

Changes may take place in labial articulation. The /ǖ/ of /mǖs/, which was fronted in pre-Old English times, later lost its lip rounding and coalesced with /ī/, so that in Middle English the vowel of *mice* fell together with that of *wife*. This change is stated as follows:

Rule 7a.   early OE ȫ ǖ > late OE ĕ ĭ
Rule 7b. $\begin{bmatrix} +\text{voc} \\ -\text{back} \end{bmatrix} \rightarrow [-\text{round}]$

That is, all front vowels were unrounded.

The examples given here illustrate changes that have taken place in the Indo-European languages. Examples of the processes illustrated here can also be cited from other languages that have been thoroughly investigated.

10.3.3 Assimilation and other processes The discussion of processes involved in sound change has examined the effects of change involving one or more distinctive features. Processes also follow general kinds of change. One of the most widely observed of these is **assimilation**, a change in the articulation of a sound to one more like that of neighboring sounds. To illustrate it, we may note changes in the consonant of Latin *ad* 'to' when it was prefixed to morphs beginning with consonants. Lat. *apparātus* 'apparatus,' from *ad + pārāre* 'make ready,' illustrates assimilation in place of articulation; the dental *d* was changed to a labial. Lat. *assimulātio* 'assimilation,' from *ad + simulāre* 'resemble,' illustrates assimilation in manner of articulation; the stop *d* was changed to a fricative. Lat. *annexus* 'annex,' from *ad + nectere* 'bind,' illustrates assimilation in position of the velum; the oral *d* was changed to a nasal. Lat. *attempto* 'attempt,' from *ad + temptāre* 'try,' illustrates assimilation in attitude of the glottis; the voiced *d* has become unvoiced.

As in these four examples, the preceding element is commonly assimilated, and the articulation of the second element is anticipated. This type of assimilation is referred to as **regressive**.

The articulation of the prior element may also be maintained, as in [sévm̩]; in this pronunciation the labial articulation is maintained for the nasal from the preceding fricative. This type of articulation is referred to as **progressive**.

The articulation of both elements may be modified, by **reciprocal assimilation**, as in [sébm]; in this pronunciation the closure of the second element is anticipated in the *b*, and the position of the *b* is maintained for the nasal.

The assimilated sound may not always be contiguous with the sound to which it is changed. An example is Eng. *orangutang*, which was taken over from Malay *orang* 'man' + *ūtan* 'forest; wild.' The nasal of *ūtan* was modified to the velar position of the nasal in *utang* by **assimilation at a distance**, or **distant assimilation**. Umlaut is an example of assimilation at a distance; as in OE *fǣt* < *fōti*, the back vowel *ō* was assimilated to the place of articulation of the following front vowel *i*.

Assimilation may be complete, resulting in two identical sounds, as in *annexus*, or partial, as in [sévm̩].

Assimilation varies greatly from language to language. The Slavic languages have undergone repeated palatalization, that is, assimilation of sounds to palatal articulation. English, too, has examples from several periods; as noted in 10.8.7. But German exhibits little palatalization. We might expect that speakers would find it easier to articulate neighboring sounds alike, and that they would accordingly introduce assimilation.

But the structure of individual languages varies so greatly that we cannot propose such a generalization. Before we assume that any one process may have led to specific changes or may be expected to, we must note the characteristic articulation in a given language, as for the following processes.

Changes in word-ending position may lead to development of an additional consonant, as in the pronunciation [sinst] for *since*. In this pronunciation the tongue makes a closure against the alveolar ridge before articulation of the word is completed. The hearer may interpret this hold as a stop [t]; he may then imitate the pronunciation, adding the stop, release and all. Such additional consonants are referred to as **excrescent**. Further examples may be taken from English, e.g., *varmint* < *vermin*, or from German; compare Germ. *Axt*, Eng. *ax*; Germ. *Sekt* 'champagne,' Eng. *sack* 'dry sherry'; Germ. *Habicht*, Eng. *hawk*.

Moreover, final vowels may be lost, a process known as **apocope**. In Old English the first singular present ended in *-e*, for example, *helpe*; in the late Middle English period such final vowels were lost. Apocope, and **syncope**, the loss of medial vowels, are prominent in languages with a strong stress accent on initial syllables. In the Germanic languages many medial and final vowels have been lost, until in present-day English many native words have become monosyllabic. The Old English first singular preterite of *temman* 'tame' was *temede*; both weakly stressed vowels have been lost, to yield NE *tamed* [teymd].

Vowels may also be introduced, a process called **epenthesis**. We find epenthetic vowels, for example, in OE *æcer*, cf. OIcel. *akr* 'acre,' OE *ofen*, cf. OIcel *ofn* 'oven,' and in many other words before *r l m n*; we find epenthetic consonants in OE *bræmbel* beside *brēmel* 'bramble,' OE *gandra* beside *ganra* 'gander,' and so on. If initial, such vowels are called **prothetic**. Prothetic vowels were introduced in French before *s* plus consonant, as in Fr. *école* < OGr. *escole* from Lat. *schola, scola* 'school'. Similar developments may be noted in Span. *escuela*, Port. *escola*, though in these langu-ages the development of the prothetic vowel is more narrowly circum-scribed.

10.4   The patterns of sound change

In discussing examples and processes of sound change, we have observed that sound change only occurs when there is a disruption of the phono-logical system. Such disruption may occur in one of two ways, either by merger or split.

Merger occurs when sounds change so completely that they fall together with the sounds of another phoneme, e.g., NE *t* as in *bitter* merging with /d/, as in *bidder*. It was the pattern by which ME /ō/, as in *roote*, became established as NE /uw/; for reflexes of ME *ō* merged with those of ME *eu*, as in *fruit* and *virtue*. Other examples are given below.

By means of **split**, one or more allophones of a phoneme may move away from the other allophones of that phoneme, e.g., ME [ŋ] split off of the ME /n/ phoneme upon loss of a following /g/, as in *young*. By means of split, new phonemes may be introduced, as was NE /ŋ/, or the diverging allophones may merge with another phoneme as did the reflexes of PGmc. /z/ with pre-OE /r/, as in *were*.

Merger is the more important of these patterns; for often when a sound change results from split, the rearrangement has taken place in such a way that one of the split allophones has merged with allophones from another source. The [e], which split off from pre-OE /a/ before *i ī j*, for example, merged with /e/ as in *men*. Moreover, allophones may become phonemes when their conditioning entities merge with others; pre-OE short and long [ö] and [ü] became phonemes when following *i ī j* merged with reflexes of other weakly stressed vowels or were lost. Merger may therefore be considered the central mechanism of sound change.

Merger may be conditioned or unconditioned. Unconditioned merger, when a phoneme merges completely with another phoneme, is relatively infrequent. An example is PGmc. /z/, which merged in pre-Old English and other Germanic dialects with PGmc. /r/. When such mergers take place, we cannot determine the earlier forms solely from one language, unless we have enough linguistic material to use the method of internal reconstruction. By comparing *was* with *were*, for example, we can distinguish the source of the *r* in *were* (PIE *s*) from that of the *r* in *four* (PIE *r*). Examples of other unconditioned mergers are: that of PIE /o/ with PIE /a/ to PGmc/a/; PIE /bh dh gh/ with /b d g/ in Iranian, Baltic, Slavic, and Celtic.

Much more frequent is conditioned merger, as when NE [t] merged with /d/ after stressed vowels preceding other vowels plus consonants, but not /n/; *bitten* did not become a homophone of *bidden*. Numerous instances of such merger can be cited: NE /u:/ in closed syllables merged with earlier ME /u/, as in *blood*, ME *blōd*, cf. Germ. *Blut* [blu:t], and *nut*, ME *nute*, cf. Germ. *Nuss* [nus]. As another example, NE /ž/ from [zy] merged with /ž/ in borrowings from French, like *rouge*.

Often after such mergers we find alternations that reflect the earlier situation, such as the /ž/ in *vision*, which alternates with the /z/ in *visible*. As noted in Chapter 6, these alternating entities are used in applying the method of internal reconstruction.

Since split may be brought about in two different ways, we distinguish two kinds of split. **Primary split** results from a change of some of the members of a phoneme, which then merge with a different phoneme. In this way the fricative reflex of OHG /t/ merged with OHG /s/ from PGmc. /s/, as in NHG *hassen*, cf. Engl *hate*; the phoneme /t/ was maintained as in MHG *treu*, cf. NE *true*. As another example, allophones of ME /ū/ merged with short ME /u/ before consonants, as in late-ME *blud* 'blood,' but ME /u:/ was maintained, as in *cū* 'cow.' As these examples indicate, primary split leads to an increase in the number of occurrences of one phoneme; after the merger of late ME /u/ from /ū/ with ME /u/, /u/ occurred more frequently. But primary split does not generally introduce new phonemes.

Secondary split results from a change in the conditioning features of allophones. Such a change may lead to the introduction of new phonemes in a system. In this way the pre-Old English front rounded allophones [ö ȫ ü ǖ] of /o ō u ū/ became phonemes when the conditioning /i ī j/ were modified. Pre-OE /o ō u ū/ were continued into Old English, but from some of their allophones, four new phonemes /ö ȫ ü ǖ/ were added to the system. Secondary split, however, does not necessarily lead to the introduction of new phonemes. For example, no new phonemes were produced from the fronted allophones of pre-OE /a ā/ when the conditioning /i ī j/ were modified; for these allophones fell together with earlier /e ē/.

In sum, disruption of phonological systems, that is, sound change, is brought about in accordance with two patterns: merger and split. In each of these patterns, the processes that lead to the change may vary, in accordance with the processes described in Section 3 of this chapter. Moreover, in languages with large numbers of speakers, the results of sound change may only be adopted over a long period of time, as we will note in the following section.

10.5 On the spread of sound change

After a sound change has taken place, it may be restricted to a given geographical area or it may be extended to other areas in which a language is spoken. In this way the spread of sound change is comparable to the spread of any linguistic innovation. We have observed in Chapter 7 that new words may be adopted throughout the area influenced by a center of prestige, as was the word *tonic*; see Chapter 8:5. Phonological innovations may be extended similarly, as demonstrated in the classical study of Kloeke's concerning the change of Middle Dutch *ū*, specifically in the words for *house* and *mouse*.

Middle Dutch *ū* changed to *ȳ*, apparently in the area around Antwerp.

The results of this change were spread to speakers who were influenced by this focal area, and in time extended virtually throughout the area in which Dutch was spoken. Near Low German territory, $\bar{u}$ was maintained, probably because of the unchanged $\bar{u}$ in Low German cognates; $\bar{u}$ was also maintained more widely in *mūs* than in *hūs*, probably because the word for 'mouse' is less widely used in communication with members of other communities than is the word for 'house, building.' The results of the change accordingly reflect both social and geographical influence. A second change of $\bar{y}$ to [øy] took place in the sixteenth and seventeenth centuries in the Antwerp area and was spread over much of the Dutch-speaking area; it became the standard pronunciation of modern Dutch *huis* and *muis*. These Dutch phenomena provide an excellent illustration of the spread of sound change, of variation from word to word in adoption of new patterns, and of the social forces at work in such spread.

Dialect geographers have carried out many studies which demonstrate that the results of sound changes are extended in accordance with communication patterns among geographical and social dialects.

Among the documented examples of sound change and its spread, the High German consonant shift may be the one most thoroughly investigated. Affecting first the High German area proper, as noted in Chapter 8:3, the results of change have been adopted through more and more of the German-speaking area. With the greater centralization of government in the nineteenth and twentieth centuries, a form of German was adopted that incorporated most of these changes. Today the dialects of North Germany, that is, the dialects of Low German with unchanged obstruents as in English, are being modified or ousted by High German. The results of the changes introduced by the High German consonant shift are accordingly still being spread, though the changes themselves took place approximately 1500 years ago.

Our observations based on the spread of the Old High German consonant shift and of the Dutch change of $\bar{u}$ may help us to understand other such phenomena in language, such as the spread of the results of the Great Vowel Shift.

When we investigate the adoption of the changes introduced in the GVS, we find that they were introduced gradually and over a long period of time. Instances of ME $\bar{\varepsilon}$, which now rhymes with $\bar{e}$, were for example treated differently in the sixteenth and seventeenth centuries. Dryden rhymed *dream* with *shame*, *sea* with *obey*. Pope rhymed *weak* with *take*, *eat* with *state*; Swift rhymed *seat* with *weight*, *meat* with *say't*, and so on. Much earlier the pronunciation [i:] for $\bar{\varepsilon}$ is reported by grammarians, but not favored by them. We assume it was used by Queen Elizabeth I, for she wrote 'biquived' for *bequeathed*. Although this pronunciation is known from the sixteenth century, still in 1747 Johnson was troubled about rhyming *great*, whether with *seat* [i:] or with *state* [e:].

We may ascribe Johnson's perplexity in part to the variation of usage among various dialects in Britain, in part to the gradual and slow extension of the EVS. As we noted in Chapter 8, sound change may take place in a focal area and be carried to other areas under its cultural influence through many centuries. The change of ME ε̄ and other long vowels must have been similar to the change of intervocalic *t* in contemporary American English, in which some speakers pronounce *butter* [bə́dər], others [bɔ́tər], still others [bɔ́tər]. As sounds are modified, the new articulation is extended gradually until words containing them reach a stabilized position in the phonological system of the standard language, as have *dream* and *great* today. Yet even today we find variation in English dialects, some of which preserve the pronunciation /diyf/ rather than the shortened /def/ of standard English. We also find considerable variation in the pronunciation of words like *roof, hoof, root*. This variation illustrates that even after six centuries the effects of the GVS have not become stabilized in English.

Just how and when sound changes are adopted in any individual speech community is a complicated problem, which requires detailed study. Our information about speech communities of the past is less detailed than is our information on contemporary languages and their use. For this reason our interpretations of the spread of sound changes in the past rely largely on studies of interrelationships between geographical dialects; Kloeke's observations of the difference in extent between the spread of the changed pronunciations in *hūs* and *mūs*, however, also involved consideration of social dialects. In this century several important investigations have been made of linguistic communities in which sound changes have been documented; these investigations provide details about the spread of change among various age groups of speakers and various social as well as geographical configurations.

The most comprehensive survey made of a speech community for historical purposes has provided important information on the gradual spread of the results of sound change. In his investigation of the French-speaking village of Charmey, Switzerland, published in 1905, L. Gauchat found differences in the speech of various age groups of the village (*L'Unité phonétique dans le patois d'une commune*. Halle). For example, where speakers 60–90 years of age used the back vowel å, speakers 30–60 years of age used both å and ao, and younger speakers used only *ao*. Further, children were also beginning to diphthongize ǫ to *ao*. Moreover, palatalized *l* was in part replaced by *y* among speakers 30–60 years of age, and totally replaced among speakers under 30. In 1929 E. Hermann published a follow-up study of Charmey, in which he examined the situation regarding some of Gauchat's conclusions at that time (Lautveränderungen in der Individualsprache einer Mundart." *Nachrichten der Gesellschaft der Wissenschaften zu Göttingen*, philos-hist. Kl. 9.195–214.) Hermann found that the change of ǫ to *ao* and other diphthongizations had become even more general. Other sound changes noted by Gauchat, however, had not been generally adopted, apparently because of contrary influence from standard French. The studies by Gauchat and Hermann show that sound changes, when adopted, are spread gradually among a community of speakers, as we have noted for the changes of the Great Vowel Shift.

Alf Sommerfelt found similar results concerning differences among speakers of varying age groups in Welsh and Irish-speaking communities (see his "Sur la propagation des changements phonétiques" in *Diachronic and Synchronic Aspects of Language*. The Hague: Mouton, 1962, pages 158–97). Besides supporting the evidence for gradual spread of the results of sound changes, Sommerfelt provided data that illustrate how such gradual shifting takes place. He found that the change was completely carried out in some words, but not yet in others. Sommerfelt's findings remind us of the situation in English after the GVS. A change may not affect all words immediately; but in time it is carried out in all words of similar phonological structure unless social conditions direct the adoption of other patterns.

We may accordingly conclude from the situation in English, in Charmey and in Wales and Ireland, how sound change takes place and is generalized in relatively small communities. After a sound change has been carried out, it is generalized so that eventually all occurrences of a linguistic element undergo the change, if its environment is the same and if the prestige of the focal area is adequate. If the linguistic community is small and homogeneous, the change may be carried out with complete consistency. This was the situation for the Proto-Germanic consonant shift; we know of no exceptions. If a change were carried out in a small, homogeneous community today, we would expect the same results. At the time of the High German consonant shift, however, the linguistic community that spoke High German was so large that the results of the shift were adopted only in a part of the area, presumably the focal area, and those neighboring areas under its influence. A similar situation existed for English in the fifteenth century, so that today "exceptions" to the GVS are found in the language side by side with the reflexes we expect from the shift as indicated in 10.1.

None of these communities approaches in size and complexity the linguistic community speaking English today, or even such a portion of this community as the New York City area. The population of the New York City area is much larger than that of England in the fifteenth century, and the speakers are also far more unlike. Recent immigration of Blacks into New York, and of Puerto Ricans, is also far more extensive than were any immigrations in Britain at any time, including the fifteenth century. It is instructive to examine how phonological systems change in such a large and complex community.

William Labov has carried out such studies, concentrating on linguistic variables, that is, items which are not found consistently among all speakers. One such variable is [r].

In his study of the status of [r], as in *guard*, in New York City speech, Labov found that it has high prestige. When speakers wish to be accepted in certain social contexts, they use the [r]. They also extend [r] and other patterns of high prestige to words in which they do not belong, producing in this way hyperforms. From his observations of the spread of variant forms with high prestige, Labov has proposed that such forms may be adopted more widely by speakers outside the focal area.

This observation has also been made for languages of the past, though only for occasional forms. Bloomfield, *Language* 479–80, cites an instance of a hyperform in Rhaeto-Romance. Another example is Old Saxon *tins* 'taxes.' This word is ultimately from Latin *census*, through Old High German *zins*. When Old Saxon speakers adopted the word from Old High German, they apparently assumed that it belonged to the patterns they observed for the Old High German consonant shift, which differentiated their own word *tolna*, from OHG *zollan* 'tax,' and the like. Rather than adopt the initial Latin consonant [ts], they introduced the normal Old Saxon equivalent of Old High German [ts], converting OHG *zins* to OS *tins*. In *tolna* such a conversion is etymologically justified, for the Latin word is *telōnēum*; in *tins*, however, it is not justified, for the initial Latin consonant was [ts]. For languages of the past, we find such changes only in sporadic forms. In the complex societies of contemporary culture, in which speakers master many varieties and dialects of their own language, such changes may be introduced more widely, as in the speech of New York City. As Weinreich, Labov, and Herzog have concluded, "the interpretation of the data in terms of language change depends on the entire sociolinguistic structure" (1968: 177).

In conclusion, the studies of Kloeke, Gauchat, Sommerfelt, and the numerous scholars who have concerned themselves with the High German consonant shift and the GVS, indicate that after sound changes take place, they are spread in accordance with social forces in a given community. If a community is small and compact, they may be adopted throughout it. An example we have cited is the Germanic consonant shift, which spread to all speakers of Proto-Germanic. Larger communities, on the other hand, may show only partial adoption of sound changes, as we may note from the results of the GVS or from the extension of the High German consonant shift. On the other hand, sound changes may be rejected in favor of competing phonological patterns, as occurred in Charmey. To understand the various phenomena involved in sound change, linguists have introduced increasingly precise techniques, notably rules in which the various forces involved can be specified. Linguists have also proposed various procedures for representing sound change, as we will note after we examine change that affects only a small number of words or only individual words in a language.

10.6   Sporadic change, or change by phonemes

In Section 10.3 we dealt with sound changes that arise from the rearrangements of allophones. Some allophones of one phoneme in the course of time come to resemble allophones of another phoneme and may merge with them. Allophones may also be split from the phoneme to which they formerly belonged, or they may be lost. In sound changes of this type, all allophones that are similar in articulation undergo the change. Moreover, when the change has taken place, the new alignment is maintained, until another shift occurs. NE /ŋ/, for example, has remained distinct from /n/ since the loss of a following /g/. Besides such change we find in language **sporadic changes**, which affect sounds only in some of their occurrences. As an example we may cite the change of ME *napron* to NE *apron*. We call the loss of initial *n* in *napron* a sporadic change because it occurred only in a few Middle English words.

Sporadic changes differ from allophonic changes in that they cannot be ascribed to any one phonological pattern. For example, initial *n* was not lost in phonological patterns similar to that of *napron*; it was maintained in *napkin*, *nape*, and so on. By contrast, every *n* was lost before voiceless fricatives in pre-Old English, as in OE *gōs* 'goose' from *gans-* (see page 155).

Since sporadic changes involve a direct change from one phoneme to another, with no gradual modification of allophones like that in AE -*t*-, we refer to them as **changes by phonemes**. They have also been referred to as **spontaneous**, and **saltatory**—in recognition of the immediate shift from one phoneme to another.

As an example we may cite the pronunciations of NE *seven*. One pronunciation, especially in careful speech is [sévn̩]. But commonly seven is pronounced [sévm̩], or even [sébm̩]. When this pronunciation is used, there has been no long gradual development of a final alveolar nasal to a labiodental or bilabial nasal. Speakers use either one of the two phonemes. Moreover, we find many such changes in rapid, informal speech, especially in everyday words. Although a similar change is often observed for NE *eleven* [əlévm̩] rather than [əlévn̩], it would be rare, or nonexistent, in *leaven* [lévn̩], which has the same phonetic environment for *n* but a different status in the social dialects of the language.

Speakers are often conscious of changes by phonemes, though they are unaware of the changes by allophones, as in the gradual voicing of NE *water, bottle,* and so on. Except for self-conscious speakers, who in this period of general advanced education flourish more widely than at any previous time, changes by allophone are carried through in all morphs in which the allophone occurs; the *t* in Modern English forms like *better, bottom,* for example, is consistently modified. On the other hand, a sporadic change like that of [sévn̩] to [sébm̩], or the pronunciation [irévələnt] for [iréləvənt], is often noted and frowned upon. The different attitude of speakers to change by phonemes probably results from an awareness that such phenomena are associated with specific social dialects or styles.

Many of the processes involved in sporadic change are like those involved in more general sound change. In this way many sporadic changes are assimilatory, such as those of *eleven*. Examples may also be found in the frequent palatalization of *ty* to yield *tš*, as in rapid pronunciation of words ending in -*t* before *you*, e.g., /betšə/ rather than /bet yə/; see also 10.8.7. Moreover, epenthetic vowels may be introduced, as in the pronunciation /éləm/ rather than /élm/. The same process led to the general introduction of epenthetic vowels in Old English, but in Modern English we do not introduce such vowels in all words with /-lm/; e.g., *film* /film/, *helm,* and so on.

One process that is exemplified primarily in sporadic changes is **dissimilation**, the production of sounds so that they will be more unlike one another. With the notable exception of Grassmann's law, dissimilation is attested only sporadically in languages. We find dissimilation particularly among the more complex sounds, which are also those learned last by children; such are *l* and *r*, as in NE *turtle* < Lat. *turtur*, NE *pilgrim* < Lat. *peregrinus*, NE *marble* < Lat. *marmor*. It is less commonly attested for stops, as in Germ. *Kartoffel* 'potato,' in which the initial *k* was dissimilated from *t* in the seventeenth century; the earlier term was *Tartuffeln*, which was borrowed from Ital. *tartuffeli*. (When the plant was imported to Italy from Peru in the sixteenth century, it was named after the truffle.) As in all these examples, in dissimilation it is usually the sound of the unaccented syllable that is modified.

Dissimilation may also involve the loss of a syllable; this is called **haplology**. As examples we may cite the Modern English adverbs in *-ly* made from adjectives ending in *-le*. In these, one syllable has been lost, as in *gently* rather than **gentlely*, *simply* rather than **simplely*. Another example is *England < Engla lond* 'land of the Angles.' Haplology is relatively infrequent.

Another type of change that is primarily sporadic is **metathesis**, the interchange of phonemes. Although few examples can be cited from Modern English, metathesis was remarkably frequent in late West Saxon, where we find *āxian* [a:ksian] 'ask,' *dox* 'dusk,' *flaxe* 'flask,' *waxan* 'wash.' Metathesis of consonant and vowel (to which some scholars restrict the term metathesis) is also attested in Old English, as in *hors < hros*, cf. NG *Ross* 'horse,' *ðirda < ðridda* 'third,' cf. NG *dritte* and NE *three*. Reflexes of the nonmetathesized forms are also found in Modern English, as in the dialectal *aks* for *ask*, and in *wal-rus* rather than **whale-horse*. In this way the examples cited here from English illustrate the phenomena of sporadic change, which affects relatively few words of the language, and which often leaves variant forms besides them.

10.7   Interpretations of sound change

In past treatments of phonological change, and in many current treatments, sound change is interpreted as a change of elements in a phonological system, as we have noted in the discussion of the phenomena described under Grimm's law (see Chapter 5:3). For example, the first of the changes in the Germanic consonant shift is interpreted as a change of the Proto-Germanic elements *p t k k^w* to *f θ χ χ^w*. The elements in question are taken to be abstract elements in the phonological system. As linguistic theory became more explicit, these abstract elements were precisely defined, and labeled phonemes, that is, classes of sounds with specific relationships to other classes of sounds in a given language. Each class was assumed to have one or more allophones, that is, subclasses of the abstract elements labeled **phonemes.** Sound change takes place in such subclasses, except in the rare instances when it is not combinatory (see 10.3.). In such instances the entire phoneme is changed. The event was stated by Grimm in the form of a rule, and has subsequently been stated by the same device. When interpreting sound changes as changes of abstract elements in a phonological system, linguists also undertook to analyze the components of these elements. Such study led to an analysis of phonemes as bundles of distinctive features. When change occurred, one or more of these components was assumed to have been modified. Thus in the Proto-Germanic change of *p t k k*ʷ to *f θ χ χ*ʷ, the manner of articulation was modified from that of a stop to a fricative. Phonological changes could in this way be interpreted as addition, alteration, or loss of a feature. Thus the feature [+front] was added to the articulation of pre-OE *a* by umlaut. In the umlaut of pre-OE *o u*, the feature [+back] was altered to [+front]. The resulting OE phonemes *ö ü* subsequently lost the feature [+rd] to merge with *e i*. By interpreting sound change as a change in features, we can specify more precisely the components of phonemes that are involved in change than if we simply use symbols for the phonemes. But whether depicted as change of subclasses of phonemes, like PIE *p t k k*ʷ, or as change of features, sound change is interpreted as a change of elements in the phonological system of a language.

10.7.1 Change as interpreted by change in rules.

With the development of transformational grammar, some linguists have introduced a view of language that shifts from a focus on elements to one on rules. This shift of focus is related to a shift in the aims of grammars. Grammars for these linguists are to account for the competence of speakers, that is their "organized body of linguistic knowledge" (King, HLGG, p. 14). The resultant grammar is then a set of rules. For many transformational grammarians such a set corresponds to the competence of an ideal speaker–hearer in an ideal linguistic community. The linguists holding this point of view base it on a generative approach to the study of language.

In order to interpret properly the grammars of generative transformationalists, one must recognize that the assumed ideal language is described by means of an elaborate set of metaphors. Moreover, the rules of the grammar, corresponding to segments of a speaker's competence arc reified and interpreted as the real essence of language.

In the course of this shift of focus, transformationalists have also introduced new terminology. To understand their terminology, students must be prepared for modification in the use of long-established terminology, as well as for neologisms in their writings.

Since to a generative transformational grammarian a grammar is a set of rules, when sound change involves innovations, the event is described as **rule addition**. Thus, the changes described in Grimm's law, in pre-OE umlaut, and in the GVS are examples of rule addition.

When, on the other hand, the application of a rule is no longer maintained in a grammar, the event is referred to as **rule loss**. As an example,

Gothic regularized the fricatives in most inflected sets; it shows voiceless fricatives where the other Germanic languages maintain voiced fricatives, as in the cognate of *choose*:

Gothic	kiusan	kaus	kusum	kusans
cf. OE	cēosan	cēas	curon	coren

Since other evidence has led many linguists to assume that the Gothic verbs at one time had had such voiced fricatives, the presence of *s* and other voiceless fricatives in the preterite plural and the preterite participle is ascribed to rule loss.

Voiced fricatives as reflexes of Proto-Indo-European voiceless stops are found in Gothic, as in the form *fadar* 'father,' and in auxiliaries like *aih* : *aigum* 'own.' Transformational grammarians account for such exceptions to rule loss by stating that words like *fadar* and *aigum* have been entered in the lexicon. Lexicalized forms may escape modification when a rule is lost.

A third type of change is ascribed to **rule reordering**. Two languages or dialects may exhibit the same rules, but the rules may differ in order. In this way the area in Central Germany that incorporated some changes from the north and others from the south has different surface forms from those of other dialects but is said to incorporate the same rules (see Chapter 8:9). The differing surface forms are said to result from the order in which the rules apply.

Besides reinterpreting sound change, and the results of sound change, in this way, grammarians with a generative point of view have introduced terms for rules that can be related to other rules. For example, if a rule describes changes that expand the scope of subsequent rules, the earlier rule is labeled a **feeding** rule, and the group of rules are said to stand in a **feeding relationship**. In this way the rules that describe the lengthening of short vowels before the GVS are labeled feeding rules. For, with the addition of more instances of *ī*, a larger number of words underwent the change of *ī* to *ay*.

This label indicates how transformationalists recognize the inter-relationships in the development of a language that Sapir called **drift**. Many changes in language take place in such a way that they can be interpreted as leading the language in a certain direction. If all changes occurred in this way, we could be far more assured of the sequence of changes in the past. But languages also undergo changes that conflict with the pattern of earlier changes. Such changes are referred to as **bleeding rules**; bleeding relationship is then used for diminution of scope.

10.7.2 Rules representing earlier historical forms and rules representing underlying forms.

Generative phonologists construct for their grammars underlying forms. These underlying phonological forms are posited on the assumption that the phonological component of the grammar is to be based on the syntactic component. That is, phonemes are determined by their roles in syntactic patterns, not by phonological analysis alone. The phonemes proposed are called systematic, in contrast with autonomous phonemes.

Systematic phonemes are virtually equivalent with the morpho-phonemes that have long been proposed. In verbs like *bite* (*bit*, *bitten*), a phonological construct *ī* may be assumed, from which with various rules the actual phonetic forms can be derived. Diphthongization is assumed in the form *bite*. While historical linguists have proposed reconstructed forms, and in this way dealt with the historical processes concerned in the change of ME *ī* to NE /ay/, generative phonologists propose such underlying phonological abstractions for the contemporary language. That is, they posit only systematic phonemes, not autonomous phonemes. (In Chapters 5 and 6 we have illustrated that this point of view is inadequate for understanding sound change.) Since the systematic phonemes proposed by generative phonologists often correspond to phonemes of an earlier stage of the language in question, students must distinguish carefully between them and the reconstructions of historical linguists.

Systematic phonemes are based on patterns observed in a language at any given time. Thus, besides *bite* : *bitten*, there is also variation between *divine* : *divinity*, *cycle* : *cyclical*, etc. By the procedures of generative phonology, the systematic phoneme /ī/ would be posited for the accented syllable of *divine*, *cycle*, as well as *bite*. But historically the vowel of *bite* is derived from ME *ī*, OE *ī*, and PGmc. *ey*: the accented vowel of *divine*, on the other hand, is derived from OFr. *-i(n)-* of *divine*, Lat. *dīvīnus*. The two have totally different origins historically.

The close analysis carried out in generative phonology can uncover patterns of earlier states of the language, as illustrated by the proposed *ī* of *bite*. But since borrowed words or newly coined words may also conform to the pattern, one must carefully distinguish the underlying forms of generative phonology from those of reconstructions made in historical linguistics. Often they coincide, and accordingly historical linguists can use underlying forms for internal reconstruction. But these forms must be used with care, for, as historical linguists have long known, words may be modified by analogy in such a way that they fit into the patterns of historically inherited words; this is one of the chief reasons for hesitation in reconstructing earlier forms, as for PIE. For the reconstruction of earlier forms of subsequently introduced words is comparable to proposing artifacts for the earlier stage of the language, such as *hamburgers, baseball,* and *hondas.*

10.7.3 On formalization of rules.   Whether one views language transformationally, the written rules representing phonemes by distinctive features are strictly regulated. This formalization makes possible greater accuracy in discussing historical developments than was observed in the past. As yet, few publications have observed the recommended standards. If they did, treatments of historical phenomena would be highly elaborate; for, as we have noted above, most rules apply only in restricted environments. Until grammars are written by linguists who have mastered both the data involved and then the format of rules, we will have no descriptions surpassing those of Carl Luick for English, or Eduard Schwyzer for ancient Greek, and many others in which the events are described rather than formulated in rules that must conform to strict patterns. The production of such accurate grammars is one of the pressing needs of historical linguistics. For example, the change of PGmc. f θ s χ χ^w to PGmc. $\bar{b}$ $\eth$ z g g^w is stated as the addition of a rule to the grammar of Proto-Germanic (King, HLGG, page 48):

$$\begin{bmatrix} +\text{obstruent} \\ +\text{continuant} \end{bmatrix} \rightarrow [+\text{voice}] \ \Bigg/ \begin{bmatrix} +\text{voice} \\ -\text{accented} \end{bmatrix} - [+\text{voice}]$$

In order to understand the publications that deal with sound change as rule change, students must be aware of their basis, and their difference from earlier descriptions and historical treatments. The use of rules is not distinctive, for, as we noted above, rules have been used since the days of Grimm. Nor is the use of distinctive features in stated sound changes restricted to such treatments, for even linguists of the nineteenth century dealt with changes by means of features. Rather, it is the identification of linguistic phenomena with rules, and the discussion of linguistic changes as rule changes, that are characteristic of this approach.

The rules of the past expressed in terms of phonemes and the rules expressed in terms of distinctive features are equivalent, if both types of rules meet the requirements of observational adequacy and descriptive adequacy. Meeting these requirements is still a greater problem in historical linguistics than is the revision of traditional terminology. For example, the rule on p. 141 is descriptively inadequate as it does not observe the "unchanged" forms of PGmc. p t k k^w after fricatives.

Other inadequacies in rules result from our lack of information about the distinctive features of phonemes in languages of the past. For example, we do not know the distinctive features of PIE *bh dh gh g^wh*. By one interpretation, they were tense voiced stops as opposed to the lenis voiced stops labeled *b d g g^w*. In attempts to understand the changes of the early Germanic consonant system, we must face such problems. By simply rewriting proposed rules formulated by earlier linguists, no new insights into the phenomena themselves are acquired.

10.8   Proposed explanations for sound change

Besides studying the processes and patterns by which phonological systems are modified, historical linguists have also attempted to determine the causes of modification and to predict its directions.

Some linguists have attempted to account for sound change by proposing that it leads to greater simplicity in language. We have already noted shortcomings of this point of view in Chapter 1:10; what is "simple" for speakers of some languages and in specific stages of a language may seem difficult in others, as we note when we compare sound changes in a given language with the phenomena in other languages. We conclude that assumptions of change toward ease of articulation in accordance with the principle of least effort is based on an inadequate view of language. For what seems easy in one language is difficult in another.

For example, German still maintains initial [kn], which has been lost in English and accordingly seems to be a very difficult consonant cluster for English speakers; compare NHG *kneten* 'knead,' NHG *Knie* 'knee,' NHG *Knoten* 'knot,' and so on. As another example we may note that in Latin there was relative freedom of occurrence of final consonants, but in Classical Greek the only final consonants to occur are *r n s*. PIE -*m* in the accusative singular, e.g., Lat. *lupum* 'wolf,' shows up as Gk. -*n*, *lúkon*. Other final consonants were lost, as illustrated by the vocative singular *paî* of *paîs*, gen. *paidós* 'boy'; Gk. *tí* 'what' corresponds to Lat. *quid*.

It is obvious from differences like these in various languages that only some sound changes tend toward simplicity and that we must look for other explanations. (See Jespersen, *Language*, pp. 319–336.)

As we have noted in Chapter 1, three major reasons have been proposed for change in language, including change in the phonological system: 1) the effect of one language on another; 2) the effects of modifications introduced when children learn their language; 3) effects of components of the system of the language concerned on other components. We will examine briefly each of these proposed explanations as they apply to sound change.

10.8.1 The proposed explanation of sound change through the effects of one language on another is based on observations of speakers who learn a second language with traces of their first language.   This is especially true if the speakers have learned the second language after their adolescence. Thus, speakers of English keep their aspirated stops when they learn French, pronouncing *peau* 'skin' as [pʰow] rather than [po·]. French speakers do the converse when they learn English. Moreover, English speakers keep their diphthongized vowels when they learn Spanish, pronouncing the Spanish *si* 'yes' as [siy], *sé* 'be' as [sey], *su* 'his' as [suw], in accordance with their own pronunciation of *see, say, sue*. By contrast, many Spanish speakers, who have only five vowels, do not distinguish between such English words as *bit* and *beet, let* and *late, pull* and *pool*. On the basis of such observations, it has been proposed that sound changes may be introduced by the carry-over of articulatory habits from the native language to a second language, with permanent effect. If, then, a large number of speakers adopts a second language, possibly as a result of conquest or migration, the sound system of the language can be modified.

The underlying language is known as a **substratum**. The proposed explanation for sound change is therefore known as the **substratum theory**. (The term **adstratum** for an adjacent influencing language, and **superstratum** for a superior influencing language, may also be used.)

Romance historical linguists especially have attempted to account for the separate developments of Spanish, French, and other Romance languages by assuming articulatory modifications carried over by speakers who adopted Latin as their second language. The French front rounded vowels are, for example, ascribed to a Celtic substratum. The changes that Latin has undergone in Rumanian are ascribed to a Dacian substratum.

One primary difficulty with proposing the substratum theory to account for sound change is the lack of evidence. We do not know what the relationships between the Celtic speakers of Gaul and the Latin-speaking settlers were. We even know little about the varieties of Celtic spoken in Gaul. The problems are similar for Spanish, Rumanian, and other languages. Until the substratum theory can be supported by observation of sound changes in contemporary languages, we must be cautious about suggesting it as an explanation for sound changes.

The effects of language interaction are determined largely by social conditions. When in some areas non-native speakers acquire a new language, the second generation masters it with rather general adequacy if the linguistic tradition is well established. In the United States, grandchildren of Italians, Germans, Spaniards, Africans, Asiatics, Irish, and Danes speak the English used by their associates without notable differences in linguistic structure. In other societies, however, different conditions may lead to different results.

When substrata have led to modifications in the pronunciation of a language, as of English in India, the linguistic tradition has been less powerful; native speakers have been outnumbered. In India relatively few native speakers were available to teach English to speakers who constantly used the indigenous languages.

There is now considerable investigation of multilingual communities such as those in India, Africa, and other areas of the world that are predominantly multilingual. The effects of one language on another may become clear after further study and may permit generalizations about sound changes resulting from the interplay of languages. Such study has indicated the effects of other languages in the component of syntax and in the lexicon, as we will note in the following chapters. From our observations to the present, however, we must conclude that sound change has as its major causes other linguistic phenomena.

10.8.2 The hypothesis that sound change is to be attributed to children learning their language is also poorly supported.   Under this hypothesis it is assumed that each new generation of speakers must master anew the grammar of their language and that, in the process, phonological change can readily be introduced. For it is apparent to anyone observing children learning their language that many of them have difficulty pronouncing certain sounds. Many children learning English, for example, pronounce the r as in rat with initial rounding, so that the word sounds like wat. Although such observations are readily supported, it is also true that children eventually overcome the difficulties.

Further, even if some young children make errors in pronunciation, there is no consistency of errors among children. Nor can we determine distinct generations of either young or old speakers who might generalize such mispronunciations. It is difficult therefore to conclude that modifications, such as those observed by Gauchat between the speech of different age groups at Charmey, were caused by inadequate learning of the phonemes in question, or of the phonological rules, by children.

Linguists who have studied sound change have observed, however, that when a change has been introduced, it is extended further by young speakers. For example, in 1943 the change of intervocalic AE t to d was carried through consistently by a group of young speakers. (See my article, "A Note on the Change of American English /t/," *American Speech* 28.271–75). And Sommerfelt observed a sound change in Wales first in a few words, and subsequently in greater numbers, until eventually all sounds in the phonological environment in question were affected (*Diachronic and Synchronic Aspects of Language*, especially pages 160–63, with reference to Henry Sweet). Apparently when a sound change is adopted, it is observed by more and more speakers in more and more words, until finally it is carried out in all the pertinent environments among a community of speakers.

We assume that if a sound change is carried out "without exceptions," as was the Proto-Germanic consonant shift, the community of speakers was homogeneous and probably small. When a sound change is carried out only partially throughout a relatively large territory, like the High German consonant shift, the community of speakers is exposed to various influences. As the effects of the High German consonant shift were spread toward Low German territory, influences from the important cultural centers of Low German-speaking northern Germany interfered with the influences leading to modification. Similarly the Great English Vowel Shift was not carried out in Scotland. We may conclude therefore that the spread of phonological changes is affected by the learning of language among children. But the initial cause of phonological changes cannot be ascribed to language learning.

10.8.3 Ascribing sound change to attempts to achieve regularity of symmetry in phonological systems seems at first blush most attractive. Examples like NE /ŋ/ can be cited that filled out the set of English nasals corresponding to the stops: /p b m t d n k g -/. While this explanation may apply for English, Italian and other languages with similar gaps in the system have not regularized in this way. Clearly this explanation, too, has its limits.

And even if we may assume a tendency toward symmetry in phonological systems, we cannot predict sound changes. For example, in Middle High German, which had a long-vowel system similar to that of Middle English, the high vowels were also changed to diphthongs, as in MHG *is* 'ice' : NHG *Eis*, MHG *hūs* 'house' : NHG *Haus*. But unlike English, the lower long vowels were not raised. The vowel of NHG *See* 'sea' is still pronounced like its Middle High German counterpart, as are the vowels of *Mond* 'moon' and *Staat* 'state.' Thus the Middle High German and Middle English vowel systems are similar in some developments, different in others. If, on the basis of these changes, we should be tempted to speculate that in long-vowel systems like those of the Germanic languages, the high vowels tend to become diphthongized, we would be dismayed by Icelandic, in which the high vowels have remained unchanged but the long low vowel has become diphthongized; the *ā* has become [au]. Similarly in Scots

English the *ā*, as in ME *hām*, was modified to *ē*, but the high vowels have not undergone the GVS.

Although we cannot flatly ascribe changes to the system, we observe that when changes occur, they are directed by the system. The Germanic reflexes of the Proto-Indo-European stops provide an excellent example of changes that seem to lead to others; after *p t k k^w* became *f θ χ χ^w*, *bh dh gh g^wh* became *b ð g g^w*, and finally *b d g g^w* became *p t k k^w*. Accordingly the elements of the system underwent changes, but in the course of these changes the system was largely maintained. Similarly in Classical Greek the system was largely maintained, though PIE *bh dh gh* became the voiceless aspirated stops *φ θ χ*. In Latin, however, the symmetry of the Proto-Indo-European system was disrupted when *bh* and *dh* coalesced to *d*, and *gh* became *g* or *h*. Further, in Celtic, Baltic, Slavic, and Iranian, the system was reduced, by the merger of *bh dh gh* with *b d g*. As these examples may illustrate, the developments in each of these languages were directed in part by the system, although from the earlier system we could not have predicted the changes in question.

After such changes take place, subsequent changes are also directed in part by the later system. Thus we find parallel series of stops and fricatives developing in English, as we have noted in Chapter 3:3. In Sanskrit, on the other hand, we find parallel series of voiceless and voiced stops, unaspirated and aspirated: *p ṭ c k ph th ṭh ch kh b d ḍ j g bh dh ḍh jh gh*. Just as the development of voiced fricatives seems natural in English, so that of voiceless aspirates seems natural in Sanskrit. Such developments in a specific direction were labeled by Sapir "drift."

But since the languages of one family may undergo a variety of changes, it is not meaningful to speak of a development toward simplicity. It is much more appropriate to observe the general articulatory patterns of the speakers of any given language, for these seem to have an effect on its changes.

This conclusion may be supported by phenomena of assimilation and other combinatory changes. For they seem to be determined by the articulatory habits of the speakers of a language and by the possibilities allowed by the structure of that language. In the history of English, we may observe many instances of assimilation of dentals and alveolars, some of which are sporadic; others are allophonic changes leading to modifications of the system. The following assimilatory changes occur sporadically in Modern English:

won't you	did you	miss you	raise you,
[wównčə]	[díjə]	[míšə]	[réyžə]

These forms may be used in rapid speech, are considered informal by some speakers, substandard by others, and have by no means replaced the more careful [wównt yùw], and so on.

Similar changes took place in early Modern English, and many of the changed forms have remained in the language. From the eighteenth century [ty] is attested with the pronunciation [š], as in *nation*; similarly [sy], as in *issue*, and especially before [yŭ], as in *sugar, sure, assure*. (This change also took place in such words as *assume, consume, suet*, but subsequently [s] was reintroduced in these words as a **spelling pronunciation**.) Similarly [zy] became [ž], as in *measure, pleasure, treasure*; [dy] became [ĵ], as in *soldier, grandeur, Indian, educate, hideous*; here, too, all words but *soldier* and *grandeur* were remodeled by spelling pronunciation. *Injun* has survived only as a pejorative term. Similarly many educators consider the regular pronunciation of the word /éĵəkèyt/ undignified and insist on the spelling pronunciation.

In early Old English, allophones of /k/ and /g/ were palatalized even more generally in the neighborhood of front vowels, so that modifications arose as follows:

cīdan 'chide'	cū 'cow'	geard 'yard'	gold 'gold'
[k'i:dan]	[ku:]	[g'ɛard]	[gold]
pic 'pitch'	bōc 'book'	dæg 'day'	longra 'longer'
[pik']	[bo:k]	[dæg']	[loŋgra]

Gradually the palatalized allophones, as in *chide, pitch, yard, day*, came to be further differentiated from the velar allophones, as in *cow, book, gold, longer*. Eventually the palatalized allophone of /k/ fell together with [tj], as in *feccan* [fetjan] 'fetch,' and the new phoneme /č/ arose; the palatalized allophone of /g/ fell together with the earlier phoneme /j/ as in OE *gear* 'year' and split from the /g/ phoneme.

Palatalization has occurred repeatedly in the Slavic languages. Some phonemes of Slavic can be ascribed to the palatalization that took place in the Indo-European speech community and gave rise to the isogloss separating the *satem* languages from the remainder of the Indo-European family. The following are examples:

OCS pĭsati 'write'	cf.	Gk. poikílos 'variegated'
OCS zrŭno 'grain'		Goth. kaurn 'grain'
OCS zemlja 'earth'		Gk. khamaí 'on the earth'

At a later time velars were again palatalized in Slavic, for example:

OCS četyre 'four'	cf.	Lat. quattuor 'four'
OCS žena 'woman'		Gk. gunḗ 'woman'
OCS žęti 'strike'		Hitt. kuenzi 'strikes'

Later still in Russian virtually all consonants were palatalized before front vowels, so that today consonants are found in two series: palatalized and nonpalatalized. The two branches of Indo-European, Germanic and Slavic, accordingly provide examples of the assimilatory change known as palatalization, as do other Indo-European languages.

In the Germanic languages assimilation also took place in the articulation of vowels. PIE /e/ before [y] became raised in Germanic, so that PIE /ey/ > PGmc. /i:/, as in OE *stīgan* 'climb,' compare Gk. *steikhō* 'come'; Modern English cognates are *sty* and *stile*. PGmc. /e/ was also assimilated to an *i* in the following syllable, as in Goth. *midjis*, OE *midd* 'mid' = Lat. *medius*.

The most far-reaching of these assimilations in the Germanic languages took place in the early period of the individual dialects, and is generally known by the term **umlaut**, or **mutation**. As we have noted in 10.1, pre-OE short and long *a o u* standing before *y* or short or long *i* of the following syllable became fronted; *a > e, o > ø*, later *e, u > y*, later *i*.

PGmc. mūsiz > OE mȳs > ME mīs > NE mice
PGmc. dōmjan 'judge' > OE døman > dēman > NE deem
Goth. satjan = OE settan 'set'

Back assimilation occurred in Old Norse. Pre-ON *a* before *u* became *o* [ɔ], e.g., ON *lǫnd* 'lands' from **landu*. Before *w* pre-ON *a > ɔ, e > ø* and *i > y*, as in ON *søkkua* 'sink' < **sekkwa*, ON *lyng* 'heather' < **lingwa*. Since the vowels are also rounded, the assimilation in these Old Norse forms involves **labialization**. The assimilation in the Germanic languages may be related to a prominent accent on words, which made them into a unit so that one pattern of articulation affected the phonemes of an entire word. Besides assimilation, we also find losses of unstressed vowels, as we illustrate below.

By contrast, in Japanese each syllable is pronounced independently. There is no stress accent; all syllables end in a vowel or *n̄*. For as long as Japanese is attested, we find maintenance of vowels; words like *Kojiki*, the name of a literary work completed in 712 A.D., are pronounced much the same way as they were over a millennium ago. (Syllable-initial consonants were assimilated to following vowels, however, as we shall note in Chapter 12.) But in Proto-Germanic, which had a syllabic structure not unlike that of Japanese before the effects of the initial stress accent were brought about, words were greatly modified. We may illustrate some of the modifications by means of the Gallehus inscription, and subsequent developments of the words it contains:

Ek HlewagastiR HoltijaR   horna tawido

Its syllabic structure, consisting primarily of open syllables, was inherited from Proto-Indo-European, which like Japanese had a pitch accent. But as we know from the effects of Verner's law, Proto-Germanic introduced a strong stress accent on the first syllable of words. This strong stress led to the loss of vowels in weakly stressed syllables. By Old English times the inscription would have read:

*Ic Hleowgiest Hylte   horn tēode

Subsequently other weakly stressed vowels were lost, leading to the mono-syllabic structure of native English words. *I, guest, Holt,* and *horn* may be related directly to the Proto-Germanic words exemplified in the inscription. Moreover, with *hlewa-* 'famous' we may compare the adjective *loud*; and with *tawido,* the noun *tool*. As these examples illustrate, English has been modified in a specific direction at least in part because of its type of accentuation.

The resulting phonological changes, which involved loss of morphological markers, also affected the syntactic patterns of English. The final syllables of Proto-Germanic indicated syntactic relationships; *horna,* for example, could have been interpreted only as an accusative or nominative singular. Since *HlewagastiR* could only be a nominative, the subject of the inscription was identifiable from the morphological markers, and the object as well. After the morphological markers were lost, word order was strictly regulated, as in Modern English. Moreover, numerous function words have been introduced, such as articles and prepositions, leading to a considerably different language from Proto-Germanic. As we have seen, the differences can be related to phonological changes, many of which in turn we ascribe to one phonological innovation: the introduction of a strong initial stress accent.

While we account for many changes in the Germanic languages by the strong initial stress accent, we do not have adequate information about Germanic in the period before our era to determine the reason for its introduction. That is to say, we cannot account for the sound change by which a stress accent was introduced. Some linguists have proposed that Proto-Germanic adopted the initial stress accent from speakers of adjacent languages whom we cannot identify. Others assume that the accent was developed within the language, and supported by no outside influences. We cannot provide an answer to these conflicting views. Possibly a combination of reasons led to the introduction of the change.

In determining the causes of sound change, we will do best to deal with less remote changes than those of Proto-Germanic, such as the change of NE -*t*- to -*d*-. By documenting fully other such changes, as Sommerfelt set out to do in Ireland and Wales, and other linguists in other areas, we may come to understand how sound change is introduced as well as how changes are extended. Linguists who have concerned themselves with sound change—for example, Sommerfelt, Weinreich, Labov, and Herzog— have pointed out the importance of relating linguistic and social phenomena. With our present knowledge of sound change, based largely on that in Indo-European dialects, we can make assured statements about its processes and patterns; about its direction or causes we can only propose hypotheses. Further study is essential to provide information in these spheres comparable to that gathered over the past century and a half on the processes and patterns of sound change.

Selected Further Readings

Sound change is one of the most widely discussed phenomena in historical linguistics. Bloomfield provides many examples and full discussion in *Language*, Chapters 20–22, pages 346–403. On pages 329–31 he interprets the data described by G. G. Kloeke, *De Hollandsche expansie* (The Hague: 1927) concerning the words for 'house' and 'mouse' in the Dutch-Flemish area, with a map on page 328. E. H. Sturtevant's *Linguistic Change* deals with sound change, pages 32–67, and elsewhere, attributing considerable influence to mistakes in speaking; since this suggested influence is disregarded here as negligible, it may be of interest to examine Sturtevant's argument. In various essays published in *Word*, some of which were later translated and published in *Économie des changements phonétiques*, A. Martinet attempts to make a point for linguistic change in accordance with the principle of least effort. Probably the most eloquent statement of language development in a specific direction is Chapter 7, "Language as a Historical Product: Drift" of Sapir's *Language*; his further chapters must also be noted, especially 8.

Specific applications of the findings from work on sound change may be found in standard handbooks such as E. Schwyzer's *Griechische Grammatik*, in which theory is also discussed at some length, or the various grammars of A. Meillet. Further information on sound change may be found in articles, such as Sapir's "Glottalized Continuants in Navaho, Nootka, and Kwakiutl," *Language* 14.248–78. For the history of English, the fullest treatment of historical phonology is given by K. Luick, *Historische Grammatik der englischen Sprache*. Leipzig, 1914–40, subsequently reprinted.

Since it is useful to observe as fully as possible the course of a sound change, reports on the voicing of intervocalic *t* in American English are of considerable interest. A phonetician's description of such *t* is provided by R-M. S. Heffner, *General Phonetics*, pages 129–30.

For additional control over the procedures necessary to understand change in language, and to employ such understanding in historical grammar, students must master Henry M. Hoenigswald's *Language Change and Linguistic Reconstruction*. This also set out to provide terminology for historical linguistics, which was employed to the extent feasible in an introductory text. Robert D. King, in *Historical Linguistics and Generative Grammar*, deals with sound change using the conventions developed in transformational grammar. The article "Empirical Foundations for a Theory of Language Change," by Uriel Weinreich, William Labov, and Marvin L. Herzog, *Directions for Historical Linguistics*, pages 95–195, is important for building on the achievements of nineteenth-century linguistics and for discussing, on the basis of rich data, the problems involved in proposing a theory of language change. Students who wish to deal further with these problems should study the article.

CHAPTER 11

Syntactic and morphological change

11.1 Change in syntactic patterns

When we examine some of the oldest materials surviving in the Indo-European languages, we find that they exhibit characteristics of OV languages. The following lines from the Rigveda illustrate several of these characteristics.

Rigveda 2.12.7   yáḥ sū́riaṃ, yá uṣásaṃ jajā́na,
            who   sun   who   dawn   created
            yó apā́ṃ netā́—sá, janāsa, Índraḥ.
            who of-waters guide—he, men, (is) Indra.

'Indra, oh men, is the one who created the sun and the dawn, and who is guide of the waters.'

This short Rigvedic passage exemplifies the following OV characteristics. The verb *jajā́na* stands at the end of its clause. The relative clauses introduced by *ya-* precede their antecedent *sa*. The genitive *apā́ṃ* precedes its noun. Moreover, the first line exhibits gapping of the type expected in OV languages; the verb is deleted from the first clause, *yáḥ sū́riaṃ*, and is found only in the second. Similar evidence for OV characteristics are found in Hittite, early Greek, and in other Indo-European languages, including Italic and the early Germanic dialects.

If we apply the principles of the comparative method to these syntactic patterns, we conclude that Proto-Indo-European was an OV language. As we have noted in Chapter 5:8.9, the comparative method is applied to abstract features, not to surface manifestations of these. In the phonological component it is applied to phonemes and to subclasses of phonemes, not to phones. Similarly in syntax, the comparative method must be applied to abstract structures. In determining the Proto-Indo-European syntactic pattern for the order of genitives, for example, we would base our reconstructions on the genitive-noun (GN) order in Vedic and in Hittite. Using the comparative method, we would propose the same pattern for Proto-Indo-European:

The reconstruction would be supported with material from other dialects. A similar illustration has been given on page 90 for the adjectival comparative construction. The procedure would be applied to any syntactic construction for which we have sufficient evidence.

To suggest further examples of syntactic change, we might note that contemporary English is a VO language, as the translation given above for the Vedic passage illustrates. The verb 'created' precedes its object. The relative clause follows its antecedent. The genitive construction 'of the waters' follows its noun. And, in gapping, the verb is maintained in the first English clause. Moreover, as we have noted in Chapter 3, most of the Indo-European languages are now VO in structure. We must conclude that there has been a comprehensive change from an OV to a VO structure, especially in the European languages of the Indo-European family.

Using a transformational framework, we would ascribe these syntactic changes to modifications of the early rules of the transformational component. Over an extended period of five millennia, the rules for syntactic constructions characteristic of OV languages underwent a fundamental syntactic change to those of VO languages.

The syntactic changes, we have illustrated so far, have to do largely with order of the constituents in constructions. Changes also occur in other syntactic features, such as the categories marked in a language and selection classes. The changes in these three syntactic characteristics will be discussed in the following sections.

11.2   Changes in order

To provide materials for changes in order, we will examine a series of texts from the Germanic languages. The following are versions of Mark 1:13 in Old and Middle English, and in early Modern English.

The King James version: 'And he was there in the wilderness forty days, tempted of Satan; and was with the wild beasts; and the angels ministered unto him.'

Wyclif's translation, made about 1380 A.D., exhibits some differences from this version, as in use of the definite article: 'And he was in desert fourty dayes and fourty niȝtis, and was temptid of Sathanas, and was with beestis, and angelis mynstriden to him.'

The Old English translation illustrates further syntactic differences, as in the OV order of the final clause: 'And hē on wēstene wæs fēowertig daga and fēowertig nihta and hē wæs from Satane gecostnod, and hē mid wilddēorum wæs, and hym englas þēnodan.'

For a more archaic example in the Germanic languages, we may recall the Gallehus inscription: *Ek HlewagastiR HoltijaR horna tawido.* As the final position of the verb indicates, the word order is still definitely OV. But by the time of the Old English translation of Mark 1:13, roughly 1000 A.D., only two of the clauses have OV word order. Four hundred years later there are no clauses with final verb. And in contemporary English the only OV patterns are those of adjective noun order, as in *wild beasts*. We also still find genitive constructions of GN order, as in *the student's books* beside *the books of the student*. But in general, English has changed fundamentally from Proto-Indo-European in its underlying syntactic structure. The change is even more thoroughgoing in the Romance languages, which place adjectives and genitives after nouns.

We conclude that languages undergo syntactic modifications comparable to the phonological modifications discussed in the preceding chapter. As in the study of phonological systems, when we deal with syntactic change, we must determine the changes, the processes involved in those changes and their spread, and where possible their causes.

The three English versions of Mark 1:13 illustrate a gradual shift from OV order to VO order in the clause. While this shift was going on, the other orders characteristic of OV languages were also being changed, such as the genitive with regard to its noun. In Old English the genitive commonly preceded nouns, as in *wuldres Wealdend* 'King of glory.' In early Middle English this order was still maintained, even in phrases with no genitive marker like *his lady grace* and *the king hand*. But in late Middle English the genitive was generally placed after its noun, as in the title of Chaucer's poem "The Parliament of Fowls."

The change took place gradually, and at different rates in various parts of England. In the north the old order was maintained longest. And to this day unmarked genitives preceding their nouns are found in petrified expressions, for example *Lady Day* and *ladybird*. For more details, see Tauno F. Mustanoja, *A Middle English Syntax* I (Helsinki, 1960) pages

71–73. But the change was thorough. As early as the fourteenth century, about 85 percent of genitive constructions consisted of a postposed genitival phrase with *of*, in contrast with about 1 percent in the tenth century. Today the percentage of *of*-constructions is even higher.

Various reasons have been proposed for the change. One is French influence. But while French exerted a strong influence on Middle English, English itself was undergoing the loss of final elements that eliminated many of the genitive endings. Moreover, as we have seen, English was adopting VO characteristics, which would require NG rather than GN order. Accordingly we cannot identify merely one cause of the change. Borrowing from French and internal influences both had an effect on the genitive construction.

Similar examples of changes in order could be cited from other languages, such as the Romance, or for other constructions, such as the development of postpositions to prepositions in Classical Latin and Greek. The change in the English genitive constructions illustrates the essential characteristics of such changes in order.

To indicate the large number of syntactic changes between Proto-Indo-European and most of the contemporary Indo-European languages, we may review some of the inflectional categories of Proto-Indo-European. Nouns in late Proto-Indo-European were inflected for eight cases, three genders, three numbers. To be sure, pronouns have preserved vestiges of a further case (*he, his, him*) and of the three genders (*he, she, it*). And the third number category, the dual (an adjectival inflection formerly used when two items were involved), is still reflected in the comparative of the adjective: *John is bigger than Judy: in fact, he is the biggest of the three children.* But the noun inflection has been sharply reduced.

Verbs in Proto-Indo-European were inflected for two voices, three aspects, four moods, three numbers, and three persons. When we compare Modern English, we find a different voice, the passive, but also the loss of the middle voice; this was used when the subject was involved in an action affecting himself, as in Gk. *édomai* 'I eat (for my own benefit).' Instead of the three aspects—present, aorist, and perfect—English has introduced two tense categories. The Proto-Indo-European moods—indicative, subjunctive, optative, imperative—have also been reduced. Except for the verb *be*, the person and number categories are reflected only in the third singular, as in *goes* versus *go*.

While many surface syntactic markers have been lost, some syntactic categories are indicated by function words, such as the genitival *of*. Phrases with *of* parallel many of the uses of the genitive in Latin and Greek, for example: the objective genitive, *criticism of Milton*; the partitive genitive, *last of all the students*; the genitive of material, *a house of cards*, and so on. And verbal phrases made up of *may* and *might* reflect subjunctives of Old English.

11.3 Change in syntactic categories and their markers

To illustrate change in syntactic categories and their markers, we may sketch briefly the history of two such changes in English: definiteness in the noun and the passive voice in the verb. In a brief sketch, many details will be omitted.

To provide a basis for comparison with earlier forms of the language, we may note that if the syntactic feature ⟨+Definite⟩ is associated with a noun in Modern English, it can be manifested by a demonstrative (*this*, *that*) or by the definite article *the*. On the other hand, ⟨−Definite⟩ can be manifested by the indefinite article *a, an* or by no overt marker. The category is applied differently to ⟨+Count⟩ and ⟨−Count⟩ nouns. A partial analysis of the phrase *the wilderness* would be represented as follows:

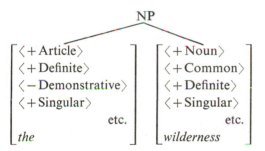

Comparing the equivalent in the Middle English and Old English translations of Mark 1:13, we note that the surface syntactic markers for definiteness have been extended in Modern English; for neither of the older passages has an article or another overt marker.

On the other hand, definiteness was an Old English category. For demonstratives were used in Old English with roughly the same meaning as those in Modern English. Moreover, other patterns indicated the category of definiteness. Old English had two declensions for adjectives, strong and weak. Weak forms of the adjective were used when definiteness was to be expressed; for example, for the expression 'in the nearby wilderness' the Old English pattern would be *in nēan wēstene* as opposed to *in nēam wēstene* for 'in a near wilderness.' As final endings were lost, the two inflections merged, and this device for indicating definiteness was lost.

Moreover, in contrast with Modern English, Old English had two demonstratives: *sē, sēo, þæt* and a more emphatic *þēs, þēos, þis*. The first has provided the forms for the Modern English definite article; the second, for the common demonstrative. That is, markers to indicate definiteness have been maintained, but they are now expressed primarily by means of preposed modifiers.

Determining the history of the syntactic category definiteness in English is then a complex syntactic study, involving its extension by means of some markers such as the definite article, its loss by means of others such as adjectival inflection, and the change in distribution of others such as *this* and *that*. When, on the other hand, we compare the syntax of Proto-Indo-European, we find no evidence for definiteness as a syntactic category. Accordingly, at some period in the history of pre-English, the category has been introduced. Its introduction represents an innovation in the underlying syntactic structure of the language. But during the history of English proper, and even from late Proto-Germanic to the present, the syntactic modifications concerning definiteness have only involved surface markers.

To provide another example of change in syntactic categories, we may survey briefly the history of the passive category. The passive was found in late Old English, as the second clause of Mark 1:13 indicates: *and hē wæs from Satane gecostnod*. The structure of this and other passive clauses in late Old English would be represented much as it is in Modern English. But there have been surface changes. One, the marker of the agentive, is obvious from the three translations of Mark 1:13. In Old English, *from* was used, as well as *mid* and *þurh*. Compare New High German, where *von* is used for a ⟨−Human⟩ agentive, and *durch*, the cognate of OE *þurh*, for a ⟨−Human⟩. A second change is in the auxiliary; in Old English, forms of *weorð-* 'become' were used (compare NHG *werden*), as well as forms of *beo-* and *wes-* 'be,' which have been maintained in Modern English. The use of *ge-* with the participle may seem to be a third surface difference, but we cannot associate this change merely with the passive or even with the participle; for *ge-* could be used with any verb form in Old English. Like other differences between Old English and Modern English, such as the loss of the dative case form, the loss of *ge-* cannot therefore be related to a change in the passive construction.

While the passive accordingly shows little change between late Old English and Modern English, in earlier stages of the language there was considerable change. As we may assume from Gothic, Proto-Germanic had an inflectional suffix for the passive: *-da*, as in *usfulljada* 'is fulfilled.' The passive inflection, however, was being lost in the language, for already in Gothic it is defective; it lacks a preterite. To represent the preterite of the passive in Gothic, a participle with the same auxiliaries as noted for Old English was used. Since the present passive is a reflex of the Proto-Indo-European middle voice, we may assume that in early Proto-Germanic it had inflections parallel with those of the active, and a broader sphere of use than in Gothic.

In Proto-Indo-European, passive constructions were subclasses of the middle voice. These were limited; instead of our passive constructions, intransitive verbs were commonly used. We must assume then that at some time in the history of late Proto-Indo-European, the passive category was introduced. The considerable differences in its markers from dialect to dialect support this assumption.

As these examples of syntactic constructions in English and its earlier stages may indicate, syntactic changes take place slowly, more slowly than do phonological changes. In the syntactic component, changes occur largely in markers of categories, particularly in inflections. The processes involved have been intensively studied for many languages. Changes in the markers for syntactic categories are largely determined by the system of a given language, as we will note in the following sections. The process by which these changes are carried out is known as analogy.

11.4   Changes in inflectionally distinct selection classes; morphological change

The history of the strong or irregular verbs in English furnishes us with excellent examples of change in selection classes. The Old English strong verbs are generally divided into seven classes in accordance with internal vocalic variation. To summarize the possible forms, principal parts are given: (I) the infinitive, (II) the first-third sg. preterite indicative, (III) the preterite indicative plural, (IV) the preterite participle. The classes are illustrated with one example for each:

	I		II	III	IV
1.	drīfan	'drive'	drāf	drifon	drifen
2.	cēosan	'choose'	cēas	curon	coren
3.	findan	'find'	fand	fundon	funden
4.	beran	'bear'	bær	bǣron	boren
5.	sprecan	'speak'	spræc	sprǣcon	sprecen
6.	standan	'stand'	stōd	stōdon	standen
7.	feallan	'fall'	fēoll	fēollon	feallen

In addition to these strong verbs, there was in Old English a large number of weak or regular verbs, which continued to expand; for almost every new verb was inflected weak. Weak verbs had fewer differing forms than did the strong verbs, as exemplified by three principal parts. Moreover, the only difference between the preterite singular and the preterite plural consisted in the endings, as for

I		II (+III)	IV
lufian	'love'	lufode	lufod

In this situation, with the largest number of verbs having relatively few forms while a small number of verbs had many more, there was reduction of the strong verb set, especially in the preterite.

The source of the preterite vowel in Modern English strong verbs, whether from the singular or plural, varied from verb to verb. In 'drive' the vowel of the preterite singular was generalized throughout the preterite, to NE *drive, drove, driven*. In *bite*, however, also of class I, the vowel of the plural was generalized to NE *bite, bit, bitten*. Other examples are given in the Workbook. Observing the development of all strong verbs in English, and the basis of selecting either singular or plural vowels in the preterite, would require considerable exposition; here we are primarily interested in demonstrating the analogical reduction of forms, on the pattern of weak verbs such as *love, loved, loved*. Yet the general principle of remodeling is an attempt to distinguish between the stem for the present and that for the preterite, in accordance with the distinction between *love*, on the one hand, and *loved, loved*, on the other. Further examples support this assumption.

In *choose*, the vowel of the preterite participle was generalized to the preterite, with *ch* and *z*, the consonants of the present and preterite singular, generalized throughout.

In *find*, the vowel of the preterite plural was generalized; in *bear*, the vowel of the preterite participle. The pattern of class IV was extended to *speak*.

In *stand*, the vowel of the preterite was generalized to the preterite participle; in *fall*, we find regular developments of the Old English forms, no new remodeled forms.

The history of the principal parts of the English strong verbs then illustrates thoroughgoing remodeling or regularization. When, as in *drāf, drifon* or *cēas, curon*, the differences in a set are regularized, we speak of **leveling**.

We may cite further forms of the Old English strong verbs to indicate the interaction between sound change and morphological regularization. The present indicative endings in West Saxon with their older forms are as follows:

Present Indicative

1. sg.   -e < pre-OE -o < -ū
2. sg.   -(e)st < pre-OE -isi (with addition of -t)
3. sg.   -(e)ð < pre-OE -iþi
   pl.   -að < pre-OE -anþi

Since -i following -e- of the stem syllable occasioned change of -e- to -i-, the forms of *beran* in West Saxon were:

1. sg.	bere	cf. Northumbrian	bero
2. sg.	bir(e)st		beres
3. sg.	bir(e)ð		bereð, -es
pl.	berað		beorað

The pre-OE sound change of *e* > *i* before *i* had taken place regularly. After the change the stem *bere*, *birest*, etc., contained two vowels, in contrast with other verbs that had no such alternation, such as *findan*, *drīfan*. As we know from the forms today, the *e* was extended throughout the present of *bear*, and the difference in vowels was leveled out.

In other ways the verbs in English have become regularized, so that today they have a maximum of five forms. Similar examples of regularization could be provided from other languages with sets of paradigms.

In the course of leveling, extensions may be made from inflected or derived, rather than from base forms. These are known as **back formations.** In Old English the verbs *flēon* 'flee' and *flēogan* 'fly' were inflected alike in all forms but the infinitive. As in *birest*, *bireð*, the vowels in the second and third singular forms underwent modification, and the present indicative was as follows:

1. sg.	flēo
2. sg.	flīehst
3. sg.	flīehð
pl.	flēoþ

The first person singular and the plural, with vowels the same as that of *flēon*, developed into NE *flee*. This should have alternated with *thou fliest*, *he flies*. Instead, a new infinitive *fly* was produced. In *flee*, the base allomorph was extended throughout the present; in *fly*, an inflected allomorph was generalized throughout the present, as a back formation.

We may cite further instances of back formations from nouns. When, in Middle English, -s came to be the general plural marker, the singular : plural contrast was based on presence and absence of s, on the pattern:

$$\frac{\text{Middle English sg. fader}}{\text{faders}} = \frac{\text{fō 'foe'}}{\text{fōs 'foes'}}$$

Some nouns that ended in *s* were interpreted as plurals, and a new singular was produced, e.g., *pes* 'pease' from the Lat, sg. *pisum*; the new singular is now commonly used, though the old has survived in the nursery rime "Pease Porridge Hot." Similarly *buriels* < OE *byrgels* 'tomb' was assumed to be plural, and a new singular was produced, which on the pattern of *funeral* was spelled with *a*, *burial*. Other such singulars were made as back formations, such as *riddle* from ME *redels* < OE *rǣdels*, compare Germ. *Rätsel*, and *cherry* from ME *cheris* < OFr. *cherise*, later reborrowed as *cerise*. In these nouns the new singular forms, rather than inflected forms, resulted from analogy.

We may illustrate a further complexity of morphological change with West Saxon *eom* 'am.' Like Gothic *im* 'am,' this should have had an *i* in the stem, for it developed from PIE /ˀés-my/ > *és-mi*, cf. Skt. *ás-mi*. In Germanic, however, the copula came to be a composite verb, with forms from the root in *be* and that in *was*, as well as that in *is*. From the northern Old English forms such as *bīom*, *bēom*, we may assume that *eom* is a combination, with the consonant from the root *es* and the vowel from the root *be*; such combinations are called **blends** or **contaminations**. Morphological change can in this way lead to forms that have a complex origin, and also to new morphological markers.

11.5 Morphological change as a source of new inflectional markers

The development of blends, as well as back formations, demonstrates that new, unpredictable forms may be produced in a language by the changes that take place in morphological sets. In this way new suffixes and grammatical markers may result. Examples are the English suffixes *-dom* and *-hood*. In Old English these were used to form compounds: *frēodom* 'freedom' < *frēo* 'free' and *dōm* 'quality,' *cynedom* 'royalty,' *camphad* 'warfare' < *camp* 'battle' and *hād* 'state,' *werhad* 'manhood,' and so on. In the course of time, these second elements of compounds were classed with elements like *-ing* in *cyning* 'king,' *æþeling* 'prince.' They then came to be treated as suffixes and distinguished from the free forms, *doom* and *hood*.

Established as independent entities, suffixes come to have a development of their own. From forms like OE *æþeling* 'nobleman,' made from *æþele* 'noble' and the suffix *-ing*, an erroneous division was made to produce a suffix *-ling*. The process has been called **suffix clipping**. From this new words were formed, as *darling*, cf. *dēor* 'dear.' Similarly, *-able* was taken as suffix in such forms as *habitable*, from Lat. *habitabilis*, and used in many new forms, such as *bearable, supportable*.

One such element that has enjoyed a wide development is *-burger*. In German, *-er* is commonly used to make adjectives of city names, such as *Berliner, Frankfurter, Wiener*. Some of these adjectives have come to characterize prepared meats. That for *Hamburg* became so completely divorced from the city that *-burger* rather than *-er* was assumed to be the element referring to the food. By chance the first syllable coincided with the name of a meat. It was quite irrelevant that ham was never used in *hamburgers*. One can now buy *fishburgers, cheeseburgers*, or even *burgers* labeled for their producer, such as *Mooreburgers*.

By the same process of improper clipping, morphological markers have been produced. One of the characteristic German plural markers is an *-er* suffix. Historically this is a derivational suffix, used to form nouns, as in Skt. *ján-as*, Lat. *gen-us* 'kind, race,' from the root PIE *gen-* 'beget.' In pre-Old High German, finals of words had been lost in such a way that *-er* survived in the plural, in contrast with no suffix in the singular, as in *kalb* 'calf' : *kelbir*. It was then taken as a plural marker, and widely extended to many neuter nouns in which the suffix had never been added, such as *Haus* 'house' : *Häuser*, and even to masculines, such as *Mann* 'man' : *Männer*. We find a similar extension in Middle Dutch, virtually none in English, only *child* : *children*.

Only by chance do we have material to determine the source of the *-er* suffix. For *kalb* is the only *er*-plural in Old High German that can be connected with the Indo-European nouns in *-es*. Moreover, the great extension of the *er*-plurals occurred in Old High German and Middle High German times, from which we have a fair number of texts. If morphological markers were produced in this way at an earlier stage of the language, we can merely hypothesize their origin and extension. The *-d-* marker for the Germanic preterite, as in Goth. *lagida* and OE *legde* 'laid.' with voiceless dental in Goth. *brahta* and OE *brōhte* 'brought,' may have originated in this way. Similarly the *v* of the Latin perfect, e.g., *amāvi* from *amō* 'love,' the *k* of the Greek perfect, e.g., *pepaídeuka* of *paideúō* 'educate,' and other morphological markers that we find in the early Indo-European dialects. In view of the absence of evidence, our support of such a hypothesis of their origin lies in general linguistic theory and the structure of the dialects after the splitting of Proto-Indo-European.

Possibly of greater amusement than significance in the development of languages are new formations that represent fanciful modification, such as

Eng. *sirloin*. This is from Fr. *sur-loin*, in which the first element derives from Lat. *super* 'upper,' so that historically the word refers to the upper part of the loin. In English, however, *sur*, which was not found in other widespread compounds, seemed aberrant and was modified to the apparently sensible *sirloin*, for the upper part of the loin is a noble piece of meat. Somewhat scornfully, this process has been referred to as **folk etymology**. It does not, however, differ essentially from the process by which a contemporary English suffix *-burger* was formed, or an Old English suffix *-ling*, or an Old High German suffix *-er*.

In folk etymology the sportive manipulation of language by individuals may be more evident than it is in less fanciful remodeling, as well as the approbation or disapprobation of fellow speakers; but what is essentially involved is the remodeling of less frequent and less favored patterns in the language in accordance with those more highly favored. When the cognate of Lat. *homo* came to be found in English only in the Old English compound *bryd-guma* 'espoused man,' see Germ. *Bräutigam*, it was modified after the more widespread though illogical *groom* to *bridegroom*. When *pentis*, from Fr. *appentis* < Lat. *appendix*, was applied to an outgrowth of a large building, it was remodeled to *penthouse*.

Just as folk etymology illustrates the inventiveness of some language users, it may illustrate the conservatism of others. The term *Welsh rabbit* for a cheese dish, like *Cape Cod turkey* for the plainest of piscatorial fare, shows an attempt by the ingenious to make simple food more palatable for the credulous. Their stolid fellow speakers may however object to this transparent outrage, and insist on *Welsh rarebit*, in much the same way that we today require inventive children to say *men* not *mans*, *better* not *gooder*, *went* not *goed*, and to banish *funner* entirely from their speech.

11.6   Reasons for syntactic change; internal influences

In accounting for phonological change, we noted that it takes place in accordance with general modifications for which no cogent reasons have been supplied. The reasons for changes in morphological markers, however, can often be ascribed to regularization of the forms in a syntactic or lexical set, as we may illustrate by means of NE *father*.

When we trace the history of NE *brother*, by successive steps we can take it back to PIE /bhrā́tēr/. Between the time of Proto-Indo-European and Modern English, the phonemes of /bhrā́tēr/ have undergone various sound changes; by noting these, we can derive all the phonemes of NE *brother* from those of its Proto-Indo-European etymon. NE *father*, however, cannot be directly related to PIE and pre-Gmc. *patér* in this way. For the Proto-Indo-European medial *t* became PGmc. *þ*, which before the accent became *ð*; this in turn became OE *d*, so that the Old English form was *fæder*; the Middle English *fader*. Without any further modification, the New English form should have *-d-*. Yet such a modification did occur. Some time after 1400, *-ð-* was substituted for *-d-*, giving rise to NE *father*. We assume that the substitution was made partly because the word *father* was associated with the word *brother* and similar words, and was remodeled after them.

Similarly we would be unable to derive the preterite participle *swelled* from a Proto-Germanic etymon, or even from an Old English form. The earlier preterite participle was *swollen*, which survives primarily as an adjective; *swelled* was made from *swell* on the pattern of

$$\frac{\text{fell}}{\text{felled}} = \frac{\text{shell}}{\text{shelled}} = \frac{\text{swell}}{\times}$$

and similar forms, and replaced the older *swollen*.

Modifications of this type illustrate the chief mode of change introduced in morphological and syntactic systems. By it the members of a morphological and syntactic set are increased or reduced in number, and the means involved in marking syntactic categories are extended. Since such changes are carried out on the pattern of those already present in the language, they are referred to as **analogical**. The process itself is called analogy.

Analogy is a process by which morphs, combinations of morphs, or linguistic patterns are modified, or new ones created, on the pattern of those present in a language.

We can observe analogy most clearly in the learning of language. Most of us have seen children learning forms such as the plural *cups* to *cup* and applying their discovery to other nouns such as

$$\frac{\text{cat}}{\text{cats}} = \frac{\text{fork}}{\text{forks}} = \frac{\text{cap}}{\text{caps}}$$

If they then see a *jet*, and learn the word, they make a plural, *jets*; if they see a particular new toy in a toy store, they make a plural, *sputniks*.

We become especially conscious of such extensions if they produce forms we consider incorrect. Just as children learn to make plurals, they make comparatives, as for

$$\frac{\text{new}}{\text{newer}} = \frac{\text{old}}{\text{older}} = \frac{\text{good}}{\text{gooder}}$$

At this point we object, and supply the correct form *better*. If we find a further extension from

That's new. = That's fine. = That's fun.
That's newer. = That's finer. = That's funner.

we may even remark on the child's cleverness after we correct him. At some time in the past, however, speakers of English were more tolerant of new comparatives, for the form *older* has replaced *elder* (except in restricted usages); *littler, littlest* have generally replaced *less* and *least* when adjectives, except in stock phrases like the bird name *least flycatcher*. In this way irregularities may be removed from grammatical sets. But by far the most important use we make of analogy in language learning is in extending forms and patterns that we have mastered.

If we learn a language like German, we do not memorize separately every inflected form. We learn a model, such as

singen   'sing'
ich singe   'I sing'
er singt   'he sings'

and expect to apply it to *ringen* 'wrestle,' *bringen* 'bring,' and so on. We may assume that native speakers learned many forms of their language in much the same way. If on the pattern of the past *ich sang*, *ich rang*, we make a form *ich brang*, we are corrected. We may even be reminded of the cognate of *ich brachte* 'I brought' to reinforce our acquisition of the irregular form. In this way we learn one of the limits of such analogical extension.

We acquire other linguistic patterns similarly. If we master the German syntactic patterns

Wir gehen heute.   'We're going today.'
Heute gehen wir.   'Today we're going.'

we do not need to learn separately every sentence beginning with *heute* or other adverbs to gain control over this type of subject position. If we have under control the normal word order, *Wir reisen heute, Wir lesen morgen*, by pattern practice we train ourselves to say

Heute reisen wir.   'Today we're traveling.'
Morgen lesen wir.   'We'll read tomorrow.'

In this way analogy is constantly applied when we use a language. As in foreign language learning, there are limits to its application, some of which we may transgress to the horror of fellow speakers; others, to their mild amusement; others, to their admiring imitation. One example of a new creation that was not adopted outside a social group is the word *focalize*, created presumably on the basis of *final : finalize : : focal :* ×. It is difficult to predict when analogical forms will be accepted, when not. We do however know some of the conditions under which analogy operates.

For the operation of analogy, some linguistic set is necessary. The set may be inflectional, like the English verbs, in which the *t/d* suffix has been replacing internal change, as it has done in *swelled*. The set may be derivational, such as the nouns with *-er* suffix, e.g., *driver*; this suffix, imported from Lat. *-arius*, has come to be used after virtually any verb. The set may also be syntactic. Several English verbs that formerly took an object in the genitive case were until quite recently followed by *of* constructions, e.g., *miss, desire, remember, forget, hope, thirst, wait*. Sir Walter Scott wrote: *I remember of detesting the man.* By contrast, the common transitive pattern in English consists of a verb followed immediately by an object; this pattern accordingly was generalized and extended to the verbs cited.

Sets may also be semantic, such as the relationship terms *brother, mother, father*. Among such sets are the numerals. In German ordinals, for example, *-te* is used from two to nineteen, e.g., *der zweite, der neunzehnte*; after that *-ste* is used, e.g., *der zwanzigste*, until the millionth, where formerly *-te* was used; today *der millionste* is being used widely, and promises to replace *millionte*. Numerous examples can be cited from the numerals in the various Indo-European dialects. The spread of Slavic *d-* to 'nine,' cf. NRuss. *d'evyat'*, from 'ten,' cf. NRuss. *d'esyat'*, is among the clearest.

Such sets are very infrequent at the phonological level. An example of analogy at the phonological level is the extension of *-r* before vowels in New England English. Since retroflection was lost before consonants but not before vowels, two forms of such words as *water* exist side by side: *watə was* . . ., but *water is* . . .; *watə wheels* . . ., but *water always*. . . Nouns with final *ə* fell into this pattern, note *soda, idea*, so that speakers with this variation say: *the idea was* . . ., but *the idea-r is.*

A type of analogy limited to literate cultures is purely graphic. ME *rīm*, for example, came to be written *rhyme* because early Modern English writers thought it was connected with *rhythm*. ME *delite* < OFr. *deliter*, Lat. *dēlectāre* came to be written in Modern English as *delight* because it was considered to be related to *light*, cf. Germ. *Licht*. Again we are most familiar with this type of analogy from language learners—from errors of students and typesetters, or from our own struggles with spelling. We may align *proceed* with *precede*, or vice versa; a part of our schooling is spent differentiating among *to*, *too*, *two*, *their*, *there*, and like sets. With our contemporary regard for spelling, a great deal of social prestige is involved in producing the standard spelling; we accordingly resist analogical modifications in our spelling system, and maintain the established patterns.

11.7   Occurrence and acceptance of analogical change

Essential problems of analogy that require further study include the conditions (1) under which it takes place and (2) by which new patterns get established. We cannot yet provide satisfactory answers. Various linguists have proposed that analogical change leads to simplification, and that such a development is to be expected when children acquire their language. Otto Jespersen reviewed the evidence for this assumption in his book *Language* (London, 1922), pages 161–88; he concluded that the question is complex (especially pages 177–78). His own observations led him to ascribe some linguistic changes to "first learners," whether they are children or adults. But he did not ascribe a development toward simplicity to children's language, even though he believed that there has been a "tendency . . . [toward] progress, slow and fitful progress, but still progress towards greater and greater clearness, regularity, ease and pliancy" in language (pages 441–42).

Unfortunately no convincing evidence has been furnished for the view that simplification in language is to be ascribed to children, even though recent scholars have returned to this assumption. As we have noted above, and as Jespersen reported at length, children generally abandon the simplifications they introduce. Rather than unsubstantiated claims about the role of children in language change, further investigations need to be made. Weinreich, Labov, and Herzog have attributed the transmission of new patterns to the "community as a whole," rather than to "the generational gap between parent and child" ("Empirical Foundations," pages 187–88.). The procedures for change they cite are even more intricate than are those considered by Jespersen. To ascribe simplification to analogical change and to the influence of children as they acquire languages is far too simplistic. This is not to deny the findings of Gauchat and others that the younger speakers in a community extend observed changes farther than the older. The findings are to be expected, for changes that are not adopted by younger speakers are lost. But claims about the causes of change are far different than observations of their spread.

In recent studies Kurylowicz has attempted to suggest reasons for the introduction of analogy in morphological sets. He finds these reasons in the relationship of forms in a paradigm. Those forms that are basic tend to influence others. For example, in verbal systems with a present tense category and a passive voice, the present active dominates both the present passive and the perfect active; the perfect passive in turn is dominated by both the present passive and the perfect active. Kurylowicz calls the present the **founding** form, a derived form like the present passive **founded**. A founded form might then be modified in accordance with the founding forms, on the pattern of the following chart:

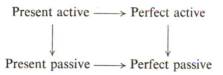

Present active ⟶ Perfect active

Present passive ⟶ Perfect passive

If, for example, the perfect active has a segment differing from that of the perfect passive, this segment may be introduced in the perfect passive.

Kurylowicz proposed this kind of conditioning in inflectional systems as the cause for a phenomenon in early Latin. In Latin, as Karl Lachmann observed more than a century ago, the past participles of stems ending in -d- and -g- have lengthened vowels, with devoicing of the stop before the participial suffix -tus. Thus the past participle of ăgō is āctus, in contrast with the short vowel in făctus from făciō; similarly lēctus from legō 'read,' ēsus < *ēssos < *ed-to-s from edō 'eat,' and so on. The phenomenon is referred to as Lachmann's law; it had been widely, and ineffectually, discussed before Kurylowicz provided a definitive explanation, explicated further by Calvert Watkins.

The explanation may be illustrated as follows:

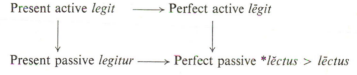

Present active *legit*   ⟶ Perfect active *lēgit*

Present passive *legitur* ⟶ Perfect passive *lĕctus* > *lēctus*

Original ĕ in the perfect passive participle was changed to long ē by analogy. The change differs from the sound changes discussed in Chapter 10 because of its motivation. Kurylowicz has definitely established that some linguistic modifications can be brought about by analogy. The reasons for such modifications are clearly the internal patterning in a language.

Kurylowicz finds many more examples of the effects of analogy in the spread of changes in morphological forms rather than in their introduction. For such extension of the results of earlier changes, he has proposed a series of rules. As the counterexamples cited below illustrate, these rules do not permit us to predict when analogy may take place in a given language, nor to determine what its direction has been under poorly known situations in the past. The rules, however, provide explanations for some instances of analogical extension.

Kurylowicz' first rule states that a twofold morphological marker tends to replace one that is single. As example he gives the *-e* plural ending of German nouns, which in some nouns was also associated with umlaut of the stem vowel, for example, *Gast* 'guest' : *Gäste*. This twofold marking has been extended as in *Baum* 'tree' : *Bäume* replacing *baume*. Many further instances can also be cited in which it does not apply; note, for instance, the German weak verb *trennen, trennte, getrennt* 'separate,' which has maintained a single marker as opposed to *rennen, rannte, gerannt* 'run.'

By Kurylowicz' second rule, analogy proceeds from the base form to derived forms. While commonly true, as in *sputnik, sputniks*, formations such as *pease* to *pea* contravene this rule.

By the third rule, any construction consisting of a constant plus a variable is used as pattern for an isolated entity of the same function. In this way constructions like *wrongly* from *wrong* were used as pattern for remodeling endingless adverbs such as *slow* to *slowly*.

In the fourth rule, which deals with the results of analogy, Kurylowicz states that a new analogical form takes over the primary function of a contrast, while the replaced form is used for secondary functions. Thus *brothers* is used for the plural of *brother*, while the replaced *brethren* maintains a peripheral function; similarly *older* versus *elder*, and so on. Yet again, contrary examples can be provided, such as analogical forms introduced in the German article *dessen* that are used today in the relative pronoun, not the article itself. The two other rules are of less interest here.

A set of such general rules would be highly advantageous if they applied to prehistoric languages, such as Proto-Indo-European and pre-Indo-European. Kurylowicz has indeed applied them in this way, especially to problems of Indo-European morphophonemic variation of vowels and to accentual problems. Yet if the rules cannot be established in contemporary languages, their application to earlier periods may be unreliable.

11.8 Syntactic change introduced on the patterns of other languages

Few, if any, morphological changes are brought about by importations. Yet syntactic means of marking categories may be imported. Thus the use of genitival phrases with *of* has been ascribed to imitation of French genitival phrases with *de*, as noted in 11.2. But even such innovations cannot be ascribed purely to borrowing. In general, borrowing has its greatest influence on the lexical segment of language, rather than on inflections. Yet evidence has been found that the influence of other languages affects patterns of order.

Such influence would be exerted by multilingual speakers. If, for example, a number of speakers spoke both an OV language and a VO language, the pattern of one might influence the other. As we have observed, many other syntactic features are closely associated with these basic orders, for example, the location of relative clauses with regard to their nouns, of adjectives and genitives with regard to their nouns, and so on. The introduction of a VO order would then have a profound effect if it were accepted by a large number of speakers.

Large-scale studies of such effects have yet to be carried out, and accordingly I will cite a personal observation of an individual speaker. This speaker, a third-generation Fijian of Indian descent, claimed to know Tamil, Fijian, and Hindi. When he produced Tamil sentences, however, they were halting and in VO order. His Fijian was correctly VO. But, of the three languages, he spoke Hindi most accurately, with consistent OV order. When questioned about Tamil, he replied with some embarrassment that it had been his grandfather's language and that he now used it rarely. Yet it is quite remarkable that he spoke it with the VO order of Fijian rather than the OV order of Hindi, in which he was most at home. One such example permits no general conclusions, inasmuch as too many variables may be involved. But the example does suggest that the basic syntactic patterns of a language may be modified on the basis of patterns in other languages.

Such modifications have been proposed for a number of languages. Akkadian, for example, is OV, in contrast with the basic VO structure of Semitic languages. It was brought into an area occupied by speakers of the OV language Sumerian, and presumably adopted by many speakers of Sumerian. For in time Sumerian became extinct. The influence it may have exerted on Akkadian, however, is our best explanation of the change in order of the Akkadian clause.

It is possible that we must ascribe the basic change in order from OV to VO structure in the Indo-European languages of Europe to a similar influence. By the time of Classical Greek, Classical Latin, and our earliest Celtic sources, these languages were adopting a VO order, or like the Celtic languages, had become VO. Explanations for this order have been proposed on the basis of the order in languages displaced by the Indo-European languages. Unfortunately we do not know the displaced languages. Yet this proposed explanation is the best that has been given. It finds support in the Indo-Aryan languages of today; for like the Dravidian languages, which are also spoken by many speakers of Indo-Aryan languages as a second language, these are now consistently OV. Yet Classical Sanskrit was ambivalent in structure.

Influence of neighboring languages has also been cited for syntactic changes in Amharic and in the early North Germanic languages, as noted in the Selected Further Readings at the end of this chapter. Further investigations of such effects on syntactic change will be among the most interesting historical linguistic studies of the future.

11.9   Interplay of changes in the syntactic and phonological components of language, and in the lexicon

As illustrated by the discussion above, analogy may be viewed as the central process in modifications introduced in syntactic and morphological systems. In Chapters 5 and 10 it was observed that sound change takes place by phonological sets, with no consideration of their morphological functioning. When it has taken place, however, its effects may be extended analogically, in morphological, syntactic, and lexical sets.

As examples of sound changes leading to change in morphological systems, we may cite instances from the Germanic languages, such as the pre-Old English umlaut change. When pre-OE *u* and *o* became *ü* and *ö* before *i ī y*, a new contrastive marker was possible between many singular and plural forms, for *i ī y* was found especially in the plural. Yet in English this sound change affected the morphological system only to a minor extent, for we have few plurals of the type *man* : *men, goose* : *geese*. In German, on the other hand, this sound change was widely extended to provide one of the prominent plural markers. In this way sound changes may contribute to the possibility of new morphological contrastive devices, which then may be extended by analogy. Such a device has recently been made available by the loss of *-t* in some English final clusters. When *-t* is lost in *slept*, a new contrast *sleep* : *slep* yields new irregular verbs. This phonological change is too recent for its results in the morphological system to be predicted.

As a result of such changes five or more millennia ago, the material was provided for one of the characteristic features of Indo-European languages, ablaut (see Chapter 6:4). It is generally assumed that the ablaut contrast between root structures of the shapes **Ce(R)C-** and **C(R)C-** resulted from a loss of vowel, which in turn was due to varying accentuation. This assumption is based on contrasts found in forms, such as those of the root PIE *derk-* 'see.' The Greek present form, with accent on the root, is *dérkomai*

'I see.' The Sanskrit past participle, however, with accent on the suffix, is *dr̥ṣṭás* 'seen.' The original situation has been obscured by many subsequent changes, so that in most forms it is opaque except to trained Indo-Euro-peanists. But the contrast has been maintained in NE *nest* (originally a compound of the adverb **ni-* and the root *sed-* 'sit'), as opposed to NE *sit*, a reflex of PIE *sed-*. The contrast has also been maintained between the present stem and the participle of many irregular verbs, such as *bit : bitten*, *choose : chosen*, *bind : bound*, *steal : stolen*. The original Proto-Indo-European sound change, which led to a loss of *e*, may have affected few forms originally. But, like the umlaut change in German, it came to be used as an inflectional marker; and the contrast was widely extended, especially in the Germanic system of irregular verbs. The contrast came to be so well established that it was introduced even into words borrowed into the Germanic languages three millennia after the sound change took place, as in the Old English verb *scrīfan* 'write (shrive)' : *scrifen* 'written (shriven).'

Another major contrast in Proto-Indo-European ablaut, that between *e* and *o*, as reflected in Greek *dérkomai* 'I see' : *dédorka* 'I have seen,' has also been explained on the basis of a sound change. As with the change of *e* to zero in some forms, the results of the original sound change, were extended by analogy. Recently, however, Kurylowicz has attempted to explain the original change itself as a result of analogical forces, somewhat as he explained the change described in Lachmann's law.

In this way the prime morphological modifications in languages are spread by analogy, though the innovations generalized may be a result of phonological change or of some other process, such as borrowing, that has provided a useful characteristic marker for a set. In the scientific termi-nology of today, certain entities have been widely spread, with a specific meaning. Thus, *-ide* is used for hundreds of chemical compounds, such as *chloride*, *fluoride*, apparently from the term *oxide*, which was borrowed from *Fr. oxygène + acide*. The suffix *-ate* is found in many names of salts and esters formed from acids with names in *-ic*, for example, *nitrate* from *nitric acid*, and so on. The suffix *-eme* has come to be used for entities in linguistics, from *phoneme* to *morpheme* to *grapheme*, and others. Analogy in this way has been useful in expanding and regularizing the derivational system of the greatly expanding vocabularies of contemporary languages as it has served to enlarge and regularize their inflectional and syntactic systems.

The source of the material used in analogy is irrelevant. Any segment of the language may be generalized, whether its origin is in sound change or borrowing, or whether it is simply a segment of the language, like OE *-ling*, which seems useful for morphological marking. When new forms are made by analogy in a language, sets of some kind undergo expansion; the process leads to larger sets, and accordingly to greater regularity in the language.

Selected Further Readings

Like sound change, analogy is one of the subjects widely treated in handbooks. Bloomfield's *Language*, pages 404–24; Sturtevant's *An Introduction to Linguistic Science*, pages 96–109; and Paul's *Prinzipien der Sprachgeschichte*, pages 106–20, have well-chosen examples. For a fuller treatment of the relations between sound change and analogy, see E. Hermann's *Lautgesetz und Analogie*.

The paper of Kurylowicz referred to, "La nature des procès dits 'analogiques,'" appeared in *Acta Linguistica*, 5.15–37 (1945–49), and has been reprinted in his *Esquisses linguistiques* (Wrocław-Kraków, 1960). Another extensive treatment of analogy, with many examples, is given by Witold Mańczak, "Tendances générales des changements analogiques," in two issues of *Lingua*, 7.298–325 and 387–420 (1958). For an excellent work making extensive use of our understanding of analogy, see O. Szemerényi's *Studies in the Indo-European System of Numerals* (Heidelberg, 1960). Reference to the various attempts to account for Lachmann's Law, including Watkins' own reformulation of the successful explanation given by Kurylowicz, may be found in "A further remark on Lachmann's law," *Harvard Studies in Classical Philology* 74.55–65 (1970). For a full explication of his views on analogy as they apply to the Indo-European languages, see Jerzy Kurylowicz, *The Inflectional Categories of Indo-European* (Heidelberg, 1964). Emmon Bach has proposed that the word order of Amharic was modified in accordance with neighboring Cushitic languages in "Is Amharic an SOV Language?" *Journal of Ethiopian Studies* 8.9–20 (1970). For my suggestions on the causes of syntactic changes in North Germanic languages, see "The Nordic Languages: Lasting Linguistic Contributions of the Past" on pages 286–305 of *The Nordic Languages and Modern Linguistics*, edited by Hreinn Benediktsson (Reykjavík, 1970).

CHAPTER 12

Semantic change and changes in the lexicon

12.1 Frameworks for understanding semantic change

In the preceding chapters we have seen that an understanding and explanation of linguistic change depends on an adequate framework. Such a framework for sound change was provided in phonological study during the nineteenth century. The well-known rules describing sound change— Grimm's law, Verner's law, and many others—were proposed when linguists increased their insights into the sound system of language and worked out a universal treatment of phonology. As information on speech sounds and the principles underlying the sound systems of various languages increased, improved formulations of phonological rules were provided. Subsequently the formulations for specific changes have been improved and are still being improved. These improvements are based on an increasingly adequate framework for dealing with changes in the phonological component of language, the groundwork for which was provided in the nineteenth century and used subsequently in interpreting sound change.

Treatment of the syntactic component of language has undergone a similar development though more recently. Eduard Sievers and other linguists of the nineteenth and early twentieth centuries dealt with an underlying phonological structure. But only recently have linguists begun to deal with underlying, or deep, structures in the syntactic component. Moreover, a framework for comprehending syntactic structures has also been produced only recently. Early in the nineteenth century linguists were able to examine the sound changes of languages in terms of phonological systems based on a small number of relationships, as those between various places of articulation, manners of articulation, and other characteristics on which the commonly used charts of sound systems are based. But only since about 1960 has a similar framework for syntax come to be understood, as we have seen in the preceding chapter. This syntactic framework is based on a small number of relationships. One such relationship is found in government constructions: the relationship of verbs, "prepositions," and comparatives with their nouns. Another is found in modifying constructions: the relationship of relative constructions, adjectives, and genitives with their nouns. Our understanding of the syntactic framework is still imperfect, as was the understanding of the phonological framework in the nineteenth century. But already we can use this framework to deal with syntactic change, as the examples in Chapter 11 and the Workbook illustrate.

In order to deal with semantic change, we need a similar framework. As in the study of phonology and syntax, we need to determine characteristic entities of semantic structures and characteristic relationships found between such entities. In the past many individual changes have been described in semantic study. For example, the Latin word for 'maternal uncle' *avunculus* is a form derived from the Latin word for 'maternal grandfather' *avus*. The derivation is quite clear, as is the development of the Latin *avunculus* to Fr. *oncle*; NE *uncle* has the same source, through borrowing from French. Although the external development of the Latin terms causes no problems, no explanation could be given for a semantic development that would lead to calling an 'uncle' something like 'little grandfather.' An explanation has recently been provided from study of the systems in language referring to kinship. For a variety of distinct systems has been determined. The system in which the mother's brother is associated with the grandfather is known as the Omaha kinship system. In a group of speakers with an Omaha kinship system one can expect to find the same or similar terms for mother's brother and for mother's grandfather. This expectation is parallel to the expectation we have observed in syntactic study of finding postpositions in a language of OV order, or of finding noun-adjective (NA) order in VO languages.

The expectation may not be fulfilled, as we have observed for English, with AN order in a VO language. If it is not, the language is in flux and we look for an explanation. Thus, the system of kinship terms in late Latin was changing to the system of terms we find in the Romance languages today, such as French, Italian, Portuguese, and Spanish. Changes in the kinship system led to changes in the kinship terms. French *oncle* is not restricted to 'maternal uncle,' nor are the further terms Italian *zio*, Spanish *tío*, or Portuguese *tío*. The kinship system has changed, and with this change the kinship terms have a different meaning from the corresponding term in Latin. But during a period in the development of the Romance languages, the meanings of these terms must have been in flux, just as in late Old English. At that time the distinctive terms for 'paternal uncle' OE *fædera* and 'maternal uncle' OE *ēam* were yielding to a single term *uncle*.

This example of the change in meaning for the term *avunculus* may illustrate the procedures we should attempt to follow in dealing with semantic change. We must attempt to determine coherent sets of terms corresponding to natural sets in language. The term **field** has often been used for such sets. For example, the German scholar Jost Trier carried out a widely influential semantic study by investigating the terms referring to the intellect in early Germanic. As yet, subclassifications of the "intellectual field" comparable to the subclassifications for kinship terms have not been determined. Nonetheless it is useful in dealing with semantic change to focus one's study on a restricted set of terms, like those for the intellectual field, for colors, or for kinship.

The observation of semantic changes in kinship systems points to a difference between the study of semantic change, on the one hand, and phonological and syntactic change, on the other. Semantic change may be intimately related to change in other social structures. For example, the shift in meaning of Latin *penna* from 'feather' to 'writing implement' is related to a change in cultural activities by which feathers were used as writing implements. As far as we have been able to determine, there is no such relationship between cultural changes and syntactic or phonological changes, even though some scholars have proposed such relationships. We may also note that not all semantic changes are related to cultural changes. For example, the restriction in meaning of the word *wife* from 'woman,' as still in German *Weib*, to 'female spouse' is unrelatable to any shift in the cultural status of women in English-speaking areas.

Nevertheless, many semantic features that are prominent in a language, and accordingly many semantic changes, are related to the physical situation of the speakers of a given language. For example, it has often been pointed out that the Eskimo language has many words for 'snow' of various kinds and that Arabic has many words for 'camel.' If these languages were transported to areas without snow or camels, the terms concerned would change in meaning or be lost. Edward Sapir provided an excellent example when he demonstrated that the Navaho of the American Southwest migrated to their present home from the Athapaskan territory in northern Canada (see his article "Internal Linguistic Evidence Suggestive of the Northern Origin of the Navaho," pages 213–24 of *Selected Writings of Edward Sapir*, edited by David G. Mandelbaum (Berkeley and Los Angeles, 1963). One of these examples is the Navaho verb for 'seed lies': -*sàs*, from "underlying *zàs* or *yàs*," page 216. For this word Sapir provided the etymology: Athapaskan **yàxs* 'snow lying on the ground.' This word maintained its meaning in the Athapaskan languages of the north but changed its meaning remarkably when Athapaskan speakers moved into a region with no snow. In somewhat the same way the words *robin*, (*mountain*) *lion*, and so on, changed in meaning when English speakers brought these terms to America. The relationship between semantic change and other cultural change adds a complexity to the study of change in meaning that is not found in the study of change in phonological and syntactic systems.

It is hardly surprising therefore that general principles have not been determined for semantic change. Modifications in the means of indicating meaning are associated with modifications in the lexicon, and for these we can propose some general patterns, as will be apparent later in the chapter. But general rules have only recently been proposed; they are restricted to small sets like kinship terms. Further such rules may be expected as the study of semantic change is pursued with the rigor applied to phonological and syntactic change.

To deal with the complexity of semantic change, three terms are used: 1) the **word**, or linguistic **symbol**; 2) the **referent**, denoted by a word, whether concrete like 'pen' or abstract like 'thought'; 3) the **reference**, or notion symbolized. Each of these may change, as examples given below will illustrate. A word like OE *ēam* 'uncle' may be lost. A referent like a feather may be replaced by a plastic cylinder with a point. A notion associated with an object, like a bear, may come to be associated with dread, and changes in the designation may result. In dealing with semantic changes, the meanings of words have come to be expressed increasingly by means of features.

12.2   Change in semantic features

In proposing a universal framework for semantic analysis, linguists have introduced distinctive semantic features. Semantic fields have been analyzed for the distinctive features found in any language. If we analyze the kinship system for Modern English in this way, we would propose the features: sex, generation, lineality. The basic set of kinship terms may be analyzed in a matrix as follows:

	FATHER	MOTHER	BROTHER	SISTER	SON	DAUGHTER	UNLCE	AUNT	COUSIN	NEPHEW	NIECE
SEX	0	1	0	1	0	1	0	1	–	0	1
GENERATION	0	0	1	1	2	2	0	0	1	2	2
LINEALITY	0	0	0	0	0	0	1	1	1	1	1

Such a matrix permits ready understanding of semantic change. For example, the system of kinship terms in Modern English is not completely symmetrical; it does not have a distinction for sex manifested in the 'cousin' relationship. If this feature were extended to the term 'cousin,' a semantic change would be brought about. As in German, a further relationship term might be introduced; a male cousin in German is called *Vetter*, a female cousin *Kusine*. In Classical Greek the term *métrōs* was used for 'maternal uncle,' and for maternal relatives in general. Since the distinctive feature of consanguinity came to be more important than that for male or female consanguinity, a word for either 'father's brother' or 'mother's brother,' *theîos* 'uncle,' was introduced. The feminine form, *theía* 'aunt,' was created, replacing earlier *tēthís* 'aunt.' These words, which are assumed to be nursery words, show a different distribution of features from the earlier set, which included the words *pátrōs* 'paternal uncle' and *métrōs* 'maternal uncle.' Apparently cultural changes had led to disregarding distinctions between paternal and maternal relationships. The change in meaning in the new system can be indicated precisely if we analyze the set of relationship terms in Classical Greek into distinctive features.

Further, the use of distinctive features in a semantic field may be specified by rules that indicate the relationships among the features. For example, in Latin the word *gener* was used for 'man's sister's husband' and for 'son-in-law.' Both meanings involve no more features than those found in the English set of kinship terms. But English does not have the same rule as Latin. This situation may illustrate the need for proposing rules depicting the use of features in a given language, as well as the need for analyzing semantic entities into features. For the Latin word *gener*, Floyd Lounsbury proposed the following rule: "Let any woman's brother, as linking relative, be regarded as equivalent to that woman's son, as linking relative." (See Floyd G. Lounsbury, "The Structural Analysis of Kinship Semantics," pages 1073–93 of *Proceedings of the Ninth International Congress of Linguists*, edited by Horace G. Lunt. [The Hague: Mouton, 1964].) Formalized, in symbolism used for kinship terminology, the rule reads: ♀ B . . . → ♀ s. This rule, which Lounsbury labels an asymmetrical skewing rule characteristic of an Omaha kinship system, was replaced by bilaterally symmetrical skewing rules in Italian, French, Spanish, and Portuguese. These languages, like English, distinguish between lineal and collateral relatives, containing separate words for 'brother-in-law' and 'son-in-law.'

This example may illustrate that semantic change may be represented much as is phonological or syntactic change. Features may be added or lost; or rules expressing the relationships between features may be modified or lost.

Other semantic modifications may be understood by means of feature analysis. For example, Modern English *mother* is used not only as a kinship term, but also in such expressions as 'mother-of-pearl,' 'mother of vinegar.' In these expressions the semantic feature ⟨+ Human⟩ has been eliminated, and the feature ⟨+ Relationship⟩ aligned in a different way with other features. Extensions of use for other words may illustrate the discussion of meaning change in this way. The term 'clothes' horse' also involves the loss of a feature: ⟨+ Animate⟩. The use of the term *house* for a body of representatives, on the other hand, involves the addition of the features ⟨+ Animate⟩ and ⟨+ Human⟩. Few studies have been carried out that exemplify such rules and their role in change of meaning. The examples included in the rest of this chapter may however be examined in this way. By analysis of the words into features, and examination of the specific modification involved, the semantic change in question may be more precisely understood.

12.3   On determining change in meaning.

Change of meaning is readily apparent in any language for which we have a series of texts. As example we may cite *persona*, for which a considerable change of meaning can be substantiated in the several millennia over which it and its reflexes are found in Latin and English texts. When we first encounter *persona*, it means 'mask.' In Roman drama, masks were used on the stage, and varied in accordance with roles. Soon *persona* came to mean a 'character indicated by a mask,' thereupon a 'character' as such or a 'role in a play.' From this developed the meaning 'representative of a character,' then a 'representative in general.' For us its central meaning is 'representative of the human race.' A peripheral meaning, 'representative of the church,' has survived in the form *parson*, which was not remodeled in pronunciation after the historical spelling. The word *persona* has accordingly undergone a considerable change, from referring to an article of stage costume through designation for human roles to a general designation for human being, all of which can be attested in Latin and subsequent English texts.

Even if we lacked these texts, we could make conjectures about its development of meaning by comparing Modern English usages like 'ten persons were at the meeting,' 'the three persons of the trinity,' and 'he is a parson.' Peripheral meanings, as well as the central meaning, may be found in texts produced at one time, and may be used to infer the change of meaning a word has undergone. In the Old English *Beowulf*, for example, the etymon of *thank* is attested in a compound with the meaning 'thought,' line 1060, *fore-þanc* 'forethought.' In *Beowulf*, line 379, it means 'satisfaction, pleasure.' On the basis of further examples, we can infer a change of meaning for *thank* from 'thought' to 'recognition' to 'acknowledgment.' Again numerous examples are available for conjecturing change of meaning in this way from texts for which we have no long succession of predecessors.

As with *thank*, conjectures on meaning change may be supported by a third procedure, comparison with elements similar in form. It is scarcely hazardous to assume that *thank* is related to *think*. For internal vowel change is a common device for deriving words in the Germanic languages, as in *drink* : *drench*, *wind* : *wend one's way*, and so on. One may therefore suggest for *thank* on the basis of etymology the earlier meaning we find attested in Old English. Such suggestions, however, require caution, for, as we have observed in the two previous chapters, forms may be modified in accordance with phonological and syntactic sets. If for example we had only the form Germ. *Sündflut* for the flood that Noah survived, we would relate the first element to *Sünde* 'sin' and assume *Sündflut* to be a compound describing the long flood caused by man's sinfulness. Actually, from older forms we find the analysis wrong; the first component was modified by folk etymology from MHG *sin-*, a cognate of Lat. *senex* 'old man,' which meant the 'long-lasting' flood. Suggesting change of meaning on the basis of etymology or similarity of form may thus be erroneous. The same caution applies when we attempt to reconstruct change of meaning from forms in related languages. We would have to know considerably more than the fact of their relationship to decide that of the pair Eng. *silly* : Germ. *selig* 'blessed,' the German form preserves the earlier meaning, while of the pair Eng. *cup* : Germ. *Kopf* 'head,' the English form does. We can conclude from comparisons of related forms that differ in meaning that change of meaning has indeed taken place. For its exact course we speak with certainty only when we have texts in which the earlier, as well as the later, meanings can be established.

In discussing the changes in semantic systems, for convenience we deal with words. Actually, any morphological element may undergo semantic change. We can note it in affixes: *super-* in *superman* differs in meaning from *super-* in *superstition* or *superstructure*. In Chapter 11:5, we noted how the segment *-burger* has changed markedly in meaning. We must make the same assumption for morphemes consisting of suprasegmental material, such as intonation patterns, but with our ignorance of supra-segmental morphemes of the past, we cannot provide sure examples. In this brief introduction to change of meaning, we will deal only with well-established examples, such as the words used for illustration in this chapter. We will discuss semantic change in relation to the processes, and to the causes that have been proposed for it.

12.4   Processes by which semantic change and change in the lexicon are carried out

In a celebrated article, "Comment les mots changent de sens," *Linguistique historique et linguistique générale*, 1.230–71, Meillet proposes three processes by which semantic change takes place.

The first of these is change in the contexts in which given words are used. An example is the restriction of meaning of French *pas, personne, rien, jamais*. These words were used with *ne* 'not' to strengthen the negation; *pas*, for example, originally meant 'step.' When *ne* was omitted, they came to have a negative meaning.

The second results from a change in the object referred to, or in the speakers' view of such an object. An example of a change in the object referred to is *pen* from Latin *penna* 'feather, quill.' Used for a writing implement dispensing some kind of fluid ink, *pen* no longer means 'feather.' Among such changes Meillet classes those resulting from taboo. One can readily cite circumlocutions for nonfavored objects, such as Gk. *aristerós* 'better' for 'left (hand),' *left*, itself from an Old English word for 'weak,' Lat. *sinister* 'more useful,' itself replaced by *gauche* in French, which now also has an unfavorable connotation. The Slavs and Welsh substituted so commonly for 'bear' the circumlocution 'honey-eater, honey-pig,' that the original was lost from their languages. Through enforced disuse of the tetragrammaton JHWH, the Hebrews lost knowledge of its pronunciation. Many tabooed words are restricted in usage only in certain social situations, so that the word is not totally lost from the language. The attempts to ban

Lady Chatterley's Lover were determined in part by Lawrence's use of a term tabooed in print, even though it is widely used in the language.

Such words under only a partial taboo do not undergo a change in meaning because of the taboo, as can be demonstrated from the long history of the often cited Anglo-Saxon four-letter words, many of which can be traced back to Proto-Indo-European. If, however, a word is under complete taboo, such as the reflex of the Proto-Indo-European word for 'bear' in Germanic-speaking areas, it may be lost; the word has reflexes in dialects spoken where the bear was not a present danger, for example, Gk. *árktos*, Lat. *ursus*, Skt. *ŕkṣas*.

The third basis for semantic change, and change in the lexical component of language, Meillet found in the influence of other languages and dialects, including social dialects. The process by which words are imported into a language is known as **borrowing**. It has by far the greatest effect on the lexicon of the three processes discussed by Meillet, as will be illustrated below for English. A large number of words in English have been borrowed from French, though their earlier source is Latin or Greek. An example is *priest*. Originally a specialized use of the Greek adjective 'older' *presbúteros* became a part of the technical language of the early Christians. The English form *presbyter*, as well as the related *priest*, has retained the specialized meaning, besides leading to a modification of *elder*. Such borrowings and lexical changes result from complex historical, social, and linguistic facts. We will discuss some of these, using primarily examples from the history of English.

12.5   Semantic change resulting from change in linguistic contexts

As we have noted, the omission of a word may lead to a change in meaning of other words. In this way modifiers may be omitted, as was French *ne* in expressions with *pas*, so that *pas* alone now means 'not.' An example from English is the word *undertaker*, which once meant 'one who undertakes, an energetic promoter.' One translation of the Twenty-third Psalm began: 'The Lord is my undertaker.' A common context in which it was used was that of *funeral undertaker*; *funeral* then was omitted, and until morticians thought they could sweeten their trade with a new name, the chief context for *undertaker* was for men who assist in the obsequies for the dead. Similarly, *main* came to be used for 'main ocean,' as in *the Spanish Main*; *mainland*, on the other hand, was retained as a compound. As other examples we may cite *fall* 'autumn,' from 'fall of leaves,' and *private* 'lowest-ranking soldier,' from 'private soldier.'

Semantic change brought about by such linguistic modifications are rare. Similarly infrequent are changes resulting from similarities between forms. As examples we may cite NE *demean* and *presently*. NE *demean* 'behave' was associated with *mean* 'inferior' and today is generally used to mean 'debase.' NE *presently* 'soon' was associated with *present* 'now' and has come to be used as an adverb meaning 'at present' rather than 'in the future.' While semantic changes resulting from linguistic influence may be cited, they are far less frequent than changes resulting from modifications in the reference or referent.

12.6   Semantic change resulting from change of reference or referent

Scientific advances, or social changes, bring about extensions of words to new uses. Examples may be given from almost any field of scientific or social change. As the scale of living has improved, for example, the term *pool* has undergone a change in meaning, as earlier *garage* came to replace *stable*. In some regions *landing strip* is equally favored. Other words referring to transportation by air have undergone striking modifications in meaning. The term *plane* was formerly found largely in modest contexts of scientific materials. Until it is restricted by the knowledgeable younger generation, who scorn it in favor of *B*-57, 707, *DC*-8, and the like, it has a great frequency. Other items used in its linguistic environment, *pilot*, *jet*, *stewardess*, and so on, have a considerably different meaning from that associated with these words before the age of flight.

We can also cite examples from the past. A *picture* formerly was something painted; now we can have our *picture taken* with a Polaroid. For the Romans a *street*, *strāta via*, was a 'paved way.' In the course of time, it came to represent any passageway for vehicles.

Other examples may be observed today in the expansion of comfortable living. With the increased frequency of little homes in suburbia came increased prestige for linguistic items suggesting life in the hills outside the city. Lots on 'trails' and 'lanes' sell rapidly. While *avenues* were formerly the grand entrances for cities, they may now be the ways on which commercial firms are located, with the former favorable meaning maintained only where some modicum of urban elegance is retained, as on *Fifth Avenue* or *Pennsylvania Avenue*. In many areas the formerly humble *trail* and *lane* have in this way outdistanced *avenue*. What entrepreneurs will do in the future, when all the haves live on *trails* and the have-mores are in search of suitable housing, will provide students of semantic change further examples of changes in meaning resulting from nonlinguistic influences.

Among the greatest sources of such influences are technical changes, with resultant changes in technical dialects and consequent influences on the language in general. Intellectual historians may look to meteorology, and speak of a *climate* of opinion. This intellectual *climate* may undergo a *renaissance*, with *nerves* of communication strengthened, especially for those who are *off center*. The technical dialects of sports have been widely exploited in English. In building a strong group, one tries to avoid *bush leaguers* (baseball) or those who might *show the white feather* (cockfighting) or those with a *bias* (bowling); otherwise one may find himself *out in left field* as far as the competition is concerned. When the former meaning is still the more prominent, we may call such transfers of context **metaphors**. In the course of time, the new meanings may prevail and cause the metaphor to fade. Today we scarcely think of the former meaning of *decide* 'cut off' or *detail* 'cut in pieces' as we *bat around* a topic.

Often the shift in reference is from a serene to an emotionally active connotation, which corresponds to the **hyperbole** of literary analysis. *Astonish*, somewhat like *stun*, once meant 'strike by thunder.' In Shakespeare's *King Henry the Fifth*, Act 5, Scene 1, Gower points out to Fluellen that he astonished Pistol when he struck him a second time. Such shifts seem to lead to a less vivid meaning, as may be illustrated by words of strong assent, e.g., *certainly*, *sure*, *indeed*—which today have less force than does *yes*; similarly, words that indicate degree, especially of behavior or appearance, such as *fine*, which now is scarcely more satisfactory than *superb*, *grand*, *perfect*, *magnificent*, *great*.

Such shifts in reference are attested for terms of address as in Spanish *don*, *donna*, from spoken Lat. *domnus*, *domna* 'lord, mistress.' In French, *domina* gave rise to *dame*, *madame*. The similar German *Herr*, like Eng. *Mister*, scarcely carries the connotation of mastery today. Lofty terms, when generalized, come to take on meanings resembling their everyday contexts. Some terms, in shifting from an indication of social to moral inferiority, have undergone even less favorable change. A *villain* was once a worker at a *villa*; other terms for rural work that have developed similarly are *churl* < OE *ceorl* 'common man, farmer' and *boor*—compare the stolid Dutch farmers who settled South Africa. A *knave*, as in the *Knave of Hearts*, was a boy; see Germ. *Knabe*. Terms for government officials may also suffer, for example, *publican* 'a public servant' or *cheater*, earlier *escheater*, an officer whose duty it was to assure the return of property to the state if the owner died without heirs or without leaving a will.

Some shifts represent general cultural or geographical changes rather than those introduced by a class of imaginative speakers. When people from Britain settled in America, they gave a red-breasted thrush the name of their *robin*, a much smaller bird with similar coloring. *Holiday*, which once referred to a sacred festival day, has lost much of its religious connotation.

Other shifts follow attitudes of the speakers. When members of a society consider it essential to use a circumlocution for a tabooed term, it may change entirely to the new meaning. *Bear* is scarcely 'the brown one' for any speaker of English today. Various words were changed in meaning as they were introduced for the tabooed names for *hand*, *left*, *right* in Indo-European languages, as we may illustrate from the panoply of Indo-European words for hand—OE *folm*, Skt. *hastas*, Gk. *kheír*, Lat. *manus*, Lith. *rankà*, Goth. *handus*. The tabooed words may then be totally lost, as was the cognate of Gk. *árktos* 'bear' in Germanic and Slavic.

It should be noted that **taboo,** or avoidance of the unspeakable, varies from culture to culture, and accordingly from language to language. It is applied to clothing in Japanese; to animal names for hunters; and to names of excretory functions, death, and divinity for us.

But in cultures that absolutely forbid the use of certain words, such as any homophone of the name of a deceased person, taboo may have an effect on the lexical stock of a language. In this way the attitudes toward objects, that is, the **reference** of individual words, may be influential in bringing about semantic change.

12.7   Semantic change resulting from borrowings

By far the most important effect on the semantic component of language is brought about by the influence of other languages or dialects, a process referred to by linguists as *borrowing*. Borrowing may be viewed as cultural diffusion. In accounting for its effects, we must attempt to determine the conditions under which borrowing takes place. We may note first that borrowings of various types may take place. Some borrowings, known as **loanwords**, mirror the phonemes of the foreign language. In Eng. *poet*, for example, the French phonemes were reproduced almost exactly in English. Most recent borrowings in English are of this type; words like *oxygen*, *hydrogen*, *telephone* are made up of entities borrowed from Greek.

Other borrowings reproduce the morphemes of a foreign language, using native material. Examples are academic terms like *handbook*, a translation of Latin *manuālis liber*, which itself has survived in the abbreviated form *manual*. Other words reproduced by translation are the names for the days of the week: *Monday* = 'diēs Lunae,' *Tuesday* = 'diēs Martis, the day of Mars' and so on. These are known as **loan-shifts, loan translations**, or **calques**. In German, loan-shifts are particularly prominent;

instead of taking over the Greek components for 'acid' and 'material,' as did English in *oxygen*, German translated them to form the loan-shift *Sauerstoff*; similarly *Wasserstoff* for 'hydrogen,' *Fernsprecher* for 'telephone,' and so on.

In a further type of borrowing, only the meaning of a linguistic entity may be changed. OE *eorl* 'earl' meant 'brave warrior': the present meaning was taken over from Old Norse, where the word indicated a rank of nobility. Similarly, OE *dwellan* meant 'lead astray' but was modified in meaning by ON *dvelja* 'abide' to present-day 'dwell.' Changes in meaning under the influence of a foreign language are known as **extensions**.

To understand borrowings of various types, we must know the degree of command speakers have of the languages in question; for the extent of reproduction is often determined by the extent of control speakers have acquired of a second language, especially before conventions of borrowing have been established.

We may illustrate possible modifications by noting how English words are treated in Japanese. The English word *violin* is reproduced variously, depending on the speaker's command over English. Sophisticated speakers may use a very similar form when they speak Japanese, i.e., *vaioriñ*, even though their own language does not contain a /v/. Most speakers, however, substitute /b/ for English *v*, and say *baioriñ*. Both sets of speakers reproduce *l* as *r*. But especially among naive speakers, borrowings show substitution of phonemic, not phonetic, entities, as the examples given below indicate.

The role of phonemic structure in borrowings may be illustrated through the treatment of English *t* in Japanese. The stop [t] occurs in Japanese only before [e a o]; before [u] we find the affricate [ts]; before [i y], the affricate [tš]. If a word like *tank* is borrowed into Japanese, the result is *tañku*, different only in the mandatory final vowel. For *touring*, the Japanese form is *tsuriñgu*; for *team* and *tube*, *tšiimu and tšyuubu*. In Japanese, [t ts tš] are in complementary distribution, they are members of the same phoneme. Nàive speakers automatically substitute any of the allophones of /t/ in accordance with their distribution before following vowels in Japanese.

To illustrate a different treatment, we may note the forms of *jet* in Japanese. Like [tš], [dž] may occur in Japanese only before [i] and [y]; *jib* is then taken over with the similar pronunciation [džibu]. Before [e a o], on the other hand, [z] is found, in complementary distribution with [dž]. With these limitations of the Japanese phonological structure, the word *jet* has been borrowed in two forms: [džietto] and [zetto]. In the first the initial consonant is similar to that of English, with vowel modification; in the second the vowel is unchanged, but the initial consonant has been altered.

For the examples cited, knowledge of the phonological structure of Japanese and English is necessary to explain the Japanese forms. One must know the allophones of the English phonemes and their possible Japanese counterparts. Details are given in the Workbook. To illustrate the Japanese treatment of English *s*, the following examples may be cited. Japanese *sañmā-sōruto* corresponds to English *sommersault*; *setto-požišoñ*, to English *set position* (of a pitcher); *šinema*, to English *cinema*; *šoruda-raiñ*, to *shoulder line*; *sūpu* to *soup*. As comparison with the statement of correspondences given in the Workbook will illustrate, the English words have undergone modifications determined largely by the possibilities in Japanese.

The borrowing language also brings about morphological modifications, for borrowings generally take on the patterns of native elements. When, for example, *bask* was borrowed into Old English from Old Norse *báða sik* 'bathe oneself' and *busk* from Old Norse *búask < búa sik* 'ready oneself,' they were treated like simple verbs in English. For reflexives were not combined with verbs in English, and accordingly the speakers failed to recognize the final pronouns. To be sure, foreign inflections may occasionally be maintained, especially by sophisticated speakers. Many nouns were imported into English with their Latin or Greek plural inflections, such as *datum* : *data*, *colon* : *cola*, *skeleton* : *skeleta*, *maximum* : *maxima*, and so on. Except in learned contexts, these now make their plurals in -*s*, with the exception of the first, *data*, which is increasingly treated as a singular, as in *the data is*.

Similarly, in Japanese, borrowings are equipped with the Japanese morphological markers. Words borrowed into Japanese from Chinese such as *keñkyuu* 'study' were treated as verbs with the addition of *suru* 'do,' *shita* 'did,' e.g., *keñkyuu shita* 'studied.' When English words were borrowed into Japanese, they, too, followed this pattern. The loanword *taipu*, from English *type*, as well as others, may be accompanied by forms of *suru*. The large number of borrowings into Japanese from Chinese and English could be inflected in this way, though without introducing any new morphological markers.

Further, syntactic expressions borrowed from another language are difficult to maintain. English *marriage of convenience* < Fr. *mariage de convenance* 'marriage for advantage' may be misinterpreted today. To be sure, the phrase *it goes without saying* < Fr. *cela va sans dire* has currently become established among many speakers. Yet neither of these expressions has affected the language deeply. A more widespread example of syntactic borrowing may be the German favoring of highly complicated sentence patterns, a result of the influence of Latin syntax. As with other supposed borrowings of syntactic patterns, such as the introduction of numeral classifiers into Japanese from Chinese, the evidence is not conclusive. As in the examples cited above, the clearest instances of borrowing are in the lexical and semantic sphere. Below, however, we shall note again that general syntactic patterns may be affected by borrowing.

12.7.1 Borrowings when a language of prestige is adopted. Various situations in the history of English provide us with good examples of different results of borrowing. Various types of language contact can be attested for English, with differing effects on the language.

The first of these was contact with Celtic speakers. When English was brought to the British Isles in the fifth century A.D., presumably there were more Celtic speakers, than Germanic invaders. Yet English survived and ousted Celtic. Moreover, it adopted very few words from Celtic, a few common nouns like *bannock* 'cake' and *brock* 'badger,' and numerous place names, such as *London, Thames, Dover*. The resulting linguistic situation is much like that of American English and the American Indian languages. A few nouns from American Indian languages were borrowed: *tomahawk, skunk,* and many place names, such as *Chicago, Mississippi, Kentucky*. The two linguistic situations had much in common; from them, with the support of other parallels, we can suggest the typical situation in which few lexical borrowings are made.

When speakers learn a prestige language, they are under social pressure to acquire it without flaws. They speak the acquired language as well as possible and avoid carrying over into it items from their native language. Examples may be taken from America in the nineteenth century. Immigrants who came to this country attempted to learn accurate English. Their own language, however, was grossly modified, often with importations from English. In the German area of Chicago, a mixed German was referred to as *die schönste lengevitsch*. It consisted in great part of German structures filled with borrowings from English. On the basis of this situation, and those just cited, we may conclude that speakers modify the language they are certain of much more readily than they do a language they know imperfectly.

As a further well-documented example, we may cite Germany in the eighteenth century. At the courts French was the language of prestige; German, that of everyday communication. Frederick the Great of Prussia considered German a language fit only for peasants. He often wrote in French; when he did, he avoided German borrowings. His German letters, on the other hand, abound with French loanwords.

From these and other examples, we may view the English-Celtic relationship as a typical situation in the contact of languages. Old English was regarded as the language of cultural prestige. Although they may have been preponderant numerically, native Celtic speakers set out to learn English, gradually abandoning their native language. In the course of time an English resulted with few lexical importations. Apart from place names, only those items were borrowed from the receding into the dominant language for which the dominant language had no readily available terms.

Although we have no evidence for this type of language interrelationship in many prehistoric situations, from the results we may assume it for many areas. It is especially relevant in the spread of Indo-European languages: of Hittite into Anatolia, of Greek into the Hellenic peninsula, of Italic into Italy, even of Indic into India, although in India there was considerable phonological modification resulting from the borrowing of cacuminals. This situation applied also for the spread of Arabic, which was adopted from Iraq to Morocco with little change in grammatical structure. Except for special situations discussed below, it also applied for the spread in recent centuries of two of the most widely spoken languages today: Russian and English.

12.7.2 Borrowing when a language of prestige is used simultaneously with a surviving indigenous language.

A second typical situation, English in the eleventh century, at first glance parallels that of the fifth century. A relatively small group of invaders took over political control of an established population and continued as the ruling class. Yet the results were quite different. In the centuries after 1066, Norman French was used by a small segment of the population, but eventually it was ousted by English.

We explain the different result by noting that the type of contact was completely different from that in the fifth century. During the eleventh and subsequent centuries, the indigenous speakers adopted words for only those cultural spheres in which they maintained contact with the ruling classes. For everyday communication they used their own language. We may illustrate this restriction of contact by noting the spheres of borrowing.

One notable sphere of borrowing was government and administration. A great number of English words in these areas was borrowed from French, for examples *council, country, crown, government, minister, nation, parliament, people, state*. For titles, *prince, duke, marquis, viscount, baron* were borrowed; only the native *earl* was kept, but the earl's wife is a *countess*, and *count* is the equivalent rank for foreign nobles. In the related area of heraldry, many French terms were taken over, including those for colors such as *sable, gules, vert.* Moreover, military words were borrowed: *armor, army, banner, navy, siege, war;* similarly such legal terms as *court, crime, defendant, judge, jury, justice, plaintiff.* In the sphere of legal terminology, some French idioms were introduced and maintained, presumably because of the extended period of French influence. Although English became the official language in 1362, legal French was not given up in courts of justice until 1731. The phrase *puis né* 'later born, inferior' was borrowed as an adjective, surviving in *puisne judge,* and more widely as *puny.* Moreover, some syntactic phrases, with adjective following noun, have been maintained: *attorney general, malice aforethought.*

The difference in social status of the two languages may be illustrated in contrasting words: for a small crime, the English *theft* is used; for a serious one, the French *larceny.*

Today, foods are still commonly said to reflect the social relation between the Norman French and their English subjects. English terms are used for animals in the field: *cow, calf, ox, sheep, boar, swine;* French, for animals on the table: *beef, veal, mutton, bacon, pork.* Moreover, the humble meal *breakfast* has an English name; the more elegant *dinner* and *supper,* at which *jelly* and *pastry* may be served, have French names. The social relationship is further reflected in words for *sport < desport,* the *chase, falconry, cards,* and *dice,* where even words for numbers were taken over: *ace, deuce, tray.* As with foods, names for artisans in the lower groups are English: *baker, fisherman, miller, shepherd, shoemaker, smith;* those in contact with upper classes are Norman French in origin: *carpenter, mason, painter, tailor.*

The general situation is clear. A few upper-class invaders maintained positions of prestige for some time but were gradually replaced by speakers of English, or the invaders themselves learned English. The terms maintained in English reflect a feudal system, with various class distinctions. We conclude that the language of lesser prestige maintained itself because of the numerical, and eventually political, preponderance of its speakers. Yet the language of greater prestige has left a great effect on certain segments of the vocabulary.

Again, we find this situation in other areas as well. The Dravidian languages of India have been maintained, though with numerous borrowings from Indic languages. In early Mesopotamia, Akkadian ousted Sumerian, though it took over many words from the earlier language of prestige. When the Japanese became aware of the higher culture of China in the second half of the first millennium after Christ, they sent emissaries to China, who imported with the higher culture a large number of borrowings; but Japanese was maintained as the national language.

To a certain extent this type of contact exists today wherever Western civilization and science are being imitated or adopted. Words like electricity, telephone, airplane are being introduced as loanwords or loanshifts. We find a variety of parallels to the English–French contact, in which the invading language leaves a marked effect in the native language, without replacing it.

12.7.3 Borrowing when the languages concerned are on an equal plane.
A third typical situation is the contact between English and Scandinavian, in the ninth to eleventh centuries. Both languages existed side by side for some time, until eventually Scandinavian was lost. But unlike Celtic several centuries earlier, it left a considerable imprint on English. This imprint, on the other hand, was not in higher segments of culture, as was the later Norman French influence, but extended through much of the everyday vocabulary. To be sure, there were various martial and legal terms of Scandinavian origin in early English, but few of these have persisted; one that has remained, *bylaw* (by = village), has merely a vestige of its original sense.

The Scandinavian borrowings show no specific areas of cultural superiority. The term for a possible architectural improvement, *window* (wind-eye), merely replaced an older *eagþyrel* (eye-hole); it did not accompany a cultural innovation. Little more can be claimed for the borrowed *steak* and *knife*. Unlike French, Scandinavian furnished many elements of the common vocabulary: *gift, husband, root, skill, skin, sky, wing; happy, loose, low, same, wrong; addle, call, die, drown, gape, get, give, hit, screech, take, want*. Still others may have been borrowed but cannot be identified, for many words were alike in tenth-century Old English and Old Norse.

Most interesting are grammatical elements: *they, them, their* have taken the place of older *hīe, heom, heora*. In these borrowings the central core of the vocabulary was affected. The inflections of English nouns and verbs may even have been simplified by the contact between the two linguistic groups. We can even suggest that the type of contact existing between English and Scandinavian may have been one force in the morphological simplification of English.

This was a contrast between two languages of equal prestige. We are not certain to what extent the two were mutually intelligible; this question may also lack pertinence. For the significant point may be that the two languages were used for communication on an everyday level. The language with the larger number of speakers was maintained, though with simplification of structure.

Still further simplification is evident when speakers communicate only on simple cultural levels. A readily attested example may be found in baby-talk. Speakers, in using it, may avoid lexical items that border on the grammatical, such as pronouns: *baby like candy*? In even less unabashed utterances, such as *baby go seepee*, we find phonological as well as morphological simplification. Such simplification, used not only to infants when attempting to convey affection, is very similar to that found in the so-called Pidgin languages or Creolized languages.

Pidgins (apparently a simplification of *business*: Chinese *p* = Eng. *b*, *ž* = *z*, yielding [pižins] < [biznis]) have arisen in areas where men communicated on a very simple level. On the Chinese coast, intercommunication was carried on in English for commerce; in the Pacific islands, it was carried on for the direction of work. In South America, descendants of slaves evolved a simple common language called *taki-taki*. When such simplified languages are the sole languages of a community, as in Haiti, they are referred to as **Creolized languages**. To illustrate the changes that may take place when speakers are in contact on a low cultural level, interesting examples may be found in *Melanesian Pidgin English*, a study by Robert A. Hall, Jr.

Melanesian Pidgin is not learned as a first language by any speaker except possibly by children of parents who cannot understand each other's language. It is spoken by speakers with a Melanesian or Papuan background, and by Europeans. When spoken, it is not uniform. Speakers carry over their native speech habits. Melanesians, for example, may pronounce voiced stops with prenasalization; *nǝbawt* 'about' may be [nǝᵐbawt]. Germans may use *tæsɔl* 'but' like German *aber*, which corresponds to Engl *but* and *however*.

In Melanesian Pidgin, the sound system of English was considerably simplified. There are no /θ ð z ž/; for instance, *this* is [dis], *nose* is [nos]. Further, in speaking Melanesian Pidgin English, Melanesians generally substitute the following:

[p] for [f v] : [pinis] = [finiš] 'already';
[æp] = [hæf] 'piece'
[s] for [š č] : [masin] = [mašin]
[š] or [tš] for [dž] as in [pičin]

[h] is omitted, as in [bi ajn] 'later.' Moreover, consonant clusters may be simplified by intercalating vowels, as in [gǝris] for [gris] 'pig.'

In morphology none of the bound forms of English are attested. There are, however, characteristic bound forms. The suffix *-felə* is used as an adjective suffix for monosyllables, and also for numerals, for example:

disfelə haws i-bigfelə	'this house is large'
tufelə pikinini	'two children'
nədərfelə səmtiŋ	'another thing'

It is also added to first- and second-person pronouns to indicate plurals:

mi 'I, me'	mifelə 'we, us'
ju 'you'	jufelə 'you'

Characteristic affixes are also used with verbs; *-im* is used as objective suffix for most verbs when transitive, as in

ju faytim pig	'you strike the pig'

A predicate marker is used as prefix, unless the subject is *mi, mifelə, ju, jufelə, jumi*, for example:

mašin i-bəgərəp finiš	'the machine is ruined,'

The syntax too is simple, with sequences of coordinated clauses.

In Melanesian and other pidgins, then, we see an extreme effect of language contact. A language is stripped down for the essentials of communication, with resulting phonological and morphological simplification. How often such processes of simplification took place in the past, we do not know; whether the Assyrian merchants in Asia Minor used simplified forms of communication during the second millennium B.C., or the Romans in Gaul, the Hittities in Asia Minor, the Phoenicians in their wanderings. Observing the simplification of structure in contemporary pidgin languages, we may wonder whether a somewhat similar situation may not have led to the form of English we find spoken after the tenth century, with its progressive loss of inflections, and to other similar reductions of complexity in language structure.

12.7.4 Borrowing between dialects. In discussing these three types of contact, we have dealt only with the relations of languages to each other. We must assume, however, similar types of contact between all different forms of speech: geographical dialects, social dialects, technical dialects, and even idiolects. Borrowings are made from any such dialect to any other, from all of them into the general language. Illustrations could be given in abundance. For 'edible corn on the cob,' the northern American *sweet corn* seems to be becoming the standard term rather than the southern *roasting ears*. With the interest in jazz, many terms have been adopted into the standard language from uneducated speech, such as *the blues*. Technical dialects of the present have introduced so many new terms that we may forget the strong influence of those in the past. We are quite aware of the time of introduction of *x-ray, radium, irradiate, isotope*. Other sources in earlier times were from the technical terms of the ecclesiastical vocabulary. Our *noon* is from OE *nōn*, Lat. *nōna hōra* 'ninth hour,' the time of the nones, a service held originally at 3 P.M. but later shifted to noon.

The extent to which these have been modified may be illustrated by our use of legal terms. For us, *subpoena*, originally a phrase meaning 'under penalty' can be used as a verb. *Affidavit*, on the other hand, a Latin verb form meaning 'he has pledged his faith' can today be a noun, as can *alibi* 'elsewhere', in origin a Latin adverb.

Although genetics has changed our views on biological inheritance, we still maintain the technical language of medieval science. We may excuse a failing by saying 'it's in my blood.' Our disposition we still refer to as our 'liquid,' Lat. *humor*, for according to medieval science there were four important liquids in man: blood, phlegm, bile, black bile. If one had too much blood, he was *sanguine*; too much phlegm, *phlegmatic*; too much bile, *bilious*; too much black bile or melancholy, *melancholic*. If the liquids are in balance, one is *good-humored*. His *temperament* is also evident in the 'weaving together' of humors, and indicated on his face by his *complection*, now *complexion*.

Like those in medieval and modern English, borrowings adopted in technical dialects are generally based on a learned language. In Arabic-speaking countries, Classical Arabic is used as a source; in India, Sanskrit. In the languages of Western Europe, Latin and Greek are plundered for technical terms. Since European technology and science have been spread throughout the world, the influence of Latin and Greek has not been confined to Indo-European languages. Names of chemical elements provide examples. The word for 'hydrogen' in Japanese is *suiso* 'water-substance'; the word for 'nitrogen,' *chisso* 'suffocating substance,' and so on.

Often the translation or adaptation is not literal. In Chinese and Japanese the morph for 'electricity' is extended from the meaning 'lightning'; 'electricity' in Japanese is *deñki* 'lightning spirit'; 'telephone,' *deñwa* 'lightning speech'; 'telegraph,' *deñpoo* 'lightning report,' and so on.

Moreover, the adaptations may fail to follow forms of the model. In linguistic terminology, for example, the proper Greek suffix for terms ending in *-eme* would be *-ematic*; *phonematic* would then be the adjective for *phoneme* rather than *phonemic*, and so on. Yet the adjectival suffix *-ic* is so common, e.g., *base*, *basic*, that it is applied to terms ending in *-eme*, contrary to Classical practice. The complexities of such formations, and the attitudes of speakers toward these formations, are subjects of interest that have been inadequately explored.

In contemporary languages we may find results of borrowings made at different times from the same ultimate source. In this way *frail*, ME *freyl*, was borrowed from OFr. *fraile*, which is from Lat. *fragilis*, the source of our *fragile*; *male* is from Fr. *mâle*, OFr. *mascle*, which is from Lat. *masculus*; a derivative *masculīnus* is the source of *masculine*, and so on. Such related words are known as **doublets**.

12.7.5 Borrowings from the written language. Another contemporary source for adaptations is the written language. Abbreviations, such as *Prof.* may be used as full words. With the expansion of government agencies, many such terms have been incorporated into everyday speech; /yənéskòw/, UNESCO, from United Nations Economic, Social and Cultural Organization, may be as widely used today as /nəbískòw/, Nabisco, from National Biscuit Company; /yûw ès ès ár/, USSR, or in the Soviet Union, /és ès ès ér/. The written language has become such an important source for borrowings of this kind that new names for organizations are generally contrived so that they will provide suitable abbreviations.

Written languages have furnished other modifications for spoken languages. A slight novelty is the odd form of *ye* for the English definite article in the name *Ye olde gifte shoppe*; this arose from the use of *y* for þ when printing was introduced into England in the fifteenth century. If the form /yiy/ is only jocular and hardly more general than this context, the pronunciations /əšúwm/ or /əsyúwm/ for *assume*, /súwət/ or /syúwət/ for *suet*, exemplify deeper modifications from the written language. The historically modified /š/ < /sy/ has been maintained only in *sure*, *assure*, *sugar*, and to some extent in *sumac*, while imitation of the written form has brought about change in pronunciation in *assume*, *consume*, *ensue*, *suet*, and others.

Influences from the written language indicate a socially favorable attitude of speakers toward it. Spelling pronunciations, such as /índiyən índyən/ for *Indian* (compare Injun Joe in *Huckleberry Finn* and the British pronunciation /injə/ for India) are considered to confer dignity on the objects of the appellation.

When such influences are exerted, the effect of individual speakers may be as significant as is that of varying dialects. With the development of widespread education, the idiolects of school teachers, for example, have exerted a considerable effect on languages during the last few centuries. Modifications such as those in *assume* may serve as one illustration. Virtually anyone can supply examples from his own schooling. A favorite target in some American schools was *aunt*. It was frequently considered undignified to label such a distinguished relative with a homonym for an insect. The spelling contributes a possible distinctive pronunciation, /áhnt/, /ɔ́hnt/, or the like. Another is *buoy*; it apparently wouldn't do to suggest that a youth was floating in the water directing traffic. Again the spelling furnishes a solution for the linguistically insecure.

Teachers and the bureaucracies supporting them may be responsible for even greater modifications in the language. Since the high front offglide used in parts of New York instead of retroflection in words like *bird* and *earl* has come to seem substandard, the whole weight of the New York school system has been thrown behind an effort to restore retroflection. School teachers are also undoubtedly responsible for depriving American English speakers of a negative in the first person of the auxiliary *be* parallel to *isn't, aren't, wasn't, weren't*; again, /éynt/ has seemed undignified for the graduates of a widespread educational system.

Such exertions have given rise to **hyperforms** in contemporary languages of culture. This term is used for forms that are attempted corrections, extended erroneously. Brooklyn children taught to modify /bəyd/ to /bərd/ in *bird* may extend their new learning to /bɔyd/ in *Boyd*, or to /ɔyl/ in *oil*, and pronounce these something like *bird* and *earl*. German children, speaking dialects without rounded front vowels, may round vowels in which rounding is not present in the standard language; taught to change from [fílə] to [fýlə] in *Fülle* 'abundance,' they may also change the vowel in *bilden* 'cultivate' and speak 'gebüldetes Deutsch.' Such modifications may be introduced without aid from a teacher or a school system, merely in an attempt to speak like the folks in the city; they are therefore also known as **hyperurbanisms**.

Besides illustrating conflicting influences that result from differing dialects, hyperforms are examples of the effects of analogy. If one is taught to substitute *I* for *me* in contexts like *It wasn't me*, one may be led also to say 'with Mary and I.' The hypercorrection *I* has been taught as the prestige pattern, and as illustrated, extended in use. The authors of "Empirical Foundations for a Theory of Language Change" consider hypercorrection "an important mechanism in the . . . transmission of prestige patterns" (181).

Whether spontaneous or induced, borrowing is one of the important influences on language. In using speech, one of our aims is adequate communication. To achieve the readiest communication, we constantly modify our phonological and syntactic systems and our vocabulary to the speech of our associates. If we wish to impress a fellow speaker, we may borrow a word of his, or imitate a pattern in his grammar. If he prefers a plural verb form after *data*, we may say 'the data are.' If he prefers the spelling pronunciations /lítəratyùwr néytyùwr/, we may adopt these. We may be considered out of date unless we adopt new extensions of meaning.

Weinreich, Labov, and Herzog have re-emphasized the effects on language change of the various subsystems found in any language. They have also attempted to determine precisely how language changes; in this attempt they have assumed a model of language that consists of "discrete layers" that coexist within one speech community and that contains "intrinsic variables." Among the variables they have studied are phonological characteristics, such as the position of *r* in New York City speech, and syntactic characteristics, such as the use of the copula *BE* in the speech of young Blacks in northern cities of America.

One of the important processes they identify in linguistic change is the "embedding" of the change, both in the structure of a given language and in the social structure of the society using that language. For example, statements have been made about the lack of the copula *be* in the speech of Black children. Labov has demonstrated that it is not lacking in their grammar ("Contradiction, Deletion, and Inherent Variability of the English Copula," *Language* 45, [1949], pages 715–62). For example, *is*, the most frequently deleted form of the copula, is found in their emphatic sentences, such as: "He *is* an expert" (page 720). To deal with problems of change, precise information such as that presented by Labov is essential. Thereupon the social significance of the variable in question, such as use or absence of *be*, must be determined. After the type of embedding in the language structure and the social structure is understood, the change may be discussed with authority.

Yet such information does not provide the data for answering the question of the origin of linguistic change. Weinreich, Labov, and Herzog ascribe this to spread of a varying feature. For example, if in a subgroup of speakers, a voiced form of intervocalic -*t*- were to spread, and if it were then widely adopted, we would acknowledge a linguistic change. As further groups adopt such a variable, that is, intervocalic [ṭ] rather than [t], it would shift in status to a constant. The change then would be considered a completed linguistic change.

Such an explanation for the 'actuation' of linguistic changes applies to complex societies of today, which are made up of heterogeneous speakers like those in a large composite community such as New York City. But sound changes or other linguistic changes in the past may not have been actuated in this way. The much smaller communities of the past, like the Proto-Germanic speech community, undoubtedly were far more homogeneous than are today's large urban communities. Instead of attempting to ascribe linguistic change to one kind of cause, we may better understand language by acknowledging a variety of possible causes.

In addition to changes actuated by variation in language, we may assume that changes are brought about by the structure of a given language. Aberrant sound systems, or syntactic systems (such as OV languages with prepositions) may be modified, as we have noted in Chapter 9:6. Yakov Malkiel ascribed some sound changes to morphological sets in his article "The Inflectional Paradigm as an Occasional Determinant of Sound Change," pages 21–64 of *Directions for Historical Linguistics*.

Another possible cause for change may lie in the imagination of man. Speakers tire of expressions handed down from generation to generation, as the practice of poets indicates. In everyday speech the desire for change is especially apparent in terms of endearment or evaluation. The inventiveness of individual speakers must, however, be generally accepted, and new patterns adopted, to bring about a significant change in a linguistic community.

Van Helmont indeed added the word *gas* to his and other languages, yet his proposed *blas* 'emanation from stars' was a failure. George Eastman introduced *Kodak* as a deliberate creation, after he noted the restrictions on the letter *k* in the English writing system; other merchants have followed him in introducing names such as *Kix* for breakfast cereals, *Krax* for crackers, *Klenso* for soaps, yet these have had an effect primarily on external elements. For major linguistic changes to be carried out, social factors as well as linguistic factors are involved. Explanations for the changes must involve both factors. Fortunately, considerable attention is again being given to language change. The resultant study will lead to our understanding of the development of languages in the past, and of language as a phenomenon.

12.8   The use of changes brought about by borrowing as a diagnostic tool

Understanding of contact phenomena is important for historical linguistics as a diagnostic tool as well as the means to interpret the non-native segments of a language. For when items are introduced into a new language, they undergo different influences from those of their original language. By proper interpretation we may therefore gain information both about the imported language and the source language at a given time. For example, the [w] of Eng. wine, imported into the Germanic languages around the beginning of our era from Lat. vīnum, informs us that at this time Latin v was pronounced [w]; when imported into English later from French, the pronunciation of v had changed to that of a labiodental, as illustrated by vine, a doublet of wine.

Such information may be important in giving us means of describing a language at any given time. We have, for example, no contemporary description of Gothic, merely materials from the fifth and sixth centuries, most of which were produced by earlier translations. Apart from the alphabetic system, which was based on the Greek alphabet and therefore transparent in part, our best source of information about Gothic pronunciation is the set of words taken into Gothic from Greek and Latin, and into them from Gothic. Most of these are names. When, for example, our Gothic texts transcribe 'Ephesus' as Aifaiso, we may infer that the combination ai represented a sound something like [ɛ]. Since we know less about the spoken Greek encountered by the Gothic fourth-century translator than we would like, and about the exact sources of the Gothic alphabet, we cannot solve all of our problems about Gothic pronunciation; the importations into Gothic, however, give us some basis for proposing a solution.

Similar procedures have been applied in a variety of languages. For determining the pronunciation of early Chinese, our primary materials are importations into Japanese. Chinese rhyming dictionaries help us with the ends of morphs; for the beginnings we would be hard pressed if we could not compare the thousands of importations taken at different times from different Chinese dialects into Japanese.

Another use of borrowings for the dating of language contacts, and beyond that of language changes through analysis of the forms of importations, is highly delicate, almost treacherous. As an illustration we may consider the attempts at dating completion of the sound change [θ] > [d] in German, as illustrated by Germ. dank in contrast with Eng. thank, We associate this change with the change of obstruents in High German, though it was further extended into Low German territory than was the change of [t] to [s]. An attempted source for dating is the name of the missionary who came to Iceland from North Germany shortly before 1000 A.D. Icelandic sources give his name as þangbrandr. By the year 1000, however, the change of [θ] to [d] had been completed, and in High German documents the name is recorded as Dankbrand. We have less information about Low German at the time, and little evidence about the completion of the change from [θ] to [d] in Low German territory. From the Old

Icelandic spelling, however, it has been concluded that the Low German form of the name must still have been *Thankbrand*, and that [θ] was still maintained in Low German around 1000 A.D.

We cannot, however, be completely certain of this conclusion, for if Icelanders heard the name even after the sound change, they might have substituted their own form of it, morph by morph. Because of such complexities, dating of linguistic changes with the help of borrowings involves consideration of many possible complications, and even so must be regarded with caution.

Borrowing of syntactic features may also inform us of the type of interrelationships existing between languages. Thus the adoption of an OV structure in Akkadian suggests that speakers of Akkadian regarded Sumerian as a language of prestige. We have noted at length in Section 12.7 of this chapter the kinds of inferences we have been able to draw about the interrelationships of English with Celtic, Norman French, and Old Norse, on the basis of lexical influences. Such information enables us to draw conclusions about the interrelationships of dialects and languages, the prestige accorded them by speakers, and also the time of linguistic changes and the cultural situation of previous periods. Inferences about earlier cultures we derive chiefly from the lexicon, and from relics of earlier stages of the language that have survived after changes have taken place.

12.9 Findings of linguistic palaeontology, especially with reference to the community of speakers of Proto-Indo-European

When semantic shifts have taken place, relics of former meanings may survive in restricted usages, such as *ghost* 'spirit' in *Holy Ghost*, *meat* 'food' in *nut-meats*, and so on. These assist us to a limited extent in reconstructing earlier features of a culture; they are scarcely useful for this purpose except for linguistic groups of which the only certain surviving segment of culture is the language, for instance the original Indo-European community. Archaeology has yielded materials from the time of this community, but in the absence of literacy we cannot readily relate artifacts to speech, or determine which archeological findings are to be associated with given linguistic groups. The linguistic possibilities we have for reconstructing the culture of the Indo-European community are examined in the study known as **linguistic palaeontology**. With the uncertain bases available in a reconstructed language for reconstructing a culture, there have been many disputes over its conclusions. Yet the contributions of linguistic palaeontology for prehistory are so important that its techniques must be noted; for archeological techniques have been improved and the findings of archeology expanded, so that we can now relate some of the prehistoric communities of Eurasia with the Indo-Europeans, and in this way improve our knowledge of the history of a part of mankind. We may then apply these techniques to other prehistoric communities.

We reconstruct for Proto-Indo-European many items that tell us little about the culture of its speakers: grammatical markers, verbs like 'go, bear, taste, know,' nouns like 'eye, water, tree, father.' But besides these are words that give us cultural information. When we find terms for 'father, mother, brother, sister, son, daughter, daughter-in-law,' and others that indicate a close relationship with the son's wife but not between a man and his in-laws, we conclude that in the Indo-European community the wife joined her husband's family. The term for the father of the wife in Greek, *pentherós*—from the root in our word *bind*—by indicating an acquired relationship between the wife's family and the husband's, supports this conclusion.

Proceeding to more complex social groups, in Skt. *dámpatis* = Gk. *despótēs* 'head of the *dam* = *domus* "house"' there is evidence for a social organization governed by a petty chieftain. Similarly, from Lith. *viēšpats*, Skt. *višpatis* 'head of the dwellings,' see Gk. *oîkos* 'house.' But the absence of general terms for leaders of larger social groups requires us to conclude that social organizations in the Indo-European community were restricted in size. A word for 'ruler,' related to the Latin verb *regere* 'guide' is found in Lat. *rēx*, Ir. *rī*, Skt. *ráj-*, but other dialects have different terms, such as Gk. *basileús* and OE *cyning*. Accordingly we may posit for the Indo-European community a well-developed family system but no higher social or political organization.

Proceeding to the everyday life of the Indo-European community we find terms for 'herd, cow, sheep, goat, pig, dog, horse, wolf, bear, goose, duck, bee, oak, beech, willow, grain.' The lack of specific terms for grains or vegetables indicates a heavy reliance on animals for food.

The terms for 'beech, bee, salmon' and others have been used for the additional purpose of attempting to pinpoint the original home of the Indo-European speech community, with varying results. One problem involved may be illustrated by a word considered among the most reliable evidence, that for 'beech,' for it may have undergone shifts in meaning— Gk. *phēgós*, cognate with *beech*, means 'oak.' Yet the restricted range of the beech to north and central Europe has been widely used in locating the home of the Indo-Europeans. Another problem may be illustrated by the word, Germ. *Lachs*, which some scholars ascribe to the Indo-European vocabulary, concluding further that the salmon concerned is *Salmo salar*, which is found in the waters of northern Europe, though a similar fish exists in the waters flowing into the Caspian. Such possibilities of interpreting variously the words, and their meaning in prehistoric times, illustrate the problems involved in attempting to determine the home of the Indo-Europeans.

The time during which the Indo-European community flourished has been subject to less dispute. When we attempt to reconstruct words for metals, we can ascribe to the Indo-European vocabulary no words even for 'silver' or 'gold,' let alone 'iron,' and scarcely even a general term for 'metal, bronze, copper,' Lat. *aes* 'copper, bronze,' OE *ār* 'brass, copper,' > NE *ore*, Skt. *ayas* 'bronze,' later 'copper.' On the basis of such vocabulary, we characterize the Indo-European community as late Neolithic.

Fortunate archeological discoveries have led to the identification of this community with a culture located north of the Black Sea from the fifth millennium B.C. (see Marija Gimbutas, "Proto-Indo-European Culture: The Kurgan Culture during the Fifth, Fourth, and Third Millennia, B.C." pages 155–97 of *Indo-European and Indo-Europeans*, edited by George Cardona, Henry M. Hoenigswald, and Alfred Senn [Philadelphia, 1970]). Named after its characteristic burials in a barrow, or *kurgan*, the characteristics of this culture can readily be equated with the characteristics assumed from reconstructed Proto-Indo-European for Indo-European culture. Much evidence is found for the importance of the horse, for other animals of which the names have been reconstructed, and for assumed social arrangements. Moreover, the expansion of the kurgan culture, as determined from archeological evidence, corresponds with the expansion of the Indo-Europeans as we know it from linguistic and historical evidence. In this way linguistic evidence has been amplified by archeological evidence, and both have been combined to give us information about the early history of the most widespread language family.

This information has been corroborated by linguistic information of a different type. It has long been known that linguistic features may be extended throughout a cultural area, such as the Balkan peninsula and Western Europe. In such an area, generally known as **Sprachbund**, characteristic features may be spread by bilingual speakers. Thus, in Western Europe the article was introduced in the second half of the first millennium A.D., as were compound tenses and other linguistic characteristics. We find these characteristics spread through mutually unintelligible languages, such as early French, pre-Old High German, and pre-Old English. From these common features we can conclude that speakers of these languages were in close contact, that they belonged to a common "speech area" or *Sprachbund*.

In various publications Th. V. Gamkrelidze and G. I. Machavariani have pointed out that linguistic features of the reconstructed Caucasian language known as Proto-Kartvelian correspond to many features of Proto-Indo-European. (See *Language* 44 [1968] 404–06.) We can account for these features by assuming that the two languages belonged to one speech area, and that they were situated side by side around 3000 B.C.

In this way another kind of linguistic study, areal linguistics, makes us more certain of the findings provided by linguistic palaeontology and archeology. Historical linguistics has thus provided us with information about an important grouping of mankind five or more millennia ago, in addition to the insights it has yielded about the development of language.

Selected Further Readings

For a reliable introduction to change of meaning, see S. Ullmann, *The Principles of Semantics*, especially pages 171–257. Ullmann gives a thorough discussion of previous work, in addition to an approach of his own and a lengthy bibliography. In "Language, Society and Culture," pages 87–136 of *Diachronic and Synchronic Aspects of Language* (The Hague: 1962), Alf Sommerfelt deals broadly with meaning changes in their social settings. Gustav Stern, *Meaning and Change of Meaning*, republished by the Indiana University Press, Bloomington, 1965, is a full and excellent work on meaning change, especially in English.

J. B. Greenough and G. L. Kittredge, *Words and Their Ways in English Speech*, provides an interesting discussion of various types of meaning change in English; its prime source of interest today is its examples, some of which were used here, rather than their analysis.

Uriel Weinreich, William Labov, and Marvin L. Herzog have provided a searching examination of the causes of linguistic change in their article "Empirical Foundations for a Theory of Language Change," pages 95–195 of *Directions for Historical Linguistics*, edited by W. P. Lehmann and Yakov Malkiel (Austin: 1968).

For a thorough statement on borrowing, see Bloomfield's *Language*, pages 444–95. Otto Jespersen, who was much interested in the influence of one language on another, deals at some length with borrowings in English in his widely read book *The Growth and Structure of the English Language*. It, like many introductory histories of languages, deals especially with the external history of the language. Jespersen's views expressed more generally may be found in *Mankind, Nation, and Individual from a Linguistic Point of View*.

A full treatment of a Pidgin language is available in Robert A. Hall, Jr., *Melanesian Pidgin English; Grammar, Texts, Vocabulary*. Einar Haugen's *The Norwegian language in America: a study in bilingual behavior* deals with theory as well as the changes that Norwegian underwent in this country.

General study of the intereffects of languages can start best from Uriel Weinreich's *Languages in Contact: Findings and Problems*, which deals concisely with the synchronic problems and gives an extensive bibliography.

Any student interested in linguistics has probably made thorough use of the data available in his dictionary, whether Webster's *Collegiate* or another desk dictionary. Historical linguists should also acquire the standard etymological dictionaries for their fields of specialty, Skeat for English, Kluge for German, and so on. Because of the price, they probably will be restricted to library use of the *Oxford English Dictionary* and C. D. Buck's *A Dictionary of Selected Synonyms in the Principal Indo-European Languages*, a copious source for the study of semantic change, as well as a good portion of the Indo-European vocabulary— with sober comments on the conclusions that may be drawn about Indo-European culture. An excellent summary of many facets of Indo-European culture and the relevant archeology may be found in *Indo-European and Indo-Europeans*, edited by George Cardona, Henry M. Hoenigswald, and Alfred Senn (Philadelphia: 1970).

CHAPTER *13*

Conclusion

13.1 On the importance of dealing with language as a whole in studying change

When we deal with individual changes in language—changes in sound, form, or meaning—we may give the impression that entities in a language are undergoing change of only one type at one time. We fail to observe that as phonological changes are taking place, syntactic or semantic changes may be going on at the same time, and also that importations may be introduced; moreover, that none of these changes may be related to one another.

Further, when we deal with any problem, we generally use a single method among those established in historical linguistics. To secure our data for Old English strong verbs, we simply master the writing system of Old English and compile the essential material. If we wish to deal with Proto-Germanic strong verbs, we use the comparative method. In attempting to find an explanation for the vowel variation in Germanic strong verbs and related forms in other languages, which is already present in the reconstructed Proto-Indo-European, we use the method of internal reconstruction. Again, however, we cannot isolate one method from another. Especially if we are dealing with the history of a language rather than an isolated problem, we must be prepared to use at one time all the methods developed in historical linguistics. Even when we deal with an isolated problem, our explanation may be inadequate if we rely solely on one method. The interlocking of the various changes and our use of all possible methods may be illustrated with virtually any linguistic material. Let us use some of the developments that the English verbs *write* and *shrive* have undergone.

13.2 On changes in the phonological system

OE *wrītan* and *scrīfan* belong in the class with *drīfan* and *bītan*, having the principal parts:

wrītan	wrāt	writon	writen
scrīfan	scrāf	scrifon	scrifen

Between Old English and contemporary English, the *ī* of the first principal part underwent the same sound change to NE /ay/ as did accented *ī* in words of whatever class, nouns, e.g. *life,* pronouns, e.g., *I,* adjectives, e.g., *blind,* and so on (see Chapter 10:2). Still other sound changes affected the forms of these verbs, such as the loss of *w* before *r,* the raising of *ā* to *ō,* compare NE *home* < OE *hām,* and others. Through sound changes that modified their forms but did not affect their morphological contrasts, the Old English forms of *write* and *shrive* developed to the forms we know today: *write, wrote, written; shrive, shrove, shriven.*

13.3 On changes in the syntactic system

At the same time changes were taking place that affected the morphological system in which they belong. If the Old English forms had been continued with the intervening sound changes, we today would say *I wrote* but *we writ.* This complication of distinguishing the preterite plural from the singular through internal vowel differentiation was absent in the numerous weak verbs, and in classes 6 and 7 of strong verbs; in classes 4 and 5 of strong verbs, it was essentially a contrast of quantity, which was eliminated in Middle English as in OE *bær* 'I carried' : *bǣron* 'we carried' (see Chapter 11:4). Accordingly only the first three classes of strong verbs indicated the distinction; they were regularized in keeping with the predominant pattern. This morphological, or analogical change, was wholly unconnected with contemporary sound changes. We have noted earlier, Chapter 11:4, that in the morphological rearrangement the plural vowel was generalized in *bite, bit,* whereas in *write, wrote* like *drive, drove,* the singular vowel came to be used throughout the past.

Other morphological changes are directly connected with sound change. The Old English first singular present *write* became a monosyllable as final vowels were lost, falling together with the imperative. Moreover, the infinitive ending, OE -*an*, became -*en*, -*e* and was finally lost.

The plural of the present underwent further changes, which we cannot account for without drawing information from study of the English dialects. The Old English plural ending -*aþ*, as in *wrītaþ* 'we, you, they write,' should have been maintained as some sort of final dental today. But, as noted in Chapter 9:2, contemporary standard English is not a direct continuation of the Old English in which most texts survived, rather a reflex of the Midland dialects. In Middle English the Midland dialects generalized the subjunctive plural ending -*en* to the indicative. Chaucer, for example, who used the Midland dialect of London, says in the Prologue to the *Canterbury Tales*, line 12: *thanne longen folk to goon on pilgrimages*. Like the infinitive ending, the plural -*en* was gradually lost, though -*en* survives in the infinitive to the time of Shakespeare. Through the sound changes affecting final -*e* and -*an*/-*en*, the syntactic system was greatly modified. These sound changes are partially responsible for the reduction of the contemporary English verb system to a small number of forms.

At the same time, syntactic changes were taking place. When the first person singular was distinguished from the second and third persons singular, and the plural by endings, pronouns were not essential. In the *Beowulf*, verbs may be used, as in Latin and Greek, with no pronoun specifying the subject. Today a telegraphic statement like *wrote* is quite ambiguous, for the subject could be singular or plural, first or third person, possibly even second. Among other syntactic changes, the final verb position in the clause was being modified. The *Beowulf* still is predominantly OV, as in the initial lines:

> Hwæt, wē Gār-dena   in gēardagum
> þēodcyninga   þrym gefrūnon,
> hū ðā æþelingas   ellen fremedon!
> > 'We valiant-Danes   in days-of-the-past
> > our-people's-kings'   glory discovered,
> > how then heroes   valiant-deeds performed.

In both lines 2 and 3, the verbs are final, and in line 2 the genitive precedes its noun *þrym*; but even in late Old English this order of verbs with regard to their objects, and of genitive constructions, is being modified to the VO order found in English today.

13.4   On changes in the semantic system

As these and other shifts were taking place in the phonological and syntactic systems, entities in the semantic system were being modified. When the Germanic peoples came into contact with the Romans, they learned new activities, such as writing. With the process they took over the name, borrowing Lat. *scrībere*. Their early writing was done on wood, bone, even stone. Accordingly a native term, the etymon of *write*, meaning 'scratch,' was modified and extended as a synonym for the borrowed form of *scrībere*. In New High German its cognate *reissen* still means 'tear,' earlier 'scratch,' though compounds like *Reissbrett* 'drawing board' exemplify the meaning 'write.' NHG *schreiben*, a reflex of the borrowing from Latin, is the general term for 'write.' In English, however, *shrive* came to be restricted more and more to the technical dialect of ecclesiastics, with the meaning of 'hear confessions and give absolution.' The related *Shrove* was used primarily for the Sunday, Monday, and Tuesday preceding Ash Wednesday, when one confessed in preparation for Lent. With growing abandonment of confession, *shrive* and *Shrove* have virtually passed out of use; but nonecclesiastics may still give offenders *short shrift*.

13.5   On changes from borrowing

Shrive as loanword and *write* as extension illustrate changes that may result from contact with a foreign language. In their development both illustrate the interplay of technical dialects. One such dialect was that associated with the production of runes, which commonly were inscribed on *beech* tablets, as we know today from the modification of meaning in *book* < *bōk* 'book, beech tree.' The technical dialect subsequently involved was that of the church. At the same time forms of *shrive* and *write* were changed by the contacts between northern and southern English geographical dialects. Without a readiness to admit variables introduced in the development of a set of forms by borrowing, which (noted in the analysis of *shrive* and *write*) may be superimposed on changes in the phonological, syntactic, and semantic systems, we would be unable to account for many phenomena in language.

13.6   On the importance of dealing with changes
with relation to specific linguistic structures

Although for simplicity we are restricting our discussion here primarily to two words, we cannot account for their development if we isolate them from the structural sets to which they belong. Both *write* and *shrive* belonged in Old English to a phonological set in which the initial consonantal segment was a cluster composed of consonant plus *r*. Morphologically their roots fell into a set with roots like *bītan*, in which the initial consonantal element was followed by *ī* plus consonant. This structure characterizes strong verbs of the first class; as a result of its coinciding with this structure, the borrowed Latin *scrībere* was taken over as a strong verb. To understand phonological, syntactic, and semantic changes, we must deal with entities in the context of their structures. Historical linguistics, to be adequate, must be structural, as phonological analysis has been for some time. Recent linguistic study has extended the emphasis on structure to the syntactic and the semantic components.

In semantic study we must deal with words in their semantic fields. Unless we dealt with OE *wrītan* and *scrīfan* as members of a semantic set that were used for writing and related activities, explaining their shifts of meaning would be difficult. It may be an oversimplification to ascribe the shift of meaning found in *shrive* to its presence in a semantic set with *write*; we find this shift, however, in the Germanic area in which the term used especially for production of runes was generalized for all kinds of writing.

13.7   On the importance of dealing with changes with relation to specific social conditions

Besides coming to know the changes that elements of a language may undergo, each in its several components, we must master the techniques that give us our information. Through knowledge of the Old English writing system as it was developed from the Roman, with modifications because of strong Irish influence, we learn to know our basic Old English material. Unless we bring to the study of Old English a mastery of the lessons taught by the study of dialect geography, our understanding of it and its changes to the Middle English and the Modern English periods will be poor. We have noted complexities in the development of the English verb paradigm. More such complexities are involved in the development of the third singular present ending -*s*. Its etymon is found in northern texts in Old English times, but the reflex of Old English -*eþ* persists in southern dialects; Chaucer still uses it, e.g., *hath*. In the fifteenth and sixteenth centuries there is increasing evidence for -*s* in the speech of London, but literary texts use -*th* even later, as in the Authorized Version of the Bible. In the course of time, -*s* replaced -*th*, through influences on which scholars are not yet commonly agreed. An influence besides the northern -*s* forms may be the third singular ending in the frequent *is*.

13.8   On the use of the comparative method and the method of internal reconstruction

Since English is well attested, for information on its development we rely almost entirely on written texts. When, however, we wish to deal with the grammar of Proto-Germanic, in the absence of texts we must use the comparative method to determine our materials. Comparing OE *wrītan*, OS *wrītan*, OHG *rīzan*, the Runic ON *wrait* 'wrote,' and Goth. *writs* 'stroke,' plus other forms, we reconstruct the Proto-Germanic verb forms. With the help of the comparative method, we can assume for Proto-Germanic a strong verb system in which roots show a variation which for the etymon of *write* would be:

wreyt-   wrayt- < wroyt   writ-, writ-

We apply the comparative method further to our reconstructed Proto-Germanic forms and cognates in other dialects, such as Gk. *rhīnē* 'file,' reconstructing Proto-Indo-European in the same way as we reconstruct Proto-Germanic.

Understanding of Proto-Indo-European and its dialects is deepened in various ways, by study of texts that are available, by applying the comparative method and the method of internal reconstruction, by applying whatever findings may have been provided by typological studies. But, since Proto-Indo-European has no known cognates, the comparative method does not permit us to carry our investigations of language farther back in time.

The method of internal reconstruction enables us to analyze Proto-Indo-European itself, and to make inferences about segments of it at an earlier time. In Chapter 6:4 we noted the application we may make of the method of internal reconstruction to the vowel alternations found in Germanic strong verbs. This method has led us to conclude that the various forms of the vocalic nucleus can ultimately be related, through sound changes that we may indicate in a simplified manner as

e > o (in the form we know as preterite singular and in other derived forms)

e > ø [zero] (in the forms we know as preterite plural, in the preterite participle and in other derived forms)

Although these sound changes took place so early that very little evidence remains by which we might reconstruct the linguistic conditions for them, we assume the following environments. PIE *e* became *o* when the pitch accent was shifted to another syllable. The shift was carried out when derived forms were made with the Indo-European suffix *-eyo*, as in

Gk. *phoréō* 'bear constantly, wear' from the root *bher-* 'carry,' or Latin *moneō* 'advise < cause to think,' from the root *men-* 'think.' This form of the root has been maintained in the borrowing from Latin, *admonish*.

At a later time PIE *e* was lost when a stress accent fell on another syllable of a word. An example is Gk. *díphros* from PIE *-bhr-*, a term used for that part of a chariot that bears the driver and the warrior. Many other examples are available, although subsequent changes have obscured the original Indo-European situation. We have also observed, in Chapter 6:5, how with the method of internal reconstruction Saussure posited for pre-Indo-European laryngeal consonants for which distinct reflexes were later discovered in Hittite. The comparative method accordingly permits us to reconstruct the Proto-Indo-European language of approximately 5000 years ago; the method of internal reconstruction enables us to posit even earlier segments of the language.

13.9   Some conclusions obtained by historical linguistic study regarding the history of mankind

The methods developed in historical linguistics have in this way enabled us to push our knowledge of one language family back to 3000 B.C. and earlier. The same methods can be applied to other language families, the Finno-Ugric, Afro-Asiatic, Sino-Tibetan, even to families in which we have only contemporary materials and must rely very heavily on the method of internal reconstruction. After we have in this way reconstructed proto-languages for each of the language families from which materials are available, we may find relations between some of them. Yet, even after we reconstruct protolanguages other than Proto-Indo-European, we may find the differences between them so great that they cannot be interrelated. It is possible that the near relatives of Proto-Indo-European were all lost and that it alone was widely carried into areas where it displaced other quite unrelated languages, such as the Hattic language superseded by Hittite.

Historical linguistics in this way takes us back along a route we know to be much longer, the development of human language, from its ultimate origin. Although the question of the origin of language has encouraged historical linguists to continue arduous analyses, the origin of human speech has been demonstrated to be so remote that it is now considered quite outside the sphere of historical linguistics, and instead, included as a part of the study of early man. As we have seen from examples in this book, we can determine the origins of much of the English grammatical system and vocabulary; but such study takes us back only about 5000 years, a long time after the origin of speech. Here it is sufficient to warn of naïve theories, which have gained wide circulation, such as the bow-wow theory that language is in origin like animal cries, the ding-dong theory that imitation of natural noises sparked the first speech, and so on. The essence of language is its use by a social group as a system with a definite structure. We may speculate how such a system was first evolved, but we have even less information to support such speculation than we do on the origin of cave paintings.

Yet, though historical linguists may regard the problem of the origin of language beyond the techniques they control, there is no shortage of activities in store for them. Problems still remain in the most widely analyzed language family, the Indo-European. Indo-Europeanists are still attempting to incorporate the contributions resulting from the recently deciphered Mycenaean Greek, for which additional texts are found almost annually. The new perspectives produced by the discovery that Greek was the language of a brilliant civilization from 1450 B.C. have brought about a revision in our view of the Indo-European languages in the second millennium. These revised views must be applied in a re-evaluation of the ancient inscriptions found elsewhere, in Italy, particularly those in Asia Minor, where vigorous archeological work promises further clarification of the language interrelationships through the second and first millennia B.C. Even without new data, our study of Proto-Indo-European must deal with suprasegmental phenomena and with syntactic patterns; it must also bring previous analyses into accord with the structural approach and typological findings that promise a more complete description of Proto-Indo-European and its early dialects than that available in past works on historical linguistics.

Outside the Indo-European family, historical linguistics has many opportunities, and obligations. Historical grammars of individual languages, of language families, and of their branches are almost universally needed, as are studies in dialect geography, vocabulary, and etymology. Even in a set of languages so well known as the Arabic, historical grammars must now be produced on the basis of the descriptive grammars that are becoming available for its various dialects. When we have an adequate historical grammar of Arabic, we hope that the other West Semitic branches will be similarly equipped. Then a historical grammar of West Semitic will be possible, followed by comparison with East Semitic to yield a Proto-Semitic grammar. With this a historical grammar for even earlier stages of the language will be possible, if in the meantime Egyptian, Berber, Chad, and Cushitic have been equally well studied.

The Hamito-Semitic or Afro-Asiatic languages represent only one of the families that need such a series of studies on which syntheses will be based. As they are being produced, new insights and techniques may be developed or discoveries made, by which some of the further problems of historical linguistics will be solved, such as the decipherment of Linear A or the Mohenjo-Daro inscriptions, the discovery of cognate languages for Sumerian, demonstration of relationship between American Indian languages and those of Asia—all of which would permit us to expand our knowledge of linguistic conditions in the third and fourth millenniâ B.C. and even earlier, in much the same way as work in the first half of this century has expanded our information on the second millennium. Work in archeology, such as the discovery of Proto-Elamite inscriptions dated approximately 3500 B.C., provides optimism for the assumption that we will increase our knowledge of early civilizations and their languages.

As we work to extend our knowledge of early languages, careful control of linguistic techniques is increasingly important. This can be derived only from mastery of the techniques applied to well-known languages. Initial mastery of the principles of historical linguistics can best be obtained through control of the historical analysis of one's native language. For this reason it is essential that historical grammars of one's own and other languages be available that incorporate the current techniques of historical linguistics. On their pattern, grammars will be produced when adequate data and interest are available regarding any language.

Selected Further Readings

Probably the best historical grammar available for a language family is A. Meillet's *Introduction à l'étude comparative des langues indo-européennes*, though essentially it has been unchanged since 1934. Two monographs in which historical grammars are undertaken for languages with no long series of texts are Robert E. Longacre's *Proto-Mixtecan* and Sarah C. Gudschinsky's *Proto-Popotecan*: A comparative study of Popolocan and Mixtecan.

The bibliography on the origin of speech is huge. Alf Sommerfelt's essay, "The Origin of Language: Theories and Hypotheses," *Journal of World History*, 1.885–902 (1954), gives a concise and sober statement of the problem, and of the recent concern with it. A more vivid presentation is Charles F. Hockett's "The Origin of Speech," *Scientific American*, 203. 88–96 (1960), with scant bibliography, page 276.

Reports on discoveries about earlier forms of language are to be found in learned journals, and subsequently in journals designed for a general audience. For a report on the Proto-Elamite tablets found at Tepe Yahyā, see "An Early City in Iran," by C. C. and Martha Lamberg-Karlovsky, *Scientific American* 224.102–11 (1971). One of the most elegant introductions to any major discovery is the book summarizing the findings resulting from the decipherment of Linear B: *Documents in Mycenaean Greek* by Michael Ventris and John Chadwick (Cambridge, 1956). Cognitive origins of writing have been proposed in "Upper Paleolithic Notation and Symbol," by A. Marshack, *Science* 178. 817–828 (1972).

Annotated Bibliography

This bibliography has been highly restricted and briefly annotated because it is designed for students who are beginning their work in historical linguistics. Further references may be found in many of the books listed.

ALGEO, JOHN. *Problems in the Origins and Development of the English Language.* New York, 1972. 2d ed.
An excellent workbook, with careful exercises, questions, topics, and illustrations.

ANTTILA, RAIMO. *An Introduction to Historical and Comparative Linguistics.* New York, 1972.
A well-planned text, with copious examples.

ARLOTTO, ANTHONY. *Introduction to Historical Linguistics.* Boston, 1972.
A brief introductory text.

BLOOMFIELD, LEONARD. *Language.* New York, 1933.
A remarkably thorough introduction to linguistic study reflecting, however, historical linguistic theory developed by the neogrammarians and accordingly somewhat confining.

BUCK, CARL DARLING. *Comparative Grammar of Greek and Latin.* Chicago, 1933.
A brief, clear introduction to historical linguistics, pp. 30–67, and a concise, factual, though somewhat dated treatment of Greek and Latin historical grammar.

———*A Dictionary of Selected Synonyms in the Principal Indo-European Languages.* Chicago, 1949.
The preface, and the dictionary itself, can be read with the interest and profit one may derive from a carefully composed work.

CHOMSKY, NOAM and MORRIS HALLE. *The Sound Pattern of English.* New York, 1968.
A text of great importance for recent synchronic phonological study,

247

and as indicated in Chapter 6, pp. 99–101, also for diachronic study. Students should note that the authors follow carefully defined principles in explicating their theory of language, as indicated in their Chapter 8, pp. 330–399. This explication includes the use of terms like "simplicity" in a carefully defined sense which must not be confused with uses of the word in traditional texts. Followers of Chomsky and Halle have in many instances developed their own terminology, as in the use of the term "simplification" rather than the generally used term "analogy" and in the abandonment of the term "sound change."

DIRINGER, D. *The Alphabet*. A key to the history of mankind; 3d ed., completely revised with the collaboration of R. Regensburger, 2 vols., New York, 1968.

A general introduction to writing.

FRANCIS, W. NELSON. *The Structure of American English*. New York, 1958.

A good elementary statement of English grammar, with information on recent work in English. Chapter 9, "The Dialects of American English," by Raven I. McDavid, Jr., is a good summary on dialect geography in the United States.

GELB, I. J. *A Study of Writing: the foundations of grammatology*. Chicago, 1963. 2d ed. Phoenix P–109.

An introduction to the structural analysis of writing systems.

GRAY, LOUIS H. *Foundations of Language*. New York, 1939.

Useful now primarily for its discussion of language families.

HOENIGSWALD, HENRY M. *Language Change and Linguistic Reconstruction*. Chicago, 1960. Phoenix P–178.

A rigorous presentation especially of the comparative method and the method of internal reconstruction; not an elementary text.

JAKOBSON, ROMAN. 1968. *Child language, aphasia and phonological universals*. (Trans. A. R. KEILER.) The Hague, 1968.

A stimulating work.

———C. GUNNAR, M. FANT and MORRIS HALLE, *Preliminaries to Speech Analysis*. Cambridge, Mass., 1969, 8th printing.

The standard text on "distinctive features and their correlates."

JENSEN, HANS. *Sign, Symbol and Script*, 3d rev. and enl. ed., trans. by GEORGE UNWIN. London, 1970.

A handsome, well-illustrated text on writing.

JESPERSEN, OTTO. *The Growth and Structure of the English Language*, 9th ed. Oxford, 1946. Anchor A-46.

A well-written account of the external history of English, which reflects, however, the author's view of evolution in language development.

———*Language, Its Nature, Development and Origin*. London, 1922. Reissued as paperback, New York, 1964.

Pertinent especially for its concise history of linguistics, pp. 19–99.

————*A Modern English Grammar on Historical Principles*, vols. 1–7. Copenhagen, 1909–1949.

One of the important grammars of English.

KEILER, ALLAN R. ed. *A Reader in Historical and Comparative Linguistics.* New York, 1972.

A selection of twenty essays published after 1902, chiefly more recent.

KING, ROBERT D. *Historical Linguistics and Generative Grammar.* Englewood Cliffs, 1969.

A pioneering work.

KURATH, HANS, MARCUS L. HANSEN, JULIA BLOCH, BERNARD BLOCH. *Handbook of the Linguistic Geography of New England.* Providence, 1939.

Probably the best handbook from which to learn the complexities of undertakings in dialect geography. In addition to the findings it presents on the dialect situation in New England, it is of interest for its chapter on settlement history, for its discussion of the phonetic alphabet, and for its sketches of the individual informants.

LASS, ROGER. ed. *Approaches to English Historical Linguistics: an Anthology.* New York, 1969.

A selection of thirty previously published articles, with general pertinence for historical study.

LEHMANN, W. P. and YAKOV MALKIEL. *Directions for Historical Linguistics.* Austin, 1968.

Essays presented at a conference held in 1966.

LEUMANN, MANU, J. B. HOFMANN, A. SZANTYR. *Lateinische Grammatik*, 2 vols. Munich, 1963–1965.

An excellent, comprehensive grammar.

MEILLET, ANTOINE. *Introduction à l'étude comparative des langues indo-européennes.* Paris, 1937, 8th ed. Subsequently reprinted by the University of Alabama Press.

Though dated, still the best introduction to Indo-European historical grammar, with a concise statement on the principles of historical linguistics.

————*Linguistique historique et linguistique générale.* Paris, I, 1926, II, 1938.

Collected essays of one of the most lucid writers in linguistics.

MEILLET, ANTOINE and MARCEL COHEN. *Les langues du monde*, 2d ed. Paris, 1952.

Summaries of language families prepared by various scholars, with maps and a useful bibliography.

————*La méthode comparative en linguistique historique.* Oslo, 1925. Trans. as *The Comparative Method in Historical Linguistics*, by G. B. FORD, JR. Paris, 1967.

One of the best introductions to the comparative method.

ORTON, HAROLD and EUGEN DIETH. *Survey of English Dialects*. Leeds, 1962–.
The *Introduction* by Orton (1962) describes the survey, discusses publication and prints the questionnaire. The planned "four volumes" of *Basic Material* have now appeared, edited by Orton and collaborators (1962–1971). Students accordingly have available a large collection of dialect data from more than three hundred localities in England.

PAUL, HERMANN. *Prinzipien der Sprachgeschichte*, 5th ed. Halle, 1920. Subsequently reprinted.
The last edition of a treatise on language by one of the most eminent neogrammarians.

PEDERSEN, HOLGER. *Linguistic Science in the Nineteenth Century*. Translated by John Spargo. Cambridge, 1931. Reissued under the title: *The Discovery of Language*. Bloomington.
A readable discussion with numerous illustrations of the principles of historical linguistics as they were evolved in the course of the nineteenth century.

POP, SEVER. *La Dialectologie. Aperçu historique et méthodes d'enquêtes linguistiques*. I. *Dialectologie romane*. II. *Dialectologie non romane*. Louvain, 1950.
An authoritative introduction to projects in dialect geography throughout the world.

SAPIR, EDWARD. *Language*. New York, 1921. Harvest BH-7.
Important in historical linguistics especially for its discussion of typology, and of change in language.

SCHMIDT, PATER W. *Die Sprachfamilien und Sprachenkreise der Erde*. Heidelberg, 1926.
See especially the useful atlas.

SCHWYZER, E. *Griechische Grammatik*, 3 vols. Munich, 1939–1953.
One of the most comprehensive historical grammars available; a lengthy introduction deals with linguistic theory.

SEBEOK, TH. A., gen. ed. *Current Trends in Linguistics*. The Hague.
A comprehensive survey of work in various fields and various areas of linguistics.

STERN, G. *Meaning and change of meaning, with special reference to the English language*. Göteborg, 1931. Reprinted by the Indiana University Press.
Useful for its thorough discussion, with excellent examples drawn from English.

STOCKWELL, R. P. and R. K. S. MACAULEY. *Linguistic Change and Generative Theory*. Bloomington, 1972.
Essays based on a 1969 conference; illustrates developments in the transformational approach.

TRAUGOTT, ELIZABETH CLOSS. *A history of English syntax: a transforma-*

tional approach to the history of English sentence structure. New York, 1972.

An attempt to present transformational treatments of historical problems for students.

TRUBETZKOY, N. S. *Grundzüge der Phonologie.* Prague, 1939.

Trans. as *Principles of Phonology* by C. A. M. BALTAXE. Berkeley, 1969. Of primary importance in descriptive linguistics, but valuable for its typological statements also in historical work.

ULLMAN, STEPHEN. *The Principles of Semantics,* 2d ed. Glasgow, 1957.

Useful especially in summarizing various theories, and in providing a comprehensive bibliography.

WEINREICH, URIEL. *Languages in Contact: Findings and Problems.* New York, 1953. Republished by Mouton, The Hague.

An attempt to provide a rigorous framework for studying the interrelationships of languages, with an extensive bibliography.

From the first, students should become acquainted with journals in the field, not least for reviews of new publications. The *MLA International Bibliography* and the *Bibliographie Linguistique,* published annually, have full lists of relevant journals, as well as works throughout linguistics. As with bibliography, one will soon learn which are the profitable sources for further investigation.

Bibliographie Linguistique. Paris. Annual bibliography of linguistic publications, beginning with 1939. Volume I appeared in 1949. (Abbreviated: BL)

Bulletin de la Société de Linguistique de Paris. Useful for the views of French linguists, especially in the annual volume of reviews. (BSL)

International Journal of American Linguistics. Baltimore. (IJAL)

Journal of the American Oriental Society. New Haven. Especially for the languages of Asia. (JOAS)

Kratylos. Wiesbaden. A review journal for works in Indo-European and general linguistics.

Language. Baltimore. Journal of the Linguistic Society of America. A general journal, reflecting the views of American linguists. (Lg)

MLA International Bibliography. III. Linguistics. Annual bibliography published also as a special issue of the journal *General Linguistics.*

Voprosy jazykoznanija. Moscow. Journal presenting the views of Russian linguists. (VJa)

Transcription and Phonological Symbols

An elementary textbook should provide an introduction to the standard textbooks in a field, including the transcriptions and transliterations they use. These unfortunately vary. The symbols proposed by the International Phonetic Association were based on compromises, and have not always been adopted. For example, those, pp. xi–xvi of the introduction to *Les Langues du Monde*, do not always agree with the IPA symbols. Moreover, the IPA symbols were not necessarily adopted in new handbooks which have become standard, such as E. Prokosch's *Comparative Germanic Grammar* (Philadelphia, 1939). In addition, influential handbooks have proposed transcriptions of their own. Thus Bloomfield's *Language*, p. 91, used the symbol [e] for the vowel of *egg*, [ε] for the vowel of *add*. This value for *e* was maintained in the widely used Trager-Smith transcription, and is also used in this textbook for the vowel of *egg*. In view of the variation in use of symbols, patience and flexibility are necessary in the acquisition and interpretation of symbols. In general, the symbols used in this textbook are those found in the standard handbooks for a language or a field.

Consonant symbols: Basically there are no problems in the interpretation of symbols for the stops: *p t k b d g*; *q* may be used to indicate a velar stop, or also for a labio-velar, as in Gothic *qius* 'quick.' The capitals *K G* are used for uvular stops.

The symbols for voiceless fricatives are relatively uniform in value: *f, s*; for the voiced counterparts, *v*, or ƀ *β* (bilabial), and *z* are used. For the voiceless interdentals *þ* or *θ* are used; for the voiced, *đ* or *ð*. For voiceless velar fricatives the symbols are *x* or *χ*, for voiced g or *γ*, though *χ* and *γ* may also be used for uvular fricatives. *h* is used for the aspirate.

The symbols *c* and *j* vary widely in use from language to language; they may be used for palatal stops. In Sanskrit they represent palatal affricates;

252

commonly a superposed inverted carat is used to specify such values, e.g. *č* as in *church* and *ǰ* as in *judge*. The symbol *j* is also used for the semivowel initial in *yes*, in part because of its value in German, as in *ja*.

Resonant symbols: The symbols *l r w y* are uniform in value, though *y* may also be used to indicate a high, front, rounded vowel. The standard use of *R* is for uvular resonants; in transliteration of runes, however, it indicates a voiced fricative, a resonant in the position of *z*.

For the nasals *m n* are standard, as is *ɲ* for the palatal, and *ŋ* for the velar.

Consonantal diacritics: Of diacritics, . below a consonantal symbol indicates retracted articulation, as in Sanskrit *ṭ ḍ* for cacuminal stops. A dot, or a circle, is also used below symbols for semivowels to indicate vocalic articulation, as in Sanskrit *saṁskṛta* or *saṁskr̥ta*. The . over the *m* is a convention in Sanskrit to indicate nasalization of the vowel.

To indicate a back *l*, a cross-bar through the symbol is used: *ł*.

Vowel symbols: For the vowels, *i e a o u* generally have the "continental values." Capitals, or reduced capitals: ɪ ɛ ʋ indicate lower or laxer variants of *i e u*. The compound symbols æ (*sat*) and œ indicate front vowels; *ə* and ʌ indicate central vowels; a barred *i*: *ɨ* indicates a high central vowel.

For front rounded vowels *ü ʋ ö* are commonly used, though *y ʏ ø* are also common.

A tilde ~ over vowel symbols indicates nasalization.

A macron – over vowel symbols indicates length, ˘ shortness.

Accent symbols: The acute ′ generally indicates the chief accent; the circumflex ˄ the next most prominent; the grave ˎ a lesser accent. In Sanskrit and in Greek forms, and in Japanese, ′ indicates high pitch; ˄ indicates a compound accent (high–low) in Sanskrit and Greek; ˎ indicates low pitch in Greek.

In Chinese superposed numerals indicate tone.

As a general principle one must bear in mind when interpreting symbols that language is based on relationships. In selecting symbols linguists attempt to denote essential contrasts in a given language. Symbols cannot therefore be exact equivalents in different languages. And scholarly traditions have often compounded the problems inherent in attempts to represent language with written symbols.

Symbols used in formulas and rules

- a hyphen, with other symbols indicates their relative position:

    t- indicates a *t* in initial position;

    -*t*- indicates a *t* in medial position;

-t   indicates a *t* in final position.

\>   indicates "developed to, became"; e.g. PIE *t* > PGmc þ

<   indicates "developed from"; e.g. PGmc þ < PIE t

=   indicates "corresponds to"; e.g. PGmc þ = PItal. t

→   indicates a synchronic rule; see pp. 154ff.

*   indicates a nonattested, usually a reconstructed form, e.g. IE **treys* 'three'; placed after a form, e.g. Goth. þreis*, indicates that the form is nonattested, but that we can be reasonably certain of it from similar forms or from other inflected forms of the same paradigm. Especially in synchronic statements, * is often used to indicate a nongrammatical sequence, e.g. **A dog the.*

OHG *drīe* >   NHG *drei* 'three'

NHG *drei* <   OHG *drīe* < IE * *treys*

OHG *drīe* =   Skt *trayas* = Goth. *þreis**

[ ]   enclose material in phonetic transcription, e.g. Skt [trəy]

/ /   enclose material in phonemic transcription, e.g. Skt /tray/

| | enclose material in systematic transcription, e.g. Skt. |trɛy|; / / however are commonly used for systematic as well as autonomous phonemes.

enclose glosses, e.g. 'three'; glosses are given for identification of cited forms, not necessarily to provide the central meaning.

Italics are used to indicate a citation.

Bold-face is used to point up a term when it is defined in the surrounding text.

Technical terms

Technical terms are defined in the text and are better learned from such a context than from lists, but a few common terms are given here for convenience.

Dialect   is used in historical linguistic texts for a subdivision of a language or a language family; e.g. English is an Indo-European dialect. The Midland dialect used across a central portion of the United States is readily understood by any speaker of the English language. – In descriptive linguistic texts on the other hand the term dialect is used for a subdivision or variant which is mutually intelligible with other such variants. For example, German, though related to the Midland dialect and also an offshoot of Indo-European, is a separate language with its own dialects.

Etymon   is the form from which another developed, e.g. PIE *treys* is the etymon of NHG *drei*.

Gloss   is a word used to identify or define another word, e.g. Skt. *tráyas* 'three'.

Reflex   is a form which has developed from an earlier form, e.g. NHG *drei* is a reflex of PIE *treys*.

Terms used to designate distinctive features:
Only very brief characterizations are given here for those terms and abbreviations used in the text; for a longer discussion see Jakobson-Fant-Halle, *Preliminaries* or Chomsky-Halle, *Sound Pattern*.

Accent — greater energy
   á +act   *a*   −act
Anterior — obstruction in front of mouth
   t +ant   *š*   −ant

Back — body of tongue retracted
   o, w +back e, j −back

Consonant — closed or nearly closed vocal tract
   b +cns i −cns

Continuant — uninterrupted air flow
   f, m +cnt p, b −cnt

Coronal — blade or front of tongue raised
   θ +cor p, g −cor

High — body of tongue raised
   u +high $æ$ −high

Low — body of tongue lowered
   o +low i −low

Nasal — lowered velum
   $m, \tilde{\varepsilon}$ +nas b, ε −nas

Resonant — relatively open vocal tract; generally voiced
   r +res d −res

Round — lips rounded
   $\bar{u}$ +rd $\bar{\imath}$ −rd

Strident — friction resulting from groove articulation
   $s, š$ +std f, x −std

Tense — relatively great muscular tension, and duration; see also Jakobson-Halle, *Preliminaries*, pp. 57–61.
   $\bar{a}$ +tense a −tense

Vocalic — open vocal tract and voicing
   a +voc k −voc

Voiced — vocal cord vibration
   d, n, o +vd t, s −vd

Abbreviations for grammatical terms:

acc.	accusative
f., fem.	feminine
indic, ind.	indicative
m., masc.	masculine
nom.	nominative
nt.	neuter
pl.	plural
pres.	present
pret.	preterite
ptc.	participle; pret. ptc. preterite participle
sg.	singular
suff.	suffix

Abbreviations used in referring to languages:

Abbreviations used in dating:

M   Middle, e.g. ME   Middle English
N   New, Modern, e.g. NE   New English, Modern English
O   Old, e.g. OE   Old English
P   Proto-, used only for reconstructed languages, e.g. PGmc. Proto-Germanic. Any form labeled P could also be marked with *
pre   a prior stage, e.g. pre-OE   pre-Old English

Symbols used for geographical subdivisions:

E   East, e.g. ESem.   East Semitic
L   Low, e.g. LG   Low German
N   North, e.g. NGmc.   North Germanic
S   South, e.g. SSlav.   South Slavic
W   West, e.g. WSax.   West Saxon
H   High, e.g. HAlem.   High Alemannic

Abbreviations used for languages:

Alem.	Alemannic	IIr.	Indo-Iranian
Arab.	Arabic	Ir.	Irish
Av.	Avestan	Iran.	Iranian
Chin.	Chinese	Ital.	Italian
Crim. Goth.	Crimean Gothic	Jap.	Japanese
CS	Church Slavic	Lat.	Latin
E, Eng.	English	LG	Low German
Egypt.	Egyptian	Lith.	Lithuanian
Fr.	French	Myc. Gk.	Mycenaean Greek
Franc.	Franconian	N	Norse
Fris.	Frisian	Pers.	Persian
G, Germ.	German	Port.	Portuguese
Gk.	Greek	Rum.	Rumanian
Gmc., Gc.	Germanic	Russ.	Russian
Goth., Go.	Gothic	Sax.	Saxon
Heb.	Hebrew	Skt.	Sanskrit
HG	High German	Sl., Slav.,	Slavic
Hitt.	Hittite	Span.	Spanish
Icel.	Icelandic	Sum.	Sumerian
IE	Indo-European	Turk.	Turkish

Index

The index is arranged in accordance with the Latin alphabet; differing pronunciations are disregarded, so that Sanskrit *c* is alphabetized with English *c*; moreover, diacritics are disregarded, so that č is treated like *c*. Thorn, þ, and edh, ð, are treated like *th*. English items are unmarked. References are to pages rather than to sections.

259

THE PRINCIPAL LANGUA